SAILING WITH STRANGERS

A Story of Courage, Survival
and
Living a Dream

CHARLEY HESTER

WINGSPAN PRESS

Printed in the United States of America.

Published by
WingSpan Press
Livermore, CA
www.wingspanpress.com

The WingSpan® name, logo and colophon are
the trademarks of WingSpan Publishing.

ISBN 1-59594-018-9
EAN 978-1-59594-018-6

First Edition 2005

          Library of Congress Cataloging-in-Publication Data

Hester, Charley.
   Sailing with strangers : a story of courage, survival, and living a
dream
   / Charley Hester. -- 1st ed.
      p. cm.
    ISBN-13: 978-1-59594-018-6 (alk. paper)
    ISBN-10: 1-59594-018-9 (alk. paper)
    1. Hester, Charley--Travel. 2. Hester, Charley--Diaries. 3.
Seafaring
  life. 4. Cape Horn (Chile) 5. Sea Wolf III (Ketch)   I. Title.
  S478.H47 2005
  940.4'5--dc22
                                         2005015440

To Maureen, who understood why.

ACKNOWLEDGEMENTS

I would like to thank the following people who read all or part of this manuscript and gave me corrections, comments, constructive criticism, and encouragement: Pete Pitard, Herb, Ann, & Janet Longtin, Jim Hilton, Tim Edsel, Jib Ellis, Kevin Ledwell, Mike Bauer, Don & Robin Moye, Len Ament, and my daughter Barclay Hester.

I also want to thank Penny from Brevard Community College, Ed Carter, and Mike Perry, for helping me learn to sail and Art Johnston for teaching me how to properly anchor a boat.

Most of all I want to thank my wife Maureen, for putting up with my absence during the voyage, and for turning this project into a book.

PREFACE

Pick up an object. Any object will do, even something as small as a grain of sand. Hold it up in front of you and look at it, even lean over and look from side to side; up and down. No matter how you crane your neck, or twist and turn the object, you can never see the whole thing at any one time. There's always a side that you can't see. If somebody is sitting across the room and looking at that same object, it's a pretty good bet that they will see it somewhat differently than you do, yet their observations are no less accurate or valid than yours. The same thing can be said of the voyage of Sea Wolf III.

I have changed the names of my shipmates, the boat, and one town in the interest of privacy. Otherwise, this book is an accurate and honest chronicle of that voyage *as I saw it*. Two of my shipmates have read this manuscript and neither of them expressed any concerns or disagreements.

I have retained a journal format as a means to give you the reader, the feeling of being right beside me on the boat, or walking through the streets, over the hills, or along the beaches of the exotic places we visited, experiencing with me not only the sights, sounds and venues, but the full range of emotions that I felt, from exhilaration to despair, to frustration and fear. I hope you enjoy the trip.

"In my life, I will not trade quality for quantity."

John Steinbeck
Travels With Charley

"There is room enough for an awful lot of people to be right about things and still not agree."

Kurt Vonnegutt, Jr
Sirens of Titan.

"The countless hours I have spent on, under, and around the water give me a great deal of respect for, but never a fear of the open ocean."

Jimmy Buffett
A Pirate Looks at Fifty

CONTENTS

INTRODUCTION

Mother, Mother ocean,
I have heard you call
Wanted to sail upon your water
Since I was three feet tall...
Jimmy Buffett

I wanted to go sailing before I ever saw the ocean or a sailboat. Somewhere around the fifth grade I read a book called "Buccaneers and Pirates of Our Coasts", with stories about characters like Jean LaFitte, Henry Morgan, Blackbeard, Francis Drake and others. I can't say it became a passion at that point, but I started dreaming of being a pirate myself, and sailing to far away places and meeting different kinds of people.

As I grew up in rural Mississippi, my boating opportunities consisted of occasional fishing trips in rowboats or skiffs with small outboard motors, and I didn't see my first sailboat until I made a trip to Biloxi when I was maybe 13 or 14. The summer I turned 17, I went to Biloxi and worked as a bellhop and had my first sailing experience. It consisted of a two-hour tour of Biloxi Harbor with half a dozen other passengers on a small day-sailor. I got to take the tour free because I sent them business from the hotel where I worked. I did that three or four times over the course of the summer, and then didn't set foot on another sailboat for nearly 20 years.

During those years my dreams of sailing were dormant, but never went away. To me, sailing was for people with lots of time and money. I didn't have much of either, as I was too busy making a living, but I read a lot of books written by people like Joshua Slocum, Francis Chichester, and Thor Heyerdahl. The books were mostly about sailing long distances over endless oceans to strange lands; of shipwrecks and survival, and overcoming adversity. For several years I lived in Pascagoula, Mississippi and spent countless hours just walking around marinas, looking at the sailboats and dreaming about what

13

kind I would like to eventually own. As time passed and I began to make a little more money, I started to think that at some point I might actually buy a sailboat. Then, it occurred to me that I didn't know how to sail, and had no idea how to go about learning.

When I was 30, I took a better job in Lakeland, Florida and swore that I was going to buy a small sailboat after I moved there and learn to sail it on one of the local lakes, but time, money, and other obligations intervened so it never happened.

Finally, in 1979 I moved to Melbourne, Florida and discovered that sailing classes were offered on Saturday mornings through Brevard Community College. The fee was minimal so I signed up, and at age 36, I finally learned to sail! I was absolutely thrilled! The boats were only Sunfish 12 foot sailboats, but to take a boat out without a motor and make it go where I wanted, was big stuff.

I was content for a time to rent Sunfish or Hobie, taking them out in the Indian River Lagoon for an hour or two at a time, but then the companies renting those boats went out of business. I wanted to sail more than ever, but no little boats were available. I explained my situation to Ed Carter of Diamond 99 Marina. He solved the problem by checking my wife Maureen and me out on a 19-foot sloop, and then renting that boat to us for half days. That kept me happy and challenged for a couple of years, but then in 1986 a friend at work told me about his experiences with bareboat charters. I said "Man, that sounds like a lot of fun! I need to learn how to do that." I went back to Ed and explained my desire to sail even bigger boats. This time, he checked us out on an Irwin 28 and wrote a letter stating that we were qualified to charter that boat from him. I was *really* excited, even though I was still unsure of my sailing abilities. I looked through the advertisements in "Cruising World", and with Ed's letter in hand I approached a charter company in Plantation Key. The next thing I knew Maureen and I were doing bareboat charters in the Florida Keys! We spent several three and four day weekends chartering in the Keys, but then we got even more ambitious. In 1987, we chartered a Jeanneau 41 in St. Vincent, sailing it through the Grenadines to Grenada and back over a two-week period.

Over the next few years we did a lot of weekends in the Keys and several two-week charters out of Guadeloupe, Eleuthera, and The Abacos. In 1992, we bought our own sailboat, a 1975 Cape Dory 28 sloop, which in spite of more ambitious intentions, ended up being used mostly for day sailing in the Indian River Lagoon. We became interested in the Western Caribbean, but since there were no charter

14

companies in that area, we started taking vacations ashore instead of chartering.

When I turned 55 in the spring of 1999, I took early retirement from my career in Human Resources. We started spending summers working as Resort Managers near West Yellowstone, Montana, but the notion of doing some serious sailing stuck with me. Chartering had given me a taste for ocean sailing and the idea of actually going somewhere was more appealing than just sailing around a local area. During the summer of 2000, I saw an advertisement in "Cruising World" for crewmembers to share expenses on a 15-month circumnavigation departing in January of 2002. I answered the ad and after some correspondence and phone calls, the captain accepted Maureen and me as crewmembers. However, Maureen decided that she wasn't willing to go on a 15-month voyage on a 34-foot boat with three other people; two of whom she didn't know. I was *extremely* disappointed, as I felt this was a truly unique opportunity, but I reluctantly let the idea go.

Then, in the spring of 2001 Maureen became pregnant with our daughter Molly, and the notion of her making a long-distance sailing trip was put on hold, but for me, the dream wouldn't go away. I contacted the captain about the circumnavigation and he said yes, a crew position was still open and I could have it, but departure had slipped a year, to January of 2003. Then shortly afterward, I learned that he had died unexpectedly, and that option was gone for good.

I started looking at advertisements in "Cruising World" again, and in March of 2002 I happened to see one for a "Cape Horn Voyage", circumnavigating South America with an itinerary that included The Galapagos and Easter Island. I had been fascinated by Easter Island for a lot of years and had never even dreamed that I would have a chance to go there, so I was interested, even though I really wanted to sail around the world. My share of the expenses would be $15,000, but that would cover everything except money I spent in ports over a six-month period, so it didn't sound too bad. The boat was a cutter-rigged Morgan 46 ketch and there would be a total of six crewmembers. Departure would be around October 15, from Mobile, Alabama and the voyage would end in Key West around the middle of April. The owner/captain agreed to hire two other fully qualified and "highly experienced Coast Guard licensed captains" so there would be one captain on each watch. I called the captain and after a brief conversation, he sent me a form to fill out and return. After he reviewed the form, he called to say that he had accepted me as the first crewmember, and was sending me a contract. He also sent a request for a deposit of $7,500. I looked the captain up on the Internet and found that he had built his own trimaran and sailed it around the world in the late sixties-early seventies, so I concluded that he was for real, and knew what he was doing.

I went to see my financial adviser, who told me I could afford to do this even though the stock market had gone to hell the last couple of years. In early May, I signed the contract and sent the deposit. Maureen had some serious misgivings, but after a lot of difficult discussions over a period of several months, agreed for me to go. She was worried that I didn't do more investigating before agreeing to go, and was not looking forward to being alone with an infant for six months, so it was especially hard for her to accept. I nearly backed out just before the rest of my money was due in July, but I think she realized that this was truly an opportunity of a lifetime, and something that I *really* needed to do.

Around the first of September I learned that one of the captains would be the owner/captain's daughter who was about to turn 21, and who just received her Coast Guard license. She was still in college and would not be available until Thanksgiving, so another captain would fill in from Mobile to The Galapagos and she would join us there.

On the way from Montana to Florida we stopped in Mobile on October 10, where I saw the boat and met my shipmates for the first time. We discovered that due to two hurricanes in the Gulf of Mexico in late September-early October, they didn't get to do sea trials, but had been working on the boat all summer, so everything should be in good shape. We found that departure would probably slip a day or so while we waited for the First Mate to finish some business in Boston.

After a quick trip home to Indialantic, Florida we drove back to Pascagoula where we spent a couple of days with my oldest daughter Stephanie, and her family. We learned that departure would be the 17th, so on the afternoon of October 15 we drove to Mobile to put most of my gear on the boat. I had been on a lot of boats before, but when I saw what was to be my home for the next six months, I nearly croaked. My bunk was such that I had to slide my feet under the workbench to lie down, and I couldn't raise my knees all the way up. My storage area looked hopelessly inadequate, too. When the captain told me that I had the best quarters on the boat, I thought, "Bullshit; I got this because I was the last person to board". I was really depressed! That night I told Maureen "I may have made a real mistake, doing this, but it's too late to back out now."

16

The next afternoon, Maureen, Stephanie, and Molly took me to go aboard. I'm not ashamed to say that I cried when Maureen and Molly left me on the dock and drove away with Stephanie, and at the same time I couldn't stop thinking "I can't believe I am really doing this". It is impossible to describe the emotions that I felt as I stood there watching them drive away. When they were out of sight, I turned and walked back to the boat. I was on my way.

1 – SHIP'S COMPANY

The Crew of Sea Wolf III

Sonny Parker - Captain and owner of Sea Wolf III. He is 63 years old, married, and his wife Jane is a nurse. He has four daughters, the youngest of which is eight. He lives near Oxnard, Illinois on a hundred acre family farm, where he grew up, and his primary occupation is owner of rental apartments. He was in the U.S. Marine Corps from 1958-1961 and spent most of his service time playing football. He attended the University of Illinois and Florida State University, where he graduated with a degree in Physical Education. He played football at Illinois (linebacker) for two years until his playing career ended with a shoulder injury. He has spent a little time teaching high school. In the late 1960's, he built a trimaran "Sea Wolf", which he sailed around the world. He wrote a book "Sea Wolf's Odyssey", documenting that voyage. Later, he took nine years to build a catamaran, Sea Wolf II, which he still owns, and which he sailed around Cuba during the winter of 2001-2002. He has spent some time operating captained charters on Sea Wolf II in the Florida Keys.

Ray Riccardi - First Mate, is 56 years old and is from Martha's Vineyard, Massachusetts. He is a native of Cape Cod. He is twice divorced, with a girlfriend who is a hotel concierge, and recently relocated from Martha's Vineyard to Florida. He has some children and grandchildren, but didn't talk much about them.

Ray is a professional sailor. During the summer he is captain of a sailing catboat owned by Woods Hole Oceanographic Research Institute, which takes passengers on day-tours of Edgartown Harbor. Winters, he delivers yachts between the northeastern United States and the Virgin Islands or Florida. Ray has a degree in Marketing from Northeastern University, and said that he has enough credits in Drama to have a minor. He reads a *lot*, and likes movies and theater. He did a lot of acting in high school and college. He said that he designed kitchens for eight years, including galleys on boats, and spent some time driving taxis in Boston. He likes to cook, and is very good at it. He stated that at one point he basically did nothing for five years. He had a drinking problem at one time, but has been sober for four years. He once made the comment that for him, there is no such thing as just one beer. Ray believes that money is for spending, and he is frequently short of cash. When he does have money, he is very generous with those around him.

There is no facial resemblance, but if you gave a physical description, Ray and I would both fit the same one. He is a fun guy; very interesting to talk with, and has the best all-around sailing, seamanship, and mechanical skills in the crew.

Brad Carlson-Second Mate (Mobile to the Galapagos); is 54 years old, lives in Naperville, Illinois, and looks a lot like the character "Walter" on the old television show "Maude". He also bears some resemblance to the late Sonny Bono. He speaks with a pronounced midwestern nasal twang. He is single, but has a serious girlfriend named Lynn, who is a Marketing professional. They live separately, but spend a lot of time together. He graduated from the University of Southern Illinois with a degree in Electrical Engineering. He was caught in a large lay-off at Lucent Technology and took early retirement a couple of years ago. He went to work there when it was called Bell Laboratories, and was an Applications Engineer. He has been very valuable as the electronics and electrical specialist on the boat.

Brad met Sonny when he took a navigation course that Sonny was teaching, and sailed with Sonny last year on the circumnavigation of Cuba. He is an avid racing sailor and has participated in a lot of yacht club races on Lake Michigan for many years. He has the racing mentality of always wanting to go a little faster, and is unhappy when it becomes necessary to tack to gain position in order to sail to windward. He wants to sail directly from here to there, even though he knows that there are times when that is not possible. Brad likes to laugh, and to drink beer. He was a lot of fun, both on board and in port.

Richard Pinckney- Crew Member, is 60 years old and lives in Old Lyme, Connecticut. He has one daughter, Melissa, who is single and a third grade teacher in Montgomery County, Maryland. He is a retired Banker, said that he has "been alone" for 16 years, and had custody of his daughter as she grew up. He is a former Army Ranger, and took jungle warfare training in Panama before serving a tour in Vietnam. He is a very skinny guy with a chest that looks emaciated, but he is wiry and tough, and in good shape. He rides a bicycle a lot, 20-30 miles at a time. He talks like a candy-ass and is almost "prissy" in some ways but that is all deceiving. He sleeps with earplugs and complains about noises, cleanliness, etc., and then the ranger in him comes out and he can handle just about anything, almost a dual personality. Sometimes he won't use profanity at all, or will excuse himself when he does, and other times he will express himself with profanity used appropriately, though never to excess.

Richard has traveled a lot since retiring- snorkeled on the Great Barrier Reef, traveled up the Amazon, and chartered a sailboat in Guadeloupe, though he wasn't the skipper. He will drink a beer occasionally but I never saw him have more than one at a sitting. He said early on that he was in his "mid-fifties" but I saw his passport in Belize, and he turned 60 shortly before we sailed. He had his hair colored at the beginning of the trip, but it went back to gray. I think maybe he has a problem facing the fact that he is aging.

Mark Schmidt- Crew Member, is 65 years old, and lives in Palatine, Illinois. He is a retired lithographer, and a widower who lost his wife to cancer a couple of years ago. She was his best friend, and he has been somewhat lost without her. He has two daughters and four grandchildren, three girls and a boy, ranging from eight months to six years old. One daughter lives near him, and her husband is a high school Industrial Arts teacher. The other daughter lives in Pennsylvania, and her husband is a Speech Professor at Westminster College. He didn't mention whether his daughters work. He has dark blond, or sandy colored hair that I originally thought was colored, but it never went gray. He let his beard grow, and it was mostly gray.

Mark likes to stay busy and to work with his hands, so he is always doing little projects. From the perspective of common sense and logic, he was probably the smartest person on the boat. He was usually the first person on board to spot things, whether it was land, a whale, or another vessel. He went with Sonny to Mobile several times to work on the boat before the voyage. He also likes to drink beer, and became my beer-drinking buddy after Brad left the boat. We especially enjoyed having beers at Café Habana in Puerto Ayora, Galapagos, with Brad, and after Brad left. He has a 14-foot catboat that he sails on a lake near his home. He has three large tattoos of tall sailing ships; one on each arm between the shoulder and elbow, and one on the inside of his right forearm. Mark is totally honest, forthright, and considerate. Of all my shipmates, he was the one I respected most.

21

Naomi Parker - Second Mate (Galapagos to Rio de Janeiro) is Sonny's 21-year old daughter. She is single, and lives with her parents on the family farm. She recently completed course work for a B.S. degree in Marketing Communications from North Central Illinois University. She still must do a senior thesis to graduate. Last summer she passed the test and received a Coast Guard "Six-Pack" captain's license. She is tall, five feet, seven or so and relatively thin - wears clothes so loose that you can't really tell. The best way to describe her would be "plain". She demonstrated a remarkable level of ignorance in regard to sailing and seamanship. She was nice and polite, but not sociable. She rarely entered into any kind of conversation with anybody but her father. She usually didn't go on deck without him, and declined invitations to participate in activities (horseback riding, boat tours, snorkeling, etc.) with the rest of us. She rarely went anywhere without her father throughout her time on the voyage, and made no effort to be part of the "team".

2 – OUT TO SEA

Wednesday, October 16 - It's 10:00 P.M. and I am ready for bed. We had a great dinner at the Wharf House, across the street from the Marina. I had a cup of gumbo and an oyster basket. Also, Mark didn't want his salad and gave it to me so I had something healthy. Everyone went except Ray. Sonny didn't go for dinner, but joined us for drinks and desert.

Today was a very emotional day, though I tried hard not to show it. It's hard to leave Molly for six months, and I really will miss Maureen but this is the trip of a lifetime and I'm excited. This is the culmination of so much emotional turmoil and I can't begin to describe it because I don't understand it all myself. Somehow though, after all misgivings and second-guessing my decisions, it all feels right.

Everyone in the crew seems like they will be good shipmates. Richard and Ray are from New England; Sonny, Mark and Brad, all from Illinois, and me. We are an odd assortment, granted, but there seems to be pretty good chemistry among us.

We plan to sail around eight o'clock or so tomorrow morning, and will take roughly eight days to reach Belize. All my stuff is stowed, though not yet as well organized as I want it. It is cool tonight so I put my blanket on the bunk. Tomorrow should be exciting!

Thursday, October 17 - Day 1 of approximately 180! I got up around six o'clock as daylight came, and took the last marina shower I will have for a while. I had breakfast of Total, coffee, and V-8. We pushed away from the dock at 7:35 A.M. What a rush of emotion that is impossible to describe! We cleared the mouth of the Dog River Channel at 8:50 A.M. and headed down the Mobile Ship Channel, a total of 26 miles to the mouth of Mobile Bay. Ray took the helm after Sonny worried us down the channel, looking for markers. There is only about 6 feet of water in the Dog River Channel and we draw 5 feet 5 inches; maybe more fully loaded as we are.

It's 7:30 P.M. and I am ready for bed. I will be on watch 2:00 - 6:00, A.M. and P.M. and Sonny is my watch partner. We will stand two

23

person watches, with four hours on and eight hours off, twice a day. As of 6:30 P.M. we had covered 59 miles, with two delays during the afternoon. First, the engine died because the battery control was bumped and vibrated to the "off" position and then we stopped the engine for Brad and Sonny to work on the water maker for an hour and a half. Winds were mostly 5 knots or less so we motored most of the day. It is a beautiful night, with clear skies and an almost-full moon. I started fishing at the mouth of Mobile Bay and trolled until 6:15 but there were no signs of any fish. Maureen and Molly should be home by now, as she probably drove all the way from Pascagoula to Indialantic today.

Friday, October 18 - Our first full day at sea! At the start of my 2:00 A.M. watch we put up the main and genoa in winds of 8-11 knots, and we sailed well. Night watch was great, with a beautiful, clear, moonlight night. When the moon set about 4:30 it was like somebody had turned on a light behind all the stars. Wind and seas built through the morning and by noon the wind was 18-20 knots and seas 4-6 feet. That continued all afternoon with winds getting to 20-22 and seas 6-8' with an occasional ten-footer. We put up the mizzen at 9:30 A.M. but took it down around noon. We are on a course due south and have covered 185 miles so far.

After night watch I had coffee, took a short nap, ate some Total, did my exercises, and took a shower. About that time Ray made omelets with green peppers and onions, so I ate again, and then volunteered to wash the dishes. He has volunteered to be the primary cook and he seems to be good at it, so I think we will eat well.

I also worked some with the fishing rod that was on the boat. The reel seems to be gummed up a little but it works, so I tried trolling off the port quarter. I am using the lure that was with the rod. The hook was broken off but I replaced it, and it seems to be working well. I gave up trolling as the winds rose.

All things considered, I think Sonny was right- my bunk and storage area just might be the best on the boat. I have slept *very* well so far and there is plenty of room for my stuff. I unrolled my sleeping bag and put it under my mattress for storage. That worked out very well.

This afternoon for the first time, we looked around and didn't see anything in any direction except the sea. Until then there have always been oil drilling platforms or wellheads in sight. Some of the wellheads have helicopter pads built on top that make them look like golf tees in the distance. We saw a few porpoises yesterday, but nothing more in the way of aquatic life, and *very* few birds. We had a dove land on the stern and ride with us for a while, but that was about it.

Several of the crew are feeling queasy, including Sonny, but Richard and I have escaped so far. It has been too rough to cook, so we had sandwiches for lunch and dinner. Skies have been mostly sunny all day. It has been a great day of sailing, and afternoon watch was fun-like a carnival ride- but uneventful. It is 7:19 P.M. and I will try and go to sleep now.

Saturday, October 19 - 9:30 A.M.- Winds have diminished a little, to 15 knots or so; seas are still 6-10′ but more swell and less chop, so it is more comfortable-especially below. The wind was 20-22 knots during my watch, and only 40-50 degrees off the port bow so we were beating hard upwind. We reefed the genoa twice but left the main alone. Sonny was feeling poorly so I sat at the helm the whole time-not much to do except watch for traffic and monitor heading, wind speed, direction, etc. The auto helm did the rest. I went back to bed after my watch and slept until 8:30. I had only slept about four hours before night watch. With the choppy seas and heeling it took awhile to get to sleep.

7:05 P.M. - Four of the six crew members have been sick for two days now, including all three skippers. I have witnessed two of them hurling over the leeward rail. Only Richard and I have escaped so far. When the cook is sick nothing gets cooked, so Richard and I are fending for ourselves. I am doing O.K. with sandwiches, Total, and tuna.

The wind has dropped to 15-18 knots and seas are beginning to lay down. This afternoon the wind was cranking at 20-22 knots with gusts to 26, and the seas were 6-10 feet. Sonny decided to take down the main and put up the mizzen to slow us down and give us better balance. When he started the engine to position us for the sail change, we blew a hose, causing the engine to overheat. It has not yet been replaced due to the rough weather, so for the moment, the engine isn't working. Richard lowered the main while Ray and I rolled and tied it. That was complicated because the boom is above the dodger and bimini. I had on my life jacket and safety harness so I hooked on my tether, put one foot on the side of the cockpit and the other on the top lifeline near a stanchion. Then I could lean across the bimini to the boom and tie down the sail. It was an exhilarating experience! Maureen would have yelled at me, but I got the job done.

We are about 325 miles out now, and should approach the Yucatan coast of Mexico tomorrow.

Sunday, October 20 - 10:15 A.M. - Last night about 8:20 P.M., just after I went to bed, a squall blew in with 30-knot winds. Brad and Mark were on watch, and decided to furl the mizzen and reef the genoa. Mistakenly, Mark rolled up all the genoa, and steerage was lost. In the commotion, Mark lost control of the jib sheet and it got wrapped around a forward cleat. No real harm was done but from down below it sounded like all hell was breaking loose. All this happened with Mark and Brad both sick; in fact I had seen them both hurling over the leeward rail. After the squall passed, the wind completely died so without an engine we just bobbed around like a cork for a couple of hours-not good for sleeping! About 10:30 the wind started, the sails went up, and I went to sleep. With only three hours sleep my 2:00 A.M. watch seemed to last forever. It was a pretty night-full moon I think. I went back to sleep for two hours when my watch ended.

Sonny has started asking my opinion about some things and seems to follow my suggestions, which makes me feel good. I am settling into life at sea. It is different but not at all unpleasant, and comfortable once you get used to it. It is agreeing with me! The soap container and toothbrush container that I bought were very good purchases.

We are getting scattered showers this morning. Wind is about 10 knots and from the south-southeast so we tacked and are sailing east. We are about 88 degrees west longitude; about 160 miles north of the Yucatan coast, and have to go east anyway to get around the Yucatan Peninsula.

Monday, October 21 - 7:10 A.M.- I just had coffee and cereal while watching the sunrise as the full moon was setting in the west. The sea is spectacular, almost flat, and glassy. I was reminded of so many full moon nights that Maureen and I have enjoyed together, the most memorable of which was a Christmas dinner at the Edgewater Hotel the first year we went to Sandpoint, Idaho to ski. The food was so good, and we watched as the full moon rose over the mountains across Lake Pend-O-Reille and reflected in the water. The only negative now is that we are motoring due to lack of wind. The engine got fixed yesterday afternoon. After a lot of trouble shooting didn't find the problem, I suggested checking the seawater strainer. When they did, nothing was clogging it but it wasn't full of water. They topped off the water and re-sealed it, and afterward the engine didn't overheat any more. It was *not* a blown hose after all.

The unstable weather lasted all day yesterday with light winds from zero to 15 knots, but lots of rain. I started my afternoon watch yesterday wearing my black anorak, but the rain got heavy and my lower back got wet. Finally I switched to my foul weather jacket and it works very well! I slept great for six hours before my night watch, and am not tired this morning.

Only Brad is still sick, and he is better. Ray cooked burgers with peppers and onions, and German potato salad last night and it was very good. We dropped the main before dark last night (less of an adventure this time), and sailed on the jib and mizzen.

We are at latitude 23 degrees, 40 minutes north and longitude 87 degrees, 55 minutes west, about 120 miles north of the Yucatan. We will approach the coast and then turn east and follow it around, to avoid going against the current of the Gulf Stream. The wind died around midnight so Ray and Richard started the engine at one o'clock. We motored throughout my night watch.

Yesterday morning someone yelled that a "dorado" was up ahead, and to get the fishing rod ready. Then they said, "It's just ahead of the boat". Dorado is another name for the dolphin *fish*, so I went to the stern and grabbed the rod. I was ready to put out the lure when a dolphin mammal (porpoise) swam from under the boat! These guys really didn't know the difference! Then, about a dozen dolphins started swimming around the bow, and did so for quite a while.

Tuesday, October 22 - 9:00 A.M.- Yesterday afternoon I caught a small blue fin tuna, creating lots of excitement among the crew. It probably weighed less than three pounds, but provided enough filets for five dinners. Ray blackened it in the oven, and it was great. I cleaned and filleted it with my Swiss army knife and got blood all over the stern. I had made the mistake of fishing from the port, or windward side so instead of running overboard the blood ran up against and along the cabin and deck. Sonny got all upset and threw a little hissy fit before we had a chance to clean it up. I asked him if he wanted me to stop fishing, and he said "No, just make sure you clean up the Goddamn mess".

We are motoring east after sailing within 10 miles of the north Yucatan coast at west longitude 87 degrees, 4 minutes. Wind is from the east so we will motor about 25 miles after dropping the sails and changing course at 6:00 A.M. We will turn south at Isla Mujeres and hoist sails. There are lots of Mexican fishermen in small boats in this area, and I am trolling.

We found out last night that the refrigerator/freezer has stopped working, and is seriously, perhaps terminally ill! Sonny doesn't seem overly concerned because he sees it as a luxury, not a necessity! I agree that it is not an absolute necessity, but without it life on board would be much less pleasant. We will see.

7:30 P.M. - At the end of my afternoon watch we rounded the lighthouse on the northeast tip of Isla Coltoy, and headed south, leaving the Gulf of Mexico and entering the Caribbean. We hoisted the sails and shortly afterward Ray served a great dinner of teriyaki chicken and broccoli. Earlier today he served us key lime pie that was excellent!

Today was probably the most difficult so far. We had great weather, but motored directly into the wind all day until we finally turned south. We found out that the pump that gets cooling water to the refrigerator is dead so we are definitely without refrigeration until or unless we find a replacement, possibly in Belize but more likely in Panama. Meantime, a *lot* of meat is going to spoil. Also, the water maker is *working* but the water is still a little salty- O.K. to shower and cook, but too much to be potable. We have 40 gallons in jerry cans, so we're O.K., just a pain in the ass. *Also*, nobody has been able to get the weather fax to work, we don't have the password to check voice mail on the satellite phone, and the engine battery charger overcharges the batteries. I hope this is just the "shakedown" problems showing up, and not a trend for the entire voyage! So far it hasn't detracted from my enjoyment of the trip.

As I was trolling this morning I got sleepy and decided to go below and take a nap. Mark told me to leave the lure out, and he would watch the rod. While I was below I heard them stop the engine while they worked on the refrigerator. We bobbed around for a while and then the engine started again. When I went back up I found Mark helplessly picking at a huge tangle of twisted monofilament line. I untwisted it and found it broken in the middle. When I pulled in the loose end I found that the lure was caught under the stern, probably wrapped around the prop shaft. When the engine was stopped the lure and line sank straight down off the stern, and then when the engine was re-started, both line and lure were sucked into the prop. The engine operation was not impacted but I cut the line and tied it off to the stern pulpit. Fishing is temporarily suspended, and when I fish from now on I will reel it in any time I leave it! I was bummed out and pissed off, mostly at myself. I think mine are the only hands on the boat that have ever held a fishing rod before. I should have known better than to leave it!

Last night I slept well, but had weird dreams of an unpleasant nature - wonder if it means anything.

28

Wednesday, October 23 - 9:30 A.M. - Last night was my most enjoyable watch yet. When we put up the sails we were on a beam reach, and have been ever since. We passed offshore from Cancun around midnight and when I came on watch at two o'clock the lights of Cancun were about 11 miles away over the starboard quarter. During my entire watch the wind was 10-15 knots on the port beam and the post-full moon was spectacular. As my watch ended we were off the northeast tip of Cozumel. If the weather holds we will have no more course changes before Belize.

The fishing lure, leader, and swivel came loose from under the stern and were dragging behind the boat. I salvaged them, and should be back fishing tomorrow. A good omen!

More bad dreams (really bad!) last night on a slightly different but closely related subject- spooky!

Thursday, October 24 - 11:00 A.M. Last night was another great night of sailing! We had winds from the east at 10-14 knots, seas two to four feet, and bright moonlight most of the time. We watched as a rainsquall passed a few miles ahead of us. We reached the north end of Banco Chinchorro (Chinchorro Bank) on my watch, but didn't actually see it. As expected, the light marking the reef there wasn't working. This morning we could see on the mainland, opposite Banco Chinchorro, what appeared to be a good-sized hotel about where the old Playa Chinchorro Resort used to be.

From our charts we can't figure out how to get through the reef into Ambergris Cay, Belize so we will probably go on to Belize City, about 30 miles further. A complicating factor is that we can reach Ambergris Cay around five o'clock, but can't reach Belize City before dark. We don't want to try going through the reef in the dark, even in a marked channel and using GPS.

As I write this we are passing seven miles off the village of Xcalak. Xcalak and Playa Chinchorro, bring back memories of one of Maureen's and my best adventures. I have wanted to come back here, and always thought I would, but I never dreamed it would be on a sailboat! I get sentimental when I remember the good times we had here.

I started trolling again this morning. I didn't catch anything, but enjoyed the morning; fishing while reading, writing, and doing my exercises on the stern. I have kept up my exercise routine- took yesterday off after exercising for six consecutive days, but resumed today. I am reading "The River Why", and it is more interesting as I get further into it so I am enjoying it.

Before leaving the dock you know about the confinement and tight quarters on a boat but something you don't fully grasp until you are at sea, is that you live in a world that is tilted to some degree almost all the time and is usually bouncing up and down, too. You learn to adapt to that world, and get around without seriously injuring yourself; to anticipate the motion and use it to your advantage. I have not yet cooked, but can use a kettle on the gimbaled stove to heat water for tea, then pour it into cups and bring it up on deck without scalding myself.

9:40 P.M.- At 7:00 P.M. we dropped anchor off the town of San Pedro on Ambergris Cay, Belize! It was dark, and too late to clear in through customs and immigration so we stayed on the boat to celebrate - Brad and I each had three Capt. Morgan Cuba Libres! It was a good crossing, as we covered the 800 miles or so from Mobile in 7 ½ days.

This afternoon while I was on watch, Richard wanted to fish so I encouraged him, and showed him how. He caught a small (1-2 lb.) Yellowtail Snapper and a Barracuda about 30 inches long. Then he hooked something *big* that he fought about 5 minutes or more while the boat was under way before it finally cut the leader. The fish was still fighting after cutting the leader, as it splashed on the surface 5 or 6 times. We never actually saw the fish. While he was fighting it I kept telling him "Stay away from the windmill Richard", as he kept pumping the rod up near the windmill generator on the stern. I tied on another lure and while I was in the galley making tea, he got another strike. It was a *big* Barracuda, which jumped out of the water and spit out the hook When it did, the suddenly slack line flew upward and got tangled in the windmill. It wrapped a few times around the shaft between the blades and the housing, and the windmill stopped. We couldn't get it loose, the line was broken, and the windmill was jammed. The net result was that we lost most of the remaining line, and will have to replace it if we are to fish any more. We all shared the yellowtail after Ray cooked it.

We had been unsuccessfully looking for a way through the reef, and had expected to go another 20 miles south, to the entrance to the channel to Belize City. That would have put us there in the middle of the night, which meant hanging around outside the reef until morning. Suddenly, one of our radio calls was answered with an apology for the delay in responding. The lady said she was on a boat off San Pedro and that she could see us, 1½ miles north. She said that Eric was coming out in their 8-foot dinghy, and would lead us in through the reef. Sure enough, he did that, and we followed him in and anchored just before dark. We are very relieved not to have to bob around out there all night! No watch tonight!

3 – BELIZE

Friday, October 25 – This morning I climbed onto the dinghy davits on the stern to a point where I could reach the windmill. I managed to get hold of an end of the fishing line that was wrapped, and after about ten minutes, managed to unwrap it and get it loose. The wind generator is now working. This was not *terribly* exciting, but with about a three-foot chop here in the lagoon it was a little more challenging than it sounds.

It took all morning for us to clear customs and immigration. First, Sonny and Ray went ashore; then they came back and said all of us had to go in. We had to see two separate people and one was not in her office so we had to sit around waiting for her to return. They do things on "Island Time" here; nobody gets in a hurry.

Afterward we discovered the Shark Bar and Restaurant, and met Gaby and Susie, who work there. The Shark seems to be a fun spot, and is situated on a pier at the beach. Susie is forty-ish and just moved here from Houston. She said that she just needed to get away for a while and Rick, the owner, offered her a job. She said that she has a five-year-old son who is with her Mother in Houston. You get the feeling that there has to be some baggage with this one, like maybe she is running away or hiding from something or someone. She and Gaby both were very nice and Susie seemed to have a need to talk, and have somebody listen. After lunch at the Shark, everybody else came back to the boat while Brad and I explored San Pedro. We found a pump that will work for the fridge, and I bought new fishing line. An interesting observation is that there are no paved streets here, as they are all surfaced with hard-packed sand. They are also quite narrow, and there are no sidewalks so pedestrians have to stay alert.

Our neighbor Eric came over and got our broken pump, took it to his boat and repaired it. He said it would only last for a month or two, so it will be our backup. This is the same guy who came out in the dinghy and led us through the reef last night. He and his girl friend have been cruising the Western Caribbean for two months in

31

a 30-foot sloop, and are heading for Houston when they leave here. They have been very helpful to us and Sonny took them to dinner tonight to express our gratitude.

Tonight we went ashore and ate at The Mango, which was recommended by an artist we met on the beach, who goes by the nickname "Island Dog". He's from Windsor, Connecticut, came here on vacation 13 years ago, and never went home. He reminded me of a character in O. Henry's "Cabbages and Kings" who "had eaten of the lotus" and "was happy and content in this land of perpetual afternoon". The Mango is located right on the beach a hundred yards south of Shark's, and was very good. I had callaloo soup (a local specialty) and a salad. The waitress was a very friendly and exquisitely beautiful young woman named Maria, from Punta Gorda, in Southern Belize. She looked Polynesian.

Afterward we went to The Shark, where they had a live band. When we got there Susie was wearing a sexy little outfit with a skirt that could have been made of two handkerchiefs and a bikini top that gave a good look at her boobs. She seemed to be advertising, and Ray said to me, "She's wearing that outfit for you.", since she had talked with me more than anybody else earlier in the day.

I said, "Nah, you're single. You go ahead and give it a try." He did, but didn't get anywhere and a little later I looked up and she was wearing a different, less revealing outfit. The band was only fair and played *loud* music that was a blend of reggae and rap. Not my kind of music, but it was a fun time and a cultural experience.

Saturday, October 26 - Another day in port. I got my laundry done - $9.00 U.S. for wash, dry, and fold. I also did a lot of exploring on my own, wandering around by myself for three or four hours. I bought a T-shirt for Molly and a mesh bag to use as a laundry bag. I ate a fish sandwich for lunch at Shark's, and had a *great* dinner at The Reef, a little family-owned local place on Middle Street. I had blackened conch with red beans and rice and coleslaw with two beers included, for $11.50! During the afternoon I was having Richard take my picture on the pier next to Shark's, when Gaby and another girl (the cook at Shark's) walked up. They wanted to be in the picture so one got on each side and gave me hugs. As Richard was snapping the picture Gaby reached over and grabbed my crotch. We'll see how the picture comes out!

After dinner we got ice cream and were watching the local socializing, when it started to rain. Ray and Mark had stayed on the boat and

32

Ray had agreed to bring the dinghy in to get us at nine o'clock. Sure enough, here he came right on time through the wind and a driving rain! Nobody would have blamed him if he had waited for the rain to stop, but I have respect for somebody who does what they say they are going to do, even under adverse circumstances. I had my black anorak, and managed to stay fairly dry, but it was an adventure.

So far Richard and Mark give the impression of being pretty stiff. They don't appear to be partiers, and seem unable to give real hearty laughs. They will drink a beer or two, but are very reserved. Ray is a great guy, but doesn't drink. He quit a while back; I think maybe because he realized he was drinking too much. Brad is fun, and more of a partier than the others, but he is leaving us in the Galapagos. Sonny likes to party a little, but he is the Captain, and so is on guard. These are impressions ten days into the voyage. Oh yes, I spent an hour (and $9.00) in the Internet Café on Middle Street. It had very fast access and machines. I read two e-mails and sent eight, which was not bad for an hour!

Sunday, October 27 - I did things on the boat this morning, and went for a swim. The weather was windy, with intermittent rain. Mark and I made three runs in the dinghy to the dock, bringing back 20 gallons of water each trip, in bad weather and about a two-foot chop - not especially fun, but a necessary task.

Mark, Richard, Brad and I had lunch at The Mango. I had a fried lobster Po-Boy and it was really good. After lunch we took pictures with Maria. She is as charming as she is beautiful and the combination just knocks your socks off.

I went with the crew provision shopping and Sonny seemed to be trying to buy what everybody wanted. No taxis were readily available so we ended up carrying all that stuff about half a mile, to the beach. When we had finished that, I went t-shirt shopping, and then had a couple of beers while watching football. I had a good phone conversation with Maureen this afternoon. Tomorrow morning we clear out of Customs and Immigration, and sail for Panama.

Monday, October 28 - The weather this morning is much better than yesterday- sunny to partly cloudy with east wind around 15 knots. We are watching a weather system that is off Honduras but we think it is mostly rain, so we will probably sail early this afternoon.

Everybody went ashore for dinner last night. After dinner I brought Ray, Mark, and Richard to the boat in the dinghy, and then went back to watch the seventh game of the World Series at Shark's, with Sonny and Brad. The Angels won - too bad Gene Autry isn't alive to enjoy it. Both dinghy trips were wet, going against the wind and chop, and I got sand all up my legs and arms. I made sure I got it off before going to bed - don't need sand in my bunk!

An old-fashioned wooden gaff-rigged island sloop just sailed past our bow. It is beautiful; the traditional, salty-looking kind of boat that makes it mandatory for everybody to stop what they're doing and watch as it goes by. We all ran and got our cameras, and I think I got a couple of good pictures.

I have enjoyed a lot of things about this island but the most distinctive thing that makes it different from other places is that the transportation vehicle of choice is the four- passenger golf cart. I don't think you can rent a car here, but there must be six or eight places to rent golf carts. There are a few cars, trucks, and vans but they seem to be mostly commercial vehicles. The streets are narrow, so golf carts are very practical. They also cause minimal noise and no pollution. With the sand streets and the quietness of the golf carts, pedestrians have to stay alert to stay out of the way of traffic. We were told that the government here has bought a machine to make cobblestone blocks to pave the streets.

I woke up this morning about four-thirty and couldn't go back to sleep. There were lots of emotions bouncing around in my head. I think they were night goblins, because they went away when daylight came.

4 – PASSAGE TO PANAMA

Monday, October 28 - 6:30 P.M.- We cleared out through Customs and Immigration this morning, did last minute provisioning, topped off the water supply, and at 12:30 P.M. weighed anchor in the lagoon at San Pedro. Ten minutes later we passed through the cut in the reef and set a rhumb line course of 120 degrees for Cabo Gracias a Dios, on the Honduras-Nicaragua border. The wind has blown steady at 20-25 knots from about 100-110 degrees, so we are slogging to windward through 8-10 foot seas. The favorable tack is to the south, and we sailed a course of 155 degrees for two hours, but there are islands and reefs down that way so now we are on a heading of about 50 degrees. It is very rough, so I will write more tomorrow describing our departure from San Pedro. It was an adventure!

Tuesday, October 29 - 7:00 P.M.- When we departed from San Pedro we knew that getting through the cut in the reef would be tricky. The cut is marked only by a large PVC pipe on the north side and is 75 yards wide with breaking seas on both sides- *just keep the bow where there is no foam*! The cut runs east west and the wind was 22 knots straight out of the east. Sonny was concerned about the possibility of engine failure in the cut, so the contingency plan was to not secure the anchor until we were safely through, but just cleat it off and leave about 20 feet of chain on the foredeck. That way, if the engine failed we could drop anchor immediately, and stay off the reef. I pulled the anchor and Brad fed the line into the hawse pipe. Going through the cut was a wild ride as we stayed on the bow to drop the anchor if necessary. Seas were 8-10 feet on the outside, and built up even more as they approached the reef. Sonny later estimated that the bow was rising and falling 20-25 feet with each wave. We got safely through, and then came the issue of securing the anchor. Brad suggested that we leave the anchor cleated and secure it later, but with those winds and seas I could see that it wasn't going to get any easier so we decided to just go ahead and do it while we were on the bow, to save another trip forward in those conditions. This securing of the anchor is done to avoid an accidental dropping of the anchor while the boat is under way. Brad fed the rest of the chain into the hawse pipe while I tied off the anchor to the bow pulpit with a small piece of line. To do this, I sat down and straddled the bowsprit with my legs clamped around the point of the bow. We dipped the bowsprit in waves three times, but each time I saw it coming, and was ready. Whenever we saw or felt a big wave coming we stopped what we were doing and held on! It was exciting!

Ten minutes after we passed through the reef Mark got seasick again and took to his bunk. He is standing his watches, but is in pretty bad shape. By the end of our afternoon watch Sonny wasn't feeling well either. About midnight last night I heard violent retching topside, and when I got up and looked I discovered that it was him. I have never *heard* such heaves! I thought his stomach would just turn itself inside out and say "here, there's nothing left; just hose me down and get it over with!" He made it through our night watch but afterward he drank some water and repeated the process. He too, is in rough shape. Late this afternoon Brad got sick, but he hasn't hurled so far. I feel bad for them, but have felt fine so far, myself.

Since we left San Pedro winds have blown 20-32 knots and seas have ranged 8-15 feet. The wind has blown from 90-110 degrees and we would like to sail a course of 122 degrees, so we are zigzagging our way on a difficult and uncomfortable heading with slow progress and a very rough ride. With the weather and seasickness, no cooking is being done so we are eating cereal, fruit, juice, and sandwiches. Even making a sandwich is an adventure. Every step must be planned and you can't set anything down because it will slide away. Tonight I ate a can of peas for dinner, right out of the can! Another problem with these conditions is that you can't open any ports or hatches because of the spray, so it gets hot down below. It has not affected my sleeping though, as I have slept very well. Taking a shower is a challenge, too! The shower is hand-held with an on-off button so I just sit down and brace with my feet.

Wednesday, October 30 - 7:00 P.M.- We are approaching the north coast of the Honduran island of Roatan, and are now about 12 miles off. We saw land an hour and a half ago and it gave me a strange feeling that is hard to describe. It brings back really good memories of some very happy times in my life! It is also another place where I can provide quasi-local knowledge to aid our navigation. We will be tacking in about an hour.

Conditions improved some today, though the wind direction stayed the same. Most of the day winds were in the 14-18 knot range, except for a rainsquall on my watch that brought winds up to 28 knots. Right now winds are 16-20 with seas probably four to six feet. Mark is still really sick- spends most of the day in his bunk, and still can't eat. Sonny is still not a hundred per cent, but much better, and Brad is O.K. now.

Radar shows a small boat operating with no lights a few miles ahead of us, which makes us a little nervous. Not scared, but wary what with all the stories people told us about pirates before we sailed, and what we know about drug running in this part of the world. More than once I have heard of people on small boats being killed because they happened to be in the wrong place at the wrong time, stumbling upon some sort of drug-running transaction.

The boat gremlins are still at work, as little problems continue to crop up. The engine overheated again today and they haven't yet figured out what the problem is. Also, there was a leak of hydraulic fluid from the steering, but tightening a valve seemed to solve that one. Also, water backed up through the sink in the head. It is a gravity drain and we don't know why that happened today and not before, but to prevent a recurrence we closed the through-hull valve for the drain. Now, to use the sink we have to open the through-hull, and close it back when we are done- a pain in the ass. Hopefully that will be temporary. Sonny is frustrated with all the little problems cropping up, as he worked all summer to get the boat ready. It is too bad he didn't get to do sea trials because of the hurricanes. Hopefully, these are just "shakedown" things, and will not plague us throughout the trip!

Thursday, October 31 - 6:30 P.M.- The wind is howling at 25-30 knots and we are still beating our way upwind with a bumpy, uncomfortable ride. We are about 70 miles off, and heading toward, the coast of Honduras about 100 miles east of Trujillo, in an area known as "The Mosquitia". Tomorrow we will start a tack to the northeast that should get us clear of Cabo Gracias a Dios, after which we should be able to turn south. Then, hopefully, we will be on a beam reach to Panama.

About 10:30 this morning we saw some rain coming in and Sonny decided to strip down on the foredeck and take a rain shower. He finished his shower and was standing in the galley at the base of the companionway steps drying off when the winds hit, peaking at 37 knots. Ray and Richard were on watch and I was in the salon reading and staying dry. The wind was unexpected, and they scrambled to take in the jib. Brad was in the cockpit too, but with the strong winds, they asked for help with the winches and sheets as sails were flapping wildly and lines were all over the place. I started to go up but Sonny said "I'm already wet; I'll go", and he dropped the towel and up the steps he went! Him running around the cockpit butt naked, pulling lines and cranking winch handles with the boat rolling back and forth in 8-10 foot seas was a sight to behold! I saw the whole thing from below and while it was not a *pretty* sight, it was an impressive performance under adverse conditions, to say the least.

Mark is still sick - now into his fourth day - and spent most of the day in his bunk. He ate a small box of raisins this morning and a few saltines with half a diet coke tonight. I think that's all he has eaten since Monday, and that has to be taking a toll on him. Richard lost a pair of eyeglasses overboard during the squall, after earlier losing a hat.

The engine is working fine again. Ray changed a belt and that seems to have solved the problem. There is a leak in the cabin above Ray's bunk, the pilot bunk above the port side settee in the salon. Now his bed is wet and he is calling it his waterbed. Hopefully, he can dry it out and caulk the leak while we are in Panama, as it's nearly impossible to do something like that while we are under way.

Sonny and Brad are having trouble sleeping in the bow, too, with all the rising and falling, and Sonny says things keep falling off the shelf on his head. He needs to get a net to secure things. At different times I have seen both of them sleeping on the floor of the salon. Richard and Mark tell of the noise made by the autopilot and windmill in the stern, so I think I really do have the best bunk on the boat!

Friday, November 1 - 7:00 P.M.- We just finished a great fish dinner! At 10:15 this morning I caught another blue fin tuna; this one around 7 or 8 pounds which was enough to feed the whole crew, and provide second helpings for three of us! Ray broiled it in aluminum foil with seasoning and cooked roasted potatoes and carrots to go with it. Even Brad, who doesn't like dark fish, thought it was great.

We had a series of squalls all night last night that brought winds to 30 knots with lots of rain, and calm winds in between- the quintessential "stormy night at sea". Before my watch, even in *my* bunk I had to hold on to be able to sleep. I was afraid I might roll and break the leeboard. Anyway, we got blown off course and it looks now like we will not reach Panama until Tuesday. It is still 350 miles after we get around Cabo Gracias a Dios.

About 11:00 A.M. we saw land on the north coast of Honduras, in "The Mosquitia", about 40 miles northeast of Trujillo- brought back good memories of happy days and adventures! We approached within five miles of shore and then motored east the rest of the day because the wind is still directly from the east, and Cabo Gracias a Dios is still ahead of us. We will try to tack northeast tonight and hope to go southeast tomorrow. The coast is pristinely spectacular here with mountains toward Trujillo that taper off to the east. They look layered, with low foothills near the coast, then a higher range; then another, still higher. There is a cloudy haze along the coast, just as there was when Maureen and I were here in 1995.

Mark is much better today. He even got up and made coffee before going on watch at six this morning.

Yesterday the *new* refrigerator pump went out. Hopefully, we can use the old one that Eric repaired for us in San Pedro. There is a bit of *good* news though. Sonny got on the satellite phone and found a membrane for the water maker and it is to be shipped to us in Panama.

Saturday, November 2 - 8:45 A.M. - I just showered and am getting ready to take a nap. After watch, I ate breakfast and then trolled for a while with no success.

Well, we can't use the old refrigerator pump after all. The new one used different fittings, and now for some reason, we don't seem to have the old fittings so we will be without refrigeration until we get to Panama.

We are still beating to windward, sailing back and forth and motoring some. We spent several hours motoring east about five miles off the coast between Cabo Campbell and Punta Patuco, and it was beautiful, with miles and miles of beach, backed by palm trees silhouetted against the late afternoon sky, and no signs of people anywhere. It is so desolate out here with no roads or towns and only the occasional fisherman's house on the beach. Even the houses that are here are usually separated by a few miles. It seems to me that it takes the same mind-set to live out here as it does to live on the remote farms and ranches of the Great Plains. I guess they just like it that way. It gave me a feeling that was almost mystical. I have wanted to visit "The Mosquitia" since visiting Trujillo in 1995 and although I am not on land, it's still pretty neat from five miles out. This is probably as close as I will ever get.

39

Sunday, November 3 - 6:30 P.M.- This morning at 5:30, while still on watch, I went to the head for my morning constitutional. I pumped water in to flush as usual, but when I was drying the bowl the handle stopped, and would move no more. I tried everything I could think of but it wouldn't budge. I stopped just short of breaking it, and told Sonny. Everybody has been using the aft head because the forward head is full of Naomi's stuff. Since she is meeting us in The Galapagos to replace Brad, and is flying there, she went ahead and put most of her stuff on board and stowed it in the head because that was the only space available. Anyway, after watch Sonny took a nap and then started to work on the head pump. When he removed the pump, I guess shit ran everywhere and he called me down to clean it up and help him. I can see why he called me, because I was the last one to use it and with everything being relative, it's less revolting to clean up your own shit than somebody else's! In any case, it was *gross*, to say the least! He found calcium deposits in the cylinder of the pump, removed them, lubed the cylinder and O-ring, and thought that was it but he re-installed it and the problem was still there. Now it seems that the line is clogged between the pump and the through-hull fitting, most likely because people were not pumping it out thoroughly, thinking "if I don't see it any more, then it must be gone", not realizing that you have to pump it through ten feet of hose. Sonny had never given anybody any instructions regarding the use of a marine toilet, apparently thinking that everybody knew. I think everybody understands now! In any case, that toilet is out of service so we cleared out enough room in the forward head to use it. The boat, from midships forward, looks like a bomb went off up there.

Except for that, the day was pretty good, as we were able to sail all day. We passed Punta Patuco at 10:30 last night and the coast began falling away to the southeast so we were able to sail closer to our desired course. About six o'clock tonight we passed Cabo Falso, or False Cape, and the coast fell away more. It is still 20 miles to Cabo Gracias a Dios, but we are now on our course, and heading out to sea. Winds are 10-14 knots and have shifted slightly to the north of due east. We saw a nice sunset over the Honduran Mosquitia.

Sonny is a little grumpy, I think out of frustration over all the little things that have gone wrong with the boat. It doesn't seem to be directed at any of us, and I think he is just tired and frustrated.

This morning I sat on the stern trolling for a while, but had no strikes. Richard missed a good strike yesterday afternoon and when I checked I found that the hook was dull so I got out the stone and sharpened all the hooks. Richard has certainly won my respect since we have been out here. He is a skinny little guy and a stuffy New Englander (when he uses any profanity he says "excuse my language"; when looking at the stars, made reference to the "large dipper", etc.) but he is wiry, strong, and shows no fear or apprehension when doing things outside the cockpit under adverse conditions like rain, high winds or rough seas. He had not fished since childhood, but shows a healthy interest and aptitude while having pretty decent success.

I have learned how to make hot tea at 3:00 A.M. on a gimbaled propane stove in 8-10 foot seas–verrrry carefully! Sonny and I like to have tea during out night watch so I go down and make it. You plan each step, from turning on the gas, filling the kettle, lighting the burner, right on through. You do one step at a time, in sequence, never setting anything down except on the stove or in the sink. You make one cup, hand it off, and then make the second one. This sounds boring, but it is an adventure, dealing with boiling water under those conditions.

I got back to my exercises after skipping three days in rough weather. I did sit-ups during that time, but nothing more. I skipped today because of the head crisis. I finished reading "The River Why" today and it turned out to be pretty good after all. I need to re-read the last few chapters, as it left me a little confused on a couple of points.

We are still about 400 miles from Panama, but should make it in three or four days now that we are *finally* around Cabo Gracias a Dios. I understand why they named it "Thank God"!

Monday, November 4 - 6:25 P.M.- *Good News*: The aft head is operational again! Today Sonny decided to do some trouble-shooting and I volunteered to be his helper. He started by checking the through-hull fitting and water came in, so that wasn't the problem. I had already reached that conclusion and told him so, because he had flipped the Y-valve and tried to pump into the holding tank. That didn't work, so that meant that the problem was between the pump and the Y-valve. He found the blockage just before the Y-valve. My help was to operate the pump when he needed it, to carry a couple of buckets up top and dump them overboard, and then bleach the bucket. Getting this fixed was a *major* victory and morale boost. He seemed to appreciate my volunteering to help.

We are about 50 miles off Cabo Gracias a Dios, on the Honduras-Nicaragua border, and sailing southeast. Hopefully we will reach Panama on Thursday. I called Maureen on the satellite phone and it was good to talk with her. I ate my Total, had coffee, exercised, and then Ray served fried eggs and ham on English muffins!

I trolled for a while this morning and had a fish on for 20 or 30 seconds before it threw the hook. I saw it splash the surface, but never saw the fish. The *big* fishing news came this afternoon. Richard was fishing while I was on watch, and something *really big* grabbed the lure and took off. It was pulling so hard that Richard couldn't get the rod out of the holder and though I had the drag set pretty tight, the reel was *screaming*! Richard hurt his hand while trying to tighten the drag more. The fish took *all* the line off the reel and when it got to the end, my new 100 pound test line snapped with a pop like a rifle shot. Richard said he saw the fish jump six or seven feet out of the water, and that it looked like a barracuda but both king mackerel and wahoo have that same shape, so I'm not sure what it was. One of the guides on the rod was broken and another was bent but I think it is still usable, and I have more line, so I will try to get it re-rigged in the morning.

Today was a great day of sailing. The weather was beautiful with winds of 10 - 15 knots, and even though the seas were in the five-to-ten foot range, they were swells, not the steep waves we had a few days ago. We saw a few Nicaraguan fishing boats, but that has been the only traffic. This area is a fertile fishing ground, with shallow banks, reefs, and drop-offs. We are about 100 miles offshore, and the water depth is from 60 - 120 feet. We are choosing the deeper channels.

We have plenty of drinking water but are low on water for everything else, like showers so we take them every other day, and will have to quit even doing that. The water maker is not working at all right now and Ray and Brad's repair efforts have been unsuccessful. We will get a new membrane in Panama, and fix it there.

Tuesday, November 5 - 6:20 P.M.- When I went on watch at 2:00 A.M. the lights of the Colombian island "Isla Providencia" were easily visible nine miles off our port beam. It is yet another place that brings back really nice memories of happy days with Maureen. The lights at that distance were mostly a glow on the horizon, but I could make out individual lights in the town on the north end, along the bay at Agua Dulce, and at the military post on the south end. I remember riding a scooter through a herd of cows on the west road, and diving the wall with the people from Sonny's Dive Shop. I especially remember our 10th anniversary dinner on the porch at Buccanero's, and giving Maureen a song I had written as an anniversary present. I had thought she would be impressed, and felt kind of silly when she didn't seem to be. I'm pretty sure she never showed it to anybody, or even told anybody about it. It was a great dinner for our anniversary, anyway.

Yesterday and today have provided our best sailing yet. We have had 12-18 knot winds over the port beam, and have averaged a speed of about six knots the entire time. We should reach Panama during the night tomorrow night. I *finally* got my book out today and started brushing up on my Spanish.

Wednesday, November 6 - 6:50 A.M.- "Now this is really stupid" is the thought that occurred to me as I stood on the starboard lifeline stanchion tying up the mainsail at 1:00 A.M. in my underwear and no life jacket or light as we sailed along at five knots. "If I slip or lose my grip on the boom and fall overboard, I can just bend way over and kiss my ass good-bye!" Ray woke me to come up and help him and Richard furl the main because he had been watching a pretty good squall approach to the point where he knew it would hit us. Half asleep, and acting as a reflex, I got out of my bunk and went up right away. I didn't fall, and it turned out that we had 15 minutes before the winds arrived. If the weather looks at all threatening we usually take down the main before dark because it is such a pain in the ass, but last night we left it up, because everything looked clear. After the squall, Sonny and I sailed the rest of the watch under the mizzen and half the jib, and still averaged five knots.

I got the fishing rod re-rigged yesterday but it is really not adequate as we only have about 35 yards of line. It will have to do until we reach Panama, which should happen around ten o'clock tonight. I finished the last of the Total this morning–forsooth!

We had another great day of sailing, averaging six knots, until about 5:00 P.M. when the wind dropped and shifted to our stern. Now we are creeping along about two knots, and every swell that passes under the boat causes the sails to flop around and the booms to swing back and forth. Hopefully, this won't last long, as it is *very* uncomfortable and noisy. We still should reach Colon, Panama some time tonight!

5 – PANAMA

Thursday, November 7 - 5:10 A.M. - We are in Panama! We dropped anchor inside the breakwater at Colon just after one o'clock this morning after motoring the last 25 miles. After three great days of sailing the wind died as we got near the coast. I am on anchor watch, and enjoying the daybreak. There are lots of ships here, but only three that were under way since I came on watch at three o'clock.

11:00 A.M. - We couldn't get anybody on the radio this morning so we motored around downtown Colon to barrio Cristobal, which has the only marina in the area, only to find that all the slips are full. We anchored out in the bay, and Sonny and Ray have gone ashore in the dinghy to try and clear us in. This is a really busy shipping area, not only with Panama Canal traffic, but *lots and lots* of cargo terminals here. It is very interesting to watch, with all kinds of cargo being loaded and unloaded, and pilot boats and tugs coming and going.

I think I nearly got killed yesterday morning! I was sleeping in my bunk and Ray was working on the diesel generator engine as it was running. Richard had closed the door to the aft cabin and the head door was closed but the door to the engine room, across from my bunk, was open. The two ports above my bunk were open but shelves under them kept air from getting down to my bunk, which is under the shelves. I was sleeping soundly when my nose stopped up, and that woke me somewhat. My nose does that sometimes, so I wasn't concerned; just wanted to breathe so I could go back to sleep. It was like I had been in a really deep sleep, and wanted nothing so much as to go back to sleep- a sort of semi-conscious state. I decided to breathe through my mouth, in hopes of going back to full sleep but when I tried that I found that I couldn't get enough air. I tried that three or four times, and remember suddenly thinking *"carbon monoxide!"* I quickly got out of my bunk, and as soon as I stood up in front of a port I was able to breathe fine. Scared the *hell* out of me! I'm sure glad I didn't go back to full sleep. If I should die out here from the sea, or something to do with sailing the boat, that's O.K.- I understood and accepted those risks before we sailed, but I would be really pissed off if I died from something stupid like that!

Friday, November 8 - 5:50 P.M.- Sonny and Ray successfully cleared us into Panama, and we got a slip at the marina after all. It is the Panama Canal Yacht Club; formerly the Cristobal Yacht Club, and it is great, though not nearly as fancy as it sounds. We plan to be here about six days. There is a neat restaurant/bar/porch here with good food, low prices, (beer for $1.00; fish dinner $5.50), showers, and laundry facilities! I used all of the above yesterday afternoon and last night. People here are really nice.

Today I did exercises *and* ran. Sonny and Brad ordered a new membrane for the water maker, a new refrigerator pump, and new collection box for the muffler. All of them *should* be here by Tuesday or Wednesday. It turns out that the pump we bought in San Pedro was designed to only flow one way but none of us knew that. When it was installed, they couldn't get it to fit right side up, so they installed it upside-down, and the flow was the wrong way so it burned out!

This afternoon Richard wanted to cash a traveler's check at a bank and look for an optician, to get a replacement pair of glasses, and I agreed to go into town with him. We ended up walking about three miles through downtown Colon and accomplished both objectives. I used my limited Spanish to ask directions to an optician, and eventually found a mother and daughter, Maria and Carol, who walked with us until we found the optician, waited with us, and then advised us to take a taxi back to the boat because Colon is dangerous! They are originally from this area, but now live in Newport News, Virginia where Carol's husband is stationed with the U.S. Army. They are here because Maria's mother, age 82, broke a hip and is in the hospital. We took their advice, and the taxi ride back was $1.00. I knew where the bank was from my morning run, so that part was easy.

Later in the afternoon we ran into a guy named Jay Tolbert whose boat "Gold Run" has Cocoa, Florida as it's hailing port. He bought the boat at the marina just north of Mathers Bridge in Indian Harbor Beach. He is single-handing, and is a full time cruiser who is about my age. Also this afternoon, a boat came by and gave us 17 old tires wrapped in plastic and tape, with short lines attached, to use as fenders during our transit of the canal. They are now stacked on the foredeck.

Saturday, November 9 - Today I went with Ray, Brad, and Richard to visit the Miraflores Locks on the Panama Canal- another place that brings back really nice memories of happy days and adventures. We were there for a couple of hours and watched three ships pass through. It was really neat to see. When I went there with Maureen there were no ships, so this was a new experience. To get there we walked to the bus station, about a quarter mile from the boat, and after I used my Spanish to find the right bus, took an air-conditioned express bus to Panama City. We were told to go to Plaza Cinco de Mayo, where we could connect with a bus to the Miraflores Locks. It worked well, and the whole thing cost $2.50. For the return trip we took a taxi (50 cents per person) to the Albrook Station, and there we caught another air-conditioned express back to Colon, getting off a quarter mile from the boat and getting back to the porch/bar just before a deluge. It was a very nice day and both Ray and Richard commented on how helpful my (limited) Spanish ability was. Maureen was correct in her prediction that I would evolve into a leadership role with this group; not on the boat, but when we are off it. I have never aspired to leadership, but very often in my life, it has worked out that way. While we were gone Sonny took the alternator and got it re-wired so that now the engine will no longer overcharge the jell-cell batteries.

I almost forgot- today I re-organized my stuff in my space, and found my missing flip-flops and black running shorts- a good omen!

Sunday, November 10 - 6:30 P.M.- Today was a laid-back day. I fished off the boat a little but caught nothing. A few fish followed the lure but wouldn't eat it. I need to figure out why.

Ray, Richard and I went to an Internet Café. They charged only $1.00 per hour, amazing, after paying $9.00 an hour in Belize. It worked great so I spent an hour doing e-mail, and will definitely go back! Maureen sent me some great pictures of Molly.

Afterward, we ate lunch at a McDonald's, and then went grocery shopping at a place called "99 Supermercado". Grocery prices are unbelievably low–steak 75 cents a pound; Heineken for $3.50 a six-pack; Chilean red wines for $3.00, etc. Everything was *very* low priced.

Later, Richard and I had a beer on the porch and discussed Sonny's grumpiness. I hope it gets better when the "boat gremlin" problems are solved. It is not really a *big* deal, and he hasn't given me any crap except about the fish blood on the deck but it would be a nicer atmosphere if he was in a better mood. He has worried a lot and doesn't seem to have had as much fun as the rest of us. I think it is gradually becoming evident to him that *it's not a new boat*!

People here keep warning us about getting robbed, even in the daytime but so far, so good. When in doubt, we take a taxi, as it only costs a dollar, from one side of town to the other. Also, I only carry $50-$75 with me at any one time, so if they want it, they can have it!

We bought some steaks at "99 Supermercado", and tonight Ray is cooking them with grilled onions, green peppers, and roast potatoes.

Monday, November 11 - 7:00 P.M.- Ray, Richard, and I took down the roller-furled jib this morning to check the halyard where it was attached to the sail. Sure enough, it was frayed so we cut off a two-foot piece, re-attached it to the sail, and re-raised the jib. We certainly don't need any frayed rigging where we are going!

Later Ray, Richard, Brad and I walked to the Internet Café on 11th Avenue but it was crowded and the system went down while we were waiting, so we gave up. Ray and I ate lunch in a little local place downtown- chicken dinner and a coke for $2.25. As we were walking back to the boat with Brad and Richard we decided to stop in the bar at the International Hotel for beers, and when we walked in, hookers came out of the woodwork! They wanted us to buy them beers, which we did (for $4.00 each!), but when I told mine that I was married, and not interested, she walked away in a huff, leaving most of her beer. It was interesting watching the other guys deal with theirs, and I think Ray and Richard were tempted!

We came back to the porch at the Yacht Club where we had beers and socialized with other boat people while we watched and enjoyed the afternoon rain.

Tuesday, November 12 - 8:30 P.M.- I really *did* nearly get killed last week! Today a mechanic came to work on the diesel generator engine because after running for about 30 minutes it would slowly die, like it wasn't getting enough fuel. Ray, Brad and Sonny couldn't figure out the problem. The mechanic found that the problem was with the fuel pump. He *also* found an *exhaust leak* in the vented loop of the exhaust system! My complaints had been discounted somewhat because the exhaust problem that we *knew* about (collection box on the muffler) was with the boat engine, and it was not running at the time of my problem. I got a little pissed off, and tactfully but firmly expressed my displeasure!

Richard and I went back to the Internet Café this morning and this time we were successful. We also went to the Post Office and bank. He has begun to loosen up a bit, and seems to be a likeable guy. He was an Army Ranger, and was in Panama 35 years ago for jungle warfare training before serving a tour in Viet Nam as a combat engineer.

Sonny, Brad and Mark went to Panama City and bought a few things for the boat, but no replacement for the broken helmsman's chair or the frayed jib sheets so far.

Wednesday, November 13 - 11:15 P.M.- I stayed at the bar late tonight, talking with some local people about nothing in particular. It rained a *lot* today, from eleven o'clock this morning steadily until about six this evening. Richard and I went with Ray to the Free Zone to pay for the diesel mechanic's work. It is a duty-free shopping area; walled, and with a customs/security gate. You need your passport to get in, and it is like a small town consisting of a huge shopping area with anything you can imagine. They even have a Sak's! Later we went to a little hardware store downtown where we found a replacement fishing rod for under $40. We didn't buy it yet, but probably will.

The new collection box for the muffler isn't going to get here before we leave so Sonny did an epoxy and fiberglass tape repair job. This is the muffler for the boat engine. Both exhaust problems are now *supposed* to be fixed! We will see! The new collection box is now to be shipped to The Galapagos. Sonny and Ray are both sensitized to my concerns and have agreed to wake me up if they need to run either engine while I am sleeping. With the repairs they made, *and* if they keep the engine room door closed, I think I will be fine.

Richard has really "loosened up" since we left Mobile-"Changes in Latitude; Changes in Attitude!" I went with him to pick up his new glasses this afternoon since we generally travel in groups of two or more. Tonight he and Ray went back to the bar at the International Hotel; I think because there are hookers there and he wanted a little action. Ray was back in about a half hour, and Richard came back about an hour later. I çan't say empirically that he screwed a hooker, because I wasn't there, but he kept talking about how she graded his performance!

Thursday, November 14 - 10:00 P.M.- Ray and Sonny found a missing nut that had vibrated loose from the boat engine water pump and fallen into the bilge. This is a major deal, because without it the engine would become inoperable, and we had been unable to find one that size anywhere. They got several little things taken care of on the boat, which got Sonny into a little better mood. He was downright rude this morning, and again late this afternoon. No deliveries of parts came today but it still looks like we will depart on Saturday.

Brad nearly got robbed today. A guy tried to grab his shoulder bag (if a woman was carrying it, it would be called a purse!) and run but Brad held on to the strap and the guy ran away. I wasn't with him when it happened. I guess the people who have been warning us about crime around here knew what they were talking about.

Tonight we ate and socialized with boat people and locals on the porch. I also did laundry, and it took a long time. To accommodate people waiting, I shared a dryer with Richard, and we overloaded it so it seemed to take forever for things to get dry. When we were loading the dryer there was a little boy about ten years old hanging around the laundry room, and as he watched he told Richard "You're putting too much in there. It won't get dry". Later as we kept coming back and sticking more quarters into the slots he kept saying "I *told* you that was too much stuff in the dryer".

Richard and I have had several discussions about the series of problems with the boat, and Sonny's demeanor. We understand his frustration and are giving him the benefit of that but we don't intend to take any crap. Hopefully, there won't be any new problems, and his attitude and personality will improve.

I talked with Maureen this morning and that was not uplifting either. I know she misses me, but sometimes she cries when I call, and even though she doesn't intend it that way it makes me feel guilty about doing this and enjoying it so much!

Friday, November 15 - 2:15 P.M.- We are making preparations to leave. We got the word that we are to meet our Panama Canal pilot outside the marina tomorrow morning at five o'clock. The new pump arrived today so now we have refrigeration again. Also, the membrane for the water maker showed up, so hopefully, we will have plenty water. Even though things seem to be looking up, Sonny still has a negative, grumpy attitude- acts like he is pissed off all the time. All the others have started to talk about it; even Mark, who has been Sonny's staunch supporter. Hopefully this will improve; especially when Naomi arrives. The rest of us are tired of it. We understand his frustration with all the things that have broken, but feel that he needs to deal with it, and set a better example. He *is* the captain and it *is* his responsibility. Sonny, Ray, and Richard have gone shopping for provisions. I chose not to go because I don't want to hear any more negative bullshit right now.

Richard wanted some candid pictures so I went downtown with him to watch his back while he took the pictures. We went all through

49

downtown; even the market, and I think he got some great shots. I helped him set some of them up by watching for and pointing out people and/or things that looked like good pictures. We bought the new fishing rod for $34.95, and it is bigger around and about a foot longer than the old one. We also got new 100 pound test line, so we will be ready to fish.

I had heard and read a lot of negative things about Colon, and had some apprehensions about it when we arrived, but I have really enjoyed my visit here. The people, in spite of the crime concerns, are really nice, very attractive, and seemingly pretty happy. I haven't seen a traffic light anywhere, and most intersections don't even have stop signs but people are courteous, drivers *and* pedestrians; and vehicular and foot traffic flow very smoothly. Also, it is pretty much bug-free! I have seen *no* roaches, and very few flies, even in the outdoor market, with all that meat, fruit, and vegetables out in the open. I haven't even seen any mosquitoes!

6 – FIRST PACIFIC PASSAGE

Saturday, November 16 - 9:10 P.M.- What a day today was! Transiting the Panama Canal! We got up at 4:00 A.M.; pulled anchor (we were docked stern-to with an anchor out from the bow) at 4:30 and met our pilot at 5:00. We actually entered the canal at 5:30 and passed under the Bridge of the Americas, entering the Pacific Ocean at 4:30 P.M., taking eleven hours for the transit. We entered the Gatun Locks at about 7:00 A.M. and it took about two hours to go up the three steps to Gatun Lake. We not only were *there*, but actively participated; handling lines, letting them out or pulling in as the water levels rose or dropped, holding us in the center, and so forth. They had us raft up with a big catamaran from New York at the Gatun Locks and then we tied off to a tugboat that held us in place in the current as the gates opened and closed. *Very* neat stuff! We then reached the Pedro Miguel Lock at about one-thirty, went down one step; and on another couple of miles to the Miraflores Locks and down the final two steps. We left there about 3:45 P.M.

Tonight we are on a mooring (they don't really have slips) at the Balboa Yacht Club near Panama City. Maureen and I came here, too; actually drove out on the long peninsula by the yacht club. They have a free shuttle boat to bring you to the pier to go ashore and they monitor the radio 24 hours a day, so you can call them whenever you are ready. Their clubhouse burned years ago and was never rebuilt, but they have a swimming pool, fuel dock, and moorings. Just up the hill is an outdoor restaurant that also offers showers for boat people. We had a good seafood dinner and took one last shower ashore. Ray stayed on the boat while the rest of us went ashore. I know he is short of money, and I feel bad for him. We leave tomorrow about 7:00 A.M. for the Galapagos.

The transit of the canal was an indescribably fantastic experience-both seeing the whole thing and the marvelous way it works, and the thrill of realizing where you are and what you are doing.

Last night Ray and Richard went to the Bar Rockola in Colon to a strip-tease show that we had seen advertised, with girls from four countries! They were disappointed, and came back early. I didn't go because we had already cleared out through immigration. Technically, we were in the country illegally and when you go somewhere like that, you don't know what might happen. The rest of us had dinner at the porch, and then took pictures and said our good-byes to our friend "Amazing Grace" and the other staff members who were so nice to us.

When we passed Gamboa in the canal, with all the cranes and dredges; then passed the place where Maureen and I went for a boat ride on the canal five years ago, and later passed under the Bridge of the Americas, it all brought back still more really nice memories of happy days.

Sonny is in a much better mood. Things are looking up, and surprisingly, we even got delivery here of the new muffler/collection box! Sonny is in a lot of pain, as he twisted his knee yesterday while climbing from the dock, through the dinghy to the boat.

Sunday, November 17 - 6:20 P.M.- We just took down the main for the night and are sailing on the jib and mizzen. The weather is fine now, but unsettled, and we got surprised by a squall this morning that brought winds up to 36 knots. It had sucked wind from one direction, then hit from the opposite direction and lasted nearly an hour. It caused no real problems, but lots of scrambling around. When it hit I looked up top to see if Ray and Richard needed help, and when they didn't, I went to my bunk and took a nap! A port was left open in the aft cabin, and Richard's bunk got wet.

We cast off our mooring lines at 7:00 A.M. and set a course south by southwest, to get out of the Gulf of Panama. After that, we will sail about 230 degrees. We motored for a while, but by eight o'clock the wind picked up enough for us to sail. We sailed most of the day in winds of 10-15 knots and seas less than three feet.

About 9:30 A.M. I caught a blue fin tuna that weighed about 10 pounds, and Ray is cooking a fish dinner right now! My first day sailing in the Pacific and I caught my first fish in the Pacific! Two firsts in one day–rare at my age!

The air is a good 10-15 degrees cooler on the Pacific side, which is interesting, especially because the water temperature this afternoon was 82. We really enjoyed Panama but it's good to be back at sea! Sonny continues to be in a good mood.

Monday, November 18 - 6:45 P.M.- Ray and Sonny were successful in fixing the generator engine! The new fuel pump that we got in Panama didn't solve the problem and today it quit working altogether. The refrigerator runs off the batteries, which are charged by the generator. The alternator repair in Panama didn't work either so we can't charge the batteries with the boat engine. For a while there it looked as if we would be without refrigeration again and we were thinking "Oh shit, here we go again with the problems!" Anyway, the problem with the generator turned out to be an air leak in the fuel line, which now *appears* to be fixed. We'll keep our fingers crossed.

After motoring for twelve hours due to light winds, we sailed from nine o'clock this morning until just now. We just started motoring again due to light winds right on our nose. Seas have been only 1-3 feet so we make good progress when we motor.

My news of the day was fishing. I had five hook-ups- caught one-another blue fin tuna that weighed 10-12 pounds. I lost another tuna after it jumped twice, and a dolphin about three feet long (it jumped too). I lost the dolphin because a wire leader failed where it was crimped. I lost two others that I never saw; one of which bit *through* a wire leader! I don't feel *too* bad about losing those fish because this is not like trolling from a *fishing* boat where you stop when you get a strike, let the fish take line and run, or even follow them with the boat. With this kind of fishing you are usually moving four to six knots and you *don't* stop. You either muscle them in or they pull loose or break off, so you can't expect to catch a high percentage of them. It is great fun, regardless!

Tonight it looks like it is almost full moon, and it made me feel sentimental. Full moons have always been special times.

Tuesday, November 19 - 11:40 A.M. - Last night was one of the prettiest I have ever experienced. We motored throughout my watch with only the occasional cloud in an otherwise clear sky. The full, or almost full moon shined golden on a sea that was flat and glassy to the horizon. In the moonlight you could even see specific reflections of the few clouds that were there.

Without realizing it, over the last day or so we have slipped into the doldrums. Somehow I had always thought of the doldrums as being five degrees either side of the equator but we appear to have picked them up between six and seven degrees north. I am trolling off the stern right now as we continue to motor through low, smooth, gentle swells of one to three feet that sometimes have tiny ripples, but are mostly glassy. Winds are less than four knots.

We are 150 miles from the nearest point of land and yesterday we picked up half a dozen tiny, hitchhiker birds that look like finches or sparrows, and unlike any sea birds that I have ever seen. Five of them spent the night huddled together on a lifeline on the port quarter with a sixth about a foot away on the life sling. I took a picture of them this morning.

Ray has been fighting off a cold and I have picked up some symptoms the last day or so. I am taking some aspirin and drinking lots of juice- so far, so good. I have also started to experience a little pain in some of my knuckles. It is not there all the time, but comes and goes. I sure hope it is not the beginning stage of arthritis! Out here, so far removed from any medical facilities, you are sensitized to any physical concerns and can start to imagine things.

Wednesday, November 20 - 8:10 P.M. - We had some visitors about four o'clock yesterday afternoon. I watched through the binoculars as a small boat came over the horizon off the starboard bow and came straight toward us. As they came closer I could see that there were three men on board about a 20-foot open boat with an outboard motor and an Ecuadorian flag painted on the bow. I found that a little strange with us being more than 150 miles from any land. We had heard stories of pirates off the coast of South America and I was looking for guns, but didn't see any. Still, I was a little apprehensive. Sonny was below, so I called him and Ray topside as the boat came alongside. I couldn't make out what they were saying, but one kept holding up a piece of net so at first we thought they wanted us to change course to avoid running over their net, but that wasn't it. Then we thought they were saying that we had *already* run over their net, but that wasn't it either. Then just as they were leaving, I heard the word "perdido", which means lost. Finally, it occurred to me that they were using a drift net, and couldn't find it! Sure enough, about three or four miles further along *we* found it. We saw a long line of plastic jug floats and attached to the float on the end was a vertical stick, about eight feet high, with a flag on top. We ran over the net but it didn't catch in the prop. I thought drift nets had been banned, but one was in use here! A little later we saw two more similar boats, both of which approached us, looking for cigarettes. We also saw what appeared to be a "mother ship", about the size of an ordinary shrimp boat. That explained the small boats being way out here.

Just after noon yesterday I was trolling, and got a strike from a big fish that broke my snap swivel, and took another lure. The swivel was an old one that was on the boat so I shouldn't have been using it since I have plenty new ones! Right after that I caught another tuna that weighed about six pounds or so, providing another dinner of fresh fish for the crew last night.

About 1:00 A.M. we had a good-sized bird land on he bow pulpit. It went away, but returned just as I was coming on watch at 2:00. Richard identified it as a red-footed blue booby, which is found only on the northernmost island in the Galapagos. That island is a good 400 miles from here! We shined a light on it and sure enough, it had red feet and a medium length beak that was the color of the sky on a clear day. We took some pictures in the moonlight. It looked a lot like a really big seagull, but with the features I described. Richard had failed to see one on his trip to the Galapagos a few years ago, and said this was one of the most exciting experiences of his life! It was pretty neat, but I wouldn't go *that* far. It rode with us until about 7:30. I still find white-footed pink boobies more exciting, but that's just me!

Last night *was* full moon, but it wasn't quite as spectacular as the night before, with more ripples and small waves on the water. About 8:00 A.M. we put up the sails after motoring nearly 36 hours. Winds held at 8-12 knots all day but died again after sunset, so tonight we are motoring again. We were happy to sail for eleven hours or so- life in the doldrums. We are near latitude 4 degrees north, and longitude 83 degrees west. So far nobody has been seasick on this passage. It could be because seas have been pretty calm, or maybe they have adjusted.

Thursday, November 21 - 7:25 P.M.- We just had a dessert of Ray's Key Lime Pie. It was excellent, and the third he has made so far. He isn't feeling well so we had pasta leftovers for dinner, but he made the pie yesterday.

Yesterday Sonny and Ray cleaned the hoses and installed the rebuilt membrane in the water maker, and now it is making water! GOOD water- we tasted it! At least for the moment, all systems on the boat seem to be working! It seems like Sonny, Ray, and Brad have spent most of the trip lying on their bellies across cushions in the engine room.

Today the wind has come and gone and has been from about 160-200 degrees. Since we would like to sail a course of 225 degrees, we sail when we can and motor when we can't. From midnight through mid-morning rain- squalls were all around, but we managed to miss them. This afternoon through my watch, and so far tonight winds have been 8-14 knots and we have maintained a course of 240-250 degrees. Right now we are just over 300 miles from Santa Cruz Island, our destination in The Galapagos. No luck trolling today.

Friday, November 22 - 7:05 P.M.- I spoke too soon about seasickness. Ray was feeling too poorly to cook last night, so we fended for ourselves. He said it was a touch of seasickness since the winds and seas have picked up. He didn't hurl, and he seems fine today. Sonny's stomach was a little upset too, but he blamed it on spicy food

So much for the doldrums! Winds ranged from 12-20 knots today and we have been sailing since Sonny and I came on watch at 2:00 A.M.- 17 hours and counting. We are still sailing 15-20 degrees off course but making good progress. We are sailing close-hauled in this and are heeled sharply to starboard, dipping the rail from time to time. At 6:00 P.M. we were near 2 degrees north and 88 degrees west, about 200 miles from Santa Cruz.

About 3:00 A.M. we were on watch and sailing by the autopilot. The weather was cloudy and spitting a little rain. Sonny was lying down on the starboard side, facing forward where he could see the instruments, and I was on the port side, leaning back on a cushion and facing aft. We hadn't seen another vessel for two days, and the radar was on "stand-by" to save power. I looked up and there was a small freighter directly aft, crossing our stern about two miles away. This was not a big deal, except that we hadn't seen him coming! I asked Sonny if he thought we should turn on the radar and he said, "To tell you the truth, I don't even know how to turn the damn thing on!" This morning I asked Ray to show *me* how to operate the radar! Sonny knows how to sail and to navigate but he is "old-school"; not just disinterested in technology, but resists it. I worry about him a little. He has arthritis in his knees (tries to hide it, but Ray and Richard told me) and problems with an Achilles tendon. He is 63 years old, but sometimes he moves like a very old man- very slowly and with obvious pain. Then, he has stomach problems, and trouble sleeping in his bow berth- ends up sleeping on the settee in the salon or on a cushion on the floor. Sometimes I wonder whether he is really up to making this trip. I'm glad we have Ray!

Saturday, November 23 - 8:20 P.M.- Again, so much for the doldrums! Winds have ranged from 12-20 knots for the last two days and we have sailed for the last 42 hours on the same tack. The wind also shifted a bit to about 170 degrees, so we are sailing pretty close to the course we want.

We eat most of our meals from small, half-circle shaped bowls, five or six inches in diameter. Plates are too hard to deal with, as they slide around, or food slides off them with the motion of the boat. With the bowls it is easy to hold them with one hand and eat with the other. Clean up is easy, too. Also, we eat most of our meals in the cockpit because it is usually nice up there, and because you can't get to the dining table in the salon. It still looks like a bomb went off in there, with stuff scattered everywhere and usually a body or two lying around. Brad and Sonny still have trouble sleeping in the bow because it is too bouncy so they sleep on the settee, or around the dining table, or sometimes on a cushion on the floor. We'll see if things get neater up there when Brad leaves and Naomi joins us in the Galapagos.

The sun was out today and was welcome after we had clouds all day yesterday. Since we left Panama the sea temperature has dropped from 84 degrees to 76; not a precipitous drop, but significant. It gets pretty cool at night; enough that you need a light jacket on watch.

I trolled for over two hours this morning and Richard tried for an hour or so but no strikes for three days now. I have begun to wonder if the fish just don't like this last trolling lure that we have, but the last fish I caught, *was* on this lure.

There are no slackers in this group so far. Everybody pitches in and does their share of the work- housekeeping, dishwashing, head cleaning, garbage handling, etc. Mark does more than anybody, because he likes to stay busy doing things with his hands. In port in Panama he even took it upon himself to polish the brightwork and varnish the woodwork. Also, everybody gets along very well so far. Nobody has really "buddied-up" and there have been no personality problems. The only one that has shown any kind of attitude is Sonny, and that is at least *somewhat* understandable, with all the things that have broken. Also, he has not felt well a lot of the time.

Sunday, November 24 - 6:45 P.M.- The engine overheated again about 3:00 A.M. We had sailed for 49 hours when winds became light and variable so we decided to motor. Ten minutes later it overheated. After nine hours of fruitless trouble-shooting efforts failed to solve the problem, Ray installed a new water pump and the problem was solved. First though, Sonny had Ray and Brad try to fix the old pump, even to the extent of Brad cutting a makeshift gasket from the cardboard cover of a wire-bound notebook! We had a new pump all along, and when Ray was finally allowed to install it, everything was fine. In any case, by that time the wind was blowing 16-18 knots so we resumed sailing.

57

We *just now* spotted Genovese Island, northernmost of the Galapagos, off our starboard beam, about 15 miles away! We are seeing a lot of interesting birds that I have never seen before, doing aerobatics around the boat. They are very entertaining.

I wore sweat pants and my fleece pullover on watch, as it is getting very chilly at night, even here near the equator. I understand that this is due to the Humboldt Current, flowing north along the South American coast.

Monday, November 25 - 9:55 A.M.- At 12:15 A.M. we crossed the equator! Ray and Richard were on watch, and exchanged "high-fives". The rest of us slept through it, figuring that it was dark, so we couldn't see the "dotted line" anyway!

We are nine miles off the northeast corner of Isla Santa Cruz, beating against unfavorable winds. We need to go about 25 miles around to the harbor at the town of Puerto Ayora in Academy Bay. We may or may not make it in time to clear in today. Brad is annoyed, and wants to motor because he flies out on December 1, and has limited time to see things here. Sonny thinks motoring into the wind and chop would not be effective.

About an hour ago I was finishing my morning visit to the head when I smelled something burning. I was coming out anyway, when Sonny yelled "Get out; we need to get in there!" I met him and Ray in the passageway by my bunk, and they went in through the bulkhead and shut down the refrigerator. The belt had burned out. We have no replacement, so we are without refrigeration again. Hopefully, we can find a replacement belt on the island. Things continue to break. Richard and I have both wondered what the hell Sonny and Mark were working on all summer!

The temperature this morning is probably in the mid-70's. It is cloudy, and downright cool! On our night watch Sonny wore a shirt, a sweatshirt, and two jackets. I was dressed the same as last night. The sea temperature is now 74 degrees.

7 – THE GALAPAGOS

Monday, November 25 - 11:15 P.M.- We are in the Galapagos! We dropped anchor in Academy Bay, at Puerto Ayora on Isla Santa Cruz at 3:00 P.M. local time. We fought against headwinds until the last hour; hence the arrival later than expected. Sonny and Ray went ashore and cleared us in; then about 6:00 we all went ashore except for Ray, who wanted some time to himself. We went and met Sonny's daughters Naomi and Alexis, and said hello to his wife Jane; then went for dinner and drinks. We went to another place for ice cream after dinner, and then to a disco; a very lively place that played mostly rap music but was interesting nonetheless. The crowd was a good mix of locals and tourists and it was a great place for "people watching", which made up for the crappy, annoying music.

The island of Santa Cruz has a maximum elevation of roughly 2,500 feet and what we have seen so far looks a little barren. We are looking forward to seeing what is here.

Tuesday, November 26 - 5:30 P.M.- Today has been a day of getting things done and seeing what's here. I took laundry in this morning and it was ready by 4:00 P.M. The lady only charges $1.00 per kilo to wash, dry, and fold, so mine cost $6.00. As in Panama, the U.S. dollar is the official currency here. I also went to the bank to cash traveler's checks, and to the post office, after which I went to the Moonrise Travel Agency and got some information about local activities. We ended up arranging a horseback tour in the mountains for tomorrow, to see the giant tortoises, and a day tour to Bartolome Island for Thursday. I got information about a two-day trip to Isabella Island, and Richard and I may decide to do that as well. Except for Sonny, the others seem to follow my lead in doing things. It's not that they aren't interested, but are just waiting for somebody to get them started. Richard will take *some* initiative but even he seems to prefer following instead of coming up with ideas.

We broke another shear pin on the dinghy outboard yesterday afternoon, so we got started using the local water taxis. They charge

40 cents to take you ashore or bring you back to the boat. They are constantly going back and forth, from early morning to midnight and you just have to wave, whistle, or yell to get their attention and they will come and get you. The government encourages their use by requiring that everyone wear life jackets in private dinghies. That way, you would either have to carry the life jackets around all the time you are ashore, or risk having them stolen if they were left in the dinghy. It is easier to just pay the 40 cents, even though our dinghy is now working again.

Sonny ordered a new battery for the satellite telephone, so now we are in the familiar position of waiting for a delivery. The Thanksgiving weekend will mean that it probably won't be shipped until Monday so it is unlikely that we will sail before Thursday, the 5th.

Another issue here is showers. We can't use the water maker in the harbor because there are lots of boats anchored here, and we are concerned that any hint of oil in the water will clog the membrane again. That being the case, it will be necessary for us to find somewhere to shower ashore. Sonny said that we could use his hotel room but his wife and two daughters are there, so it would be awkward. Their room is small, with four single beds side-by-side, reminiscent of a college dormitory or army barracks. There is a hotel that lets you pay for showers, so we will probably do that.

10:10 P.M.- Tonight I had what just might be the best Pina Colada I ever had. It was at a place called Café Habana, which is owned and operated by a guy from Havana, Cuba who is also the head bartender. I watched him work for a while last night, and again tonight. You don't normally think of a bartender as an artist but if there is such a thing, this guy is it. He is in the process of training two young bartenders, a male and a female, and it is interesting to watch. He is very precise, and is slow and patient with them; shows them, and then has them do it themselves. He obviously takes great pride in his work and I admire that, regardless of the occupation.

Tonight, while walking along the waterfront on Avenida Charles Darwin, I stopped to appreciate where I am and what I am doing. People were walking, or sitting and talking and couples were sitting on benches beside the street, and I wished that Maureen was here.

Wednesday, November 27 - 10:30 P.M.- Today was a very full and outstanding day! This morning Richard, Ray, Mark, Brad and I went horseback riding in the highlands, to an area where the giant land tortoises live and they were *very* impressive. We invited Naomi to go with us but she declined. The horses were very well trained and our guide, Segundo, was excellent. He spoke no English but I was able to communicate with him pretty well in Spanish. The tortoises were amazing- looked a lot like gopher turtles but I saw no signs of burrowing- and they are *huge*. Segundo estimated that one was about 150 years old and weighed 250 kilos, or about 550 pounds. We also saw two *Vermillion flycatchers*, a bird that Richard said is found nowhere in the world but here.

From the tortoise area we rode the horses to a lava tube. It is a lava tunnel 300 meters long with steps down into the hole at each end, a few lights inside, and a little gravel on the floor but no other improvements. At the far end was a short section where the roof was only about two feet high. There was a small ladder about ten feet long, horizontal on the floor, and you crawled along it (the floor was wet and muddy there) to a section where the roof rose to about four feet. It was not a place for anyone who is claustrophobic, but is very interesting! Shortly after that you could stand up. It drizzled rain on and off throughout the ride but it wasn't bad, and everybody said that they had a great time. Ray had expressed some apprehensions initially, making some vague references to a fear of horses, and previous bad experiences but he went anyway, and said that he thoroughly enjoyed it. Some people go through life allowing fear to stop them in their tracks while others are afraid, but do things anyway. I think the second group gets a lot more out of life than the first.

After lunch, Brad, Richard, and I hiked to Bahia Tortuga, about two miles one-way, and then about a mile up a gorgeous beach. We saw lots of iguanas, some blue-footed boobies, and two seals playing in the surf. Another fantastic outing!

Tonight I again had trouble making phone calls. I *still* can't figure out how to use my A.T. & T. prepaid card, and the phones at the telephone company office didn't work either. They kept cutting off the connection as soon as the phone was answered on the receiving end. I finally had to end up calling collect, and by then I needed to go to the bathroom *really* bad so I had to make the call very short- a bad ending to an otherwise great day, and I lost a pair of underwear in the process!

Thursday, November 28   Thanksgiving, and Molly's Birthday! 10:00 P.M.- Today Brad, Mark and I took a day trip to Isla Bartolome, northwest of Santa Cruz. It cost $63.00, including breakfast and lunch. We had to go ashore and be on the dock at 5:30 A.M. A bus picked us up and took us across to the north side of Santa Cruz where we boarded a 40-foot wooden powerboat. The bus ride was 30-40 minutes and the boat ride was three hours each way. On the way, we passed a small island where we went in close and saw masked boobies nesting in the cliffs; our only opportunity to see that particular species. At Bartolome we saw sea lions, blue-footed boobies, marine iguanas, sea turtles, frigate birds, and small penguins about two feet long! Bartolome is a small, totally volcanic island composed of both heavy and light lava and ash, just off the northeast coast of the much larger Isla Santiago. There is a trail with 680 steps leading to the top of the cone, and the views from there are spectacular! There are some "secondary craters", including one that is clearly visible under water as you look down from the summit. I got to go snorkeling for about 30 minutes, and saw lots of neat tropical fish; especially the parrotfish, which were many different, pretty, pastel colors. I also saw two sea lions, one of which swam right at me, passing directly under me so close I could have touched it. I snorkeled around the base of a black, pointed needle-like rock that rose about 200 feet straight up out of the sea and it was overwhelming to look up at it from the water. Neither Mark nor Brad went in the water. On the return bus ride we stopped at "twin craters"; two large volcano craters up in the highlands, one on each side of the highway, and connected by a lava tube.

Ray said that Sonny had a guy come today and take the water maker pump and membrane, to rebuild, clean, etc. Hopefully this will solve that problem for good!

Naomi still has not set foot on the boat, to check out her living area or anything and you have to wonder why. I can't help but wonder if she really wants to do this, or has any idea what she is getting into! When she sees her living quarters for the next few months she may experience culture shock!

Friday, November 29 - Midnight- I had a very difficult telephone conversation with Maureen this afternoon. I'm sure it is not her intent but sometimes she makes it hard for me to fully enjoy what I am doing. I don't want many more conversations like that. Life is too short.

Today was a day of getting things done. I straightened up my living area on the boat, shopped, wrote post cards, did e-mail, and just rested a little after two very active days. Naomi finally came to the boat today and didn't seem overwhelmed; however I asked whether she has had much experience sailing monohulls and she said that she has never set foot on one before. Then, she asked if it heels much! Yes, she seems a little naïve.

Tonight we had a really good time. Brad, Richard and I went ashore for dinner, and then to a place called "La Taberna del Duende". It is a tiny house on a gravel back street, up the hillside, that has been turned into a bistro. We had been told that they had good live music on weekends, and they did. Two guys played acoustic guitars and sang in Spanish, and they were fantastic! One played lead and the other rhythm and they were totally together. They played some classical guitar, some Spanish guitar, and some just all-around good music. The guy who played rhythm is really an excellent singer. They didn't get started until 10:30 and we had to leave just after 11:30 because the water taxis stop running at midnight. We plan to go back tomorrow night and bring the dinghy so we can stay later.

Saturday, November 30 - 11:20 P.M.- After dinner tonight we went back to La Taberna del Duende, but it was disappointing. The musicians were there but we were the only customers so they were not playing. We waited until just before 11:00, and then gave up and left.

We went to Angermeyer Point for Brad's going away dinner- his choice. It was good, both food and ambience, but overpriced. We ate outdoors, and noticed the first mosquitoes of the trip.

Today was not really a bad day, just not a good day, with lots of semi-negative vibes in the air. Brad leaves tomorrow, as do Jane and Alexis, and Sonny and Naomi will move aboard Monday. The telephone battery has supposedly been shipped and should arrive Monday so we will probably sail Wednesday. All of us have some concerns about Naomi, and this next leg to Easter Island is long so we'll see what she is made of!

I checked my e-mail today but had nothing from Maureen so I sent one to her. Her attitude and thought processes get to me sometimes. Then I see couples together sitting along the waterfront, walking along holding hands, or just looking at each other and I feel really lonely.

Tomorrow Richard and I go on a day trip to two small islands off the eastern shore of Santa Cruz.

Sunday, December 1 - 9:25 P.M.- Today was a good day. Richard and I took a day tour to the Plaza islands and Seymour Island, all just a short distance off the coast of Santa Cruz. We took a bus to the north side of Santa Cruz at 7:30 A.M. and returned at 6:30 P.M. We took a boat from the north side; a 35-40 foot wooden power boat that looked a lot like the "Minnow" on "Gilligan's Island"! We went ashore with a guide at South Plaza Island, in a group of 14 people. We saw *lots* of sea lions, land iguanas, swallowtail gulls, etc. There are no large predators here so these critters have no fear of humans. You have to be careful not to step on them! A large yellow male land iguana decided to walk in my direction and when I didn't move, he walked right across my feet! The south side of the island has cliffs about 50 or 60 feet above the ocean, and the sea lions make their way up there to lie in the sun. We saw one make the descent back to the water, and it was amazing how it climbed down the rocks on his belly. I scarcely could have climbed down his route using hands and feet.

Seymour Island is nesting ground for the blue-footed booby and the frigate bird. Nesting season for the frigates peaked a month ago but we still saw a few of the males with the red pouches under their beaks inflated to attract females. Here too, you could walk right up to these birds. We were not allowed to leave the trail so I didn't get close-up pictures of the frigate birds with the pouches, but young blue-footed boobies were everywhere, including underfoot.

When we finished visiting South Plaza Island we went snorkeling off North Plaza. Not much there in the way of fish life but we did see an Angelfish that I had not seen before. It was a lot like the Queen Angel but instead of the "crown", it had a gold streak from just above the eyes, back to the dorsal area and had white vertical bars down each side just behind the gills. The highlight of snorkeling was that the sea lions were swimming with us. They would swim toward you, roll over on their backs, and swim under you while looking up at you, just beyond your reach. I stuck my fin out to one and it approached as if it was going to bite it, but didn't. Being in the water with them playing around you was indescribable.

When we got up this morning we discovered that the main anchor was dragging and we were getting close to another boat, so we had to first, take in the stern anchor; then the main anchor, and then move and re-anchor. A pain in the ass, but necessary.

I didn't call Maureen again today and didn't check e-mail. I just didn't feel like any more negative bullshit, and besides, I was busy. Tomorrow Sonny and Naomi move aboard, and that will be interesting. It will probably work out O.K. but I have some misgivings at this point.

Monday, December 2 - 5:05 P.M.- Sonny, Ray, Naomi and Mark took the boat out for a couple of hours today to test the water maker and it appears to be working as it is supposed to. It made three gallons of good water in an hour. Hopefully that issue is now resolved but we will still bring all he water we can, just in case. We will have 100 gallons in the tank and 40 more in jerry jugs lashed to the deck. Richard and I will help load water tomorrow morning. We still need to take on diesel and shop for provisions. I had my laundry done again today as I didn't' want to wait until the last day, in case something went wrong. This next passage will be 16-20 days so I expect to use it all. I also finished shopping, wrote post cards, and did e-mail so I, personally, am ready. The phone battery still has not arrived but we are still planning to leave Wednesday.

We all have misgivings about Naomi. Yesterday Ray was taking her and Sonny ashore in the dinghy and he said she was "jittery", and wouldn't sit on the side of the inflatable. When he asked her to sit up on the side and relax, she said, "I don't want to fall in!"

Tuesday, December 3 - Today was an interesting day. We spent the morning filling the water tank by hauling 155 gallons from the local water company, Agua Galapagos, in 12 five-gallon jugs. We took a water taxi to the dock; then a pick-up truck taxi to Agua Galapagos, filled the jugs, and then reversed the process. Ray, Richard and I did the hauling and it took three trips. Mark waited on the boat for the garbage boat to come by- they take your garbage away for a dollar a bag. Then Sonny, Ray and Naomi managed to borrow five ten-gallon jugs to haul diesel, and brought the first 50 gallons on board. Then Mark and I went with Ray on a second diesel run. It was the same process as with hauling water except that the jugs were twice as heavy. Lifting them from the water taxi on to our boat was difficult and tricky, with swells rolling in- this bay opens to the south, where prevailing winds and seas come from. Anyway, after we got the diesel jugs on board Ray and Mark started pouring it into the tank. As they finished pouring the first ten gallons into the tank it welled up and ran over a little. Just then I heard Ray shouting "FUCK, FUCK, FUCK!" as he discovered that they had poured it into the water tank. Not a good thing, to say the least but I thought Sonny took it well, considering his previous displays of emotion. He didn't even yell or curse at Ray. The water fill and diesel fill are both at midship on the starboard side of the deck and look similar, but are clearly marked "water" and "diesel". The only explanation is that they just made a mistake; those things happen! Fortunately, the water tank access in the cabin has a removable plate about a foot square on the top. Richard and I helped Ray as first he dipped out the diesel that was floating on top, and put it into a jug. Then we dipped out bucket by bucket, the rest of the 100 gallons. First we used a large coffee can, which Ray would sink straight down, dipping out the surface film that had some diesel residue. Then we used a manual bilge pump to get the rest of the water out. We added some detergent to break up any remaining diesel in each bucket, and dumped it down the sink into the sea. After that process was completed, Ray sponged out all of the tank that he could physically reach, and then flushed it and the filler hose with detergent water. Ray accepted full responsibility for this incident, and feels really bad about it. Now, we will repeat the water hauling process tomorrow. What a pain in the ass!

The phone battery still has not arrived, but we are still planning to leave tomorrow, although it looks more like Thursday to me. Nobody has been shopping for provisions yet, so that is still to be done. So far Naomi has a very good attitude and does everything she can to be helpful.

Wednesday, December 4 - 8:30 P.M.- No battery delivery today but Sonny went to our agent and paid a $139 customs charge, so it should arrive tomorrow. Now it looks like it may be Friday before we sail and nobody has yet done any shopping for provisions. I forgot to mention that if visiting boats are to transact any business while they are here, they are required to retain the services of an "agent". If you don't know one, the customs and immigration people will find one for you. I don't recall how much Sonny paid as a retainer for the agent, but I think it was $100. Anyway, it seems like a scam to me.

We made two water runs this morning to re-fill the tank and the water situation seems to be in hand. You can still detect a slight diesel smell but I think it is O.K. We will probably use another tank full for showers and dishwashing before we start drinking it.

A local form of volleyball is very popular, though it is played a little differently here. There are two courts next to the harbor, and play seems to start around four o'clock every afternoon. There appear to be two leagues, because the level of play on one court seems to be better than the other. They play in three man teams and play the same position all the time, with no rotation. The net is about 10 feet high, so there is no spiking. They do set-ups with a motion that would be called "lifting" in the U.S., almost catching the ball. The players are very athletic, and take the games seriously. A good number of people gather to watch the games, and money has been seen changing hands. Very interesting!

66

Thursday, December 5 - 8:20 P.M.- No battery delivery again today. Now the promise is tomorrow afternoon for sure, so we are planning to leave early Saturday morning. We made yet another water run this morning, and provision shopping was done this afternoon, so we are ready. I just took a shower and I have to admit that it still smells like diesel a little. It will be a while before we drink water from the tank. Staying longer than expected here, plus the tours I took has caused me to overspend my budget a little but I won't be taking this kind of tours anywhere else, so I think I am O.K. We have been taking most of our meals on the boat the last few days.

This afternoon I went with Ray and Mark to a place called "the canyon". Ray found out about it from a lady he has met here. To get there you go by water to Angermeyer Point, at the southwest entrance to Academy Bay, and then hike about 20 minutes. The first half is over a developed trail of crushed lava rock and the second half is over a marked but undeveloped trail over very rough lava rock- tough going, but well worth the effort. The canyon is no more than 15 feet wide and drops about 30 or 40 feet down to the water. Some stairs lead down about 15 or 20 feet and then you climb the rest of the way over large rocks. The water is crystal clear, and about 30-35 feet deep. The water in the canyon is connected to the ocean by an underwater tunnel and the canyon is about 200 yards long, broken into three sections by rocks. There are a few fish, but the attraction is the rock structures above and below the water. Ray and I snorkeled there for about half an hour, and Mark took pictures. Naomi is a certified diver, so we invited her to go with us but she wasn't interested. We have also invited her to go on some of the tours, but again, no interest. She doesn't stray from Sonny's side. It's almost like she is doing this to take care of him.

Maureen continues to have a difficult time, and it really detracts from my moods. She still has trouble being alone and dealing with Molly without me, and she seems jealous of me being here.

Friday, December 6 - 10:00 A.M.- We made the "final" water run this morning, topping off the tank one last time getting ready to leave early tomorrow. Sonny and Naomi are ashore now, finishing the provisioning. We have the perception that they are trying to go cheap with the provisions, and complained yesterday because they didn't get any soft drinks- cokes, 7-ups, etc. Sonny complained about the prices here but we are unsympathetic, as Richard, Mark and I contributed a total of $45,000 toward the expenses of this trip. It seems that Naomi is even cheaper than Sonny! Sonny said that he thought we were stocking up in Panama with enough to last until we reach Puerto Montt, and we reminded him that there is a physical limit to how much we can carry. He did point out correctly, that we have employed no discipline in our rate of consumption. He is right in that if you want a supply to last you have to manage your rate of consumption. The problem there is that it doesn't work unless everybody does it.

7:55 P.M.- Well, we finished our departure preparations, and then– the battery didn't come again! Now they are saying it will be here at noon tomorrow and if that happens we will leave in the afternoon. We have deflated and stored the dinghy and outboard, and Sonny has cleared us out through customs and immigration.

The web site for this voyage is finally up, but from what I hear from Ray it leaves a lot to be desired. It only mentions Sonny and Naomi in connection with the voyage, and is nowhere near up to date- not even anything about Panama. It is a half-assed job at best. Ray is hurt and angry over being left out, especially with him being the First Mate. I personally don't give a crap but when they told us there would be a web site for our families and friends to follow the voyage, they created expectations. Over this and other issues, Ray blew up at Sonny tonight in front of everybody. He said some things that needed saying but he let his emotions get away from him, and lost some effectiveness. The "F" word was flying around a lot and I think it's fair to say that Ray did a lot of yelling. I only made a couple of comments that I felt were necessary and appropriate but for the most part I kept my mouth shut and stayed out of it. I *did* say "We really need for the two of you to get along". I think this trip will be tough enough without the Captain and the First Mate fighting. To his credit, Sonny kept his cool and didn't escalate things. Hopefully, it will all blow over. My three *primary* objectives for this trip are The Galapagos, Easter Island, and Cape Horn, and I can put up with a lot of crap if necessary, to meet those objectives but when I have something to say, I will say it.

The water taxis are a critical and interesting part of the scene here in Puerto Ayora. They are about 15 feet long and powered by outboards, and operate from 6:00 A.M. until midnight. They are open except for the forward three feet at the bow, and each has a blue bimini roof. Most are painted yellow, and most but not all, have pointed bows. Old tires are fitted around the bow as bumpers, and attached to the enclosed part of the bow is a U-shaped handrail about three feet high and two feet in length, running fore and aft. This rail is used for support and balance when people are getting on and off the boat. The operator gently runs the bow into the dock or the larger boat that people are getting on or off of, and holds it there by keeping the outboard in gear and revved a little. Sometimes some pretty good-sized swells come into the anchorage and it is a little tricky getting from your boat onto the taxi, or vice-versa but the operators do a really good job. Some taxis have two handrails and most but not all, have stabilizer braces in the handrails about half way up.

I had a really good conversation with Maureen this afternoon. That will send me on this passage with a positive feeling.

8 – TO THE EDGE OF THE WORLD

Saturday, December 7 - 4:55 P.M.- We weighed anchor in Academy Bay at 1:00 P.M. and put up sails at 1:45, bound for Easter Island. We have a rhumb line course of 215 degrees, but the wind is from the south so we are heading 230 to 250 degrees as the wind shifts. It is rainy and cold, surprisingly cold for this latitude, just a few degrees south of the equator. We are experiencing first hand, the effects of the Humboldt Current. I started trolling about 2:15 and within ten minutes I lost my new eleven-dollar lure! I got a strike and the fish was taking a little line, in spurts. We were under sail and couldn't stop the boat easily. I should have let it continue as long as it was only taking a little line, to see if it would tire but I prematurely clamped down on the drag and a new snap swivel broke. It really pissed me off! It was partly my fault as I made a mistake, but the snap swivel should not have broken! I still have one decent lure, so I will try again.

The boat problems continue. Two hours after we sailed the water maker quit making fresh water! The pump works and the membrane works; seawater goes in, but no fresh water comes out. Everything goes into the drain tube, and it is salty. So far Sonny and Ray have been unable to figure out what is wrong. As it is, we have 65 gallons in the tank for washing and 55 in jugs for drinking and cooking. Unless they can solve the problem, that will have to last for 15-20 days.

Naomi and I will have the six to ten o'clock watches on this passage. Sonny asked me to take watches with her because I have more sailing experience than Mark or Richard and she has far less than either he or Ray.

Sunday, December 8 - 10:30 A.M.- When I went on watch at 6:00 A.M. we had left the Galapagos behind and it was an interesting feeling to know that we will not see land again for more than two weeks. We will probably not even see any other ships as we are going farther and farther off the beaten path. That is pretty exciting stuff to me, and a significant part of the adventure.

Last night and this morning were both easy watches with steady winds ranging from 8 to 16 knots and swells ranging 2 to 10 feet. The sea temperature is 73 degrees and the air is downright cool so I wore my fleece pullover on both watches. We have wind from 170-180 degrees and we want to sail a course of 215, so we are having to sail about 20 degrees off our course but that's not a big deal. Once we clear the doldrums, at about 5-7 degrees south latitude we will pick up the trade winds from the east, and sail directly to Easter Island. Right now we are about 1 degree, 30 minutes south latitude and 91 degrees, 3 minutes west longitude, or 1,835 miles from Easter Island. Naomi stands watch about like her dad- lies over on the side of the cockpit on some cushions and doesn't do anything. Through two watches she has yet to sit at the helm. She got seasick and aarfed once last night, but otherwise everybody is O.K. so far.

3:35 P.M.- The water maker started working again last night, and this morning we had more water than we did yesterday; however it has now stopped again! When it started, we had tacked and were on a starboard tack and it quit after we were back on a port tack. Coincidence? We don't know. The wind has shifted in our favor and we are now sailing the course we want.

Monday, December 9 - 3:45 P.M.- We had really great sailing on the morning watch, with southeast winds of 14-20 knots with swells running mostly 8-10 feet. It continues to be mostly cloudy and amazingly cool, and we are heeled pretty far to starboard, but other than that there is nothing to complain about. Shortly after beginning our watch last night I had the pleasure of watching Naomi puke into a bucket and daintily dump it over the side. She has been seasick since Saturday night and has not eaten anything since Saturday afternoon. She said that she slept a little last night between 2:00 and 3:00 A.M. She has only aarfed twice that I know of, but it's easy to see that she feels *really* bad.

Last night she did finally spend a little time at the helm. I was at the helm and she said, "You really like to sit in that chair, don't you?"

I said "Not especially, but I think *somebody* needs to be up here." After that, she volunteered to take her turns at the helm and almost immediately confirmed my opinion that she doesn't know what the hell she is doing, twice in steering and once when we tacked. She had trouble steering a compass course using the autopilot and wind indicator, and also with coming about. She unintentionally allowed the bow to pass through the wind direction, causing us to come about when we didn't want to. Then when we tacked I had trouble pulling in the jib on the new tack. When I looked up, there she was, holding on

71

for dear life to the jib sheet on the other side! I will probably never find out but I would really like to know the real reason she is out here.

We have discovered that the water maker doesn't work when the boat is sharply heeled, but will work fine when the boat is more or less level. The starboard side of the boat is much more heavily loaded than the port side, with the generator diesel on that side, and the water and fuel tank configurations. It lists to starboard even when we are at anchor in calm water. That being the case, when we are on a starboard tack the boat is relatively level but when we are on a port tack, it heels *way* over, hence the problem. With prevailing winds, we expect to be on a port tack pretty much all the way to Easter Island. We are dealing with the problem by reducing sail until the heeling abates, and making water for two or three hours. That, of course, slows us down to a speed of about two knots and costs us 10-15 miles a day. This will delay our arrival at Easter Island by about a day if it continues. So far we haven't found any other solution.

We are now near 3 degrees south latitude and 93 degrees west longitude, just over 1,700 miles from Easter Island- getting closer all the time!

Tuesday, December 10 - 4:40 P.M.- I am getting a new watch partner. Mark will be joining me on the 6:00-10:00 watches and Naomi will join Sonny on the 2:00-6:00 watches. It seems that Mark casually mentioned that he was having some trouble staying awake on the 2:00-6:00 night watch because it was new to him. He said that Naomi jumped on that right away and suggested that they trade watches. I personally am very happy, because she really doesn't know how to sail, and if she has a personality I have seen no evidence of it. Besides, I enjoy talking to Mark. I am now recognized as the Watch Captain on my watch.

Naomi showed her naivety again around nine o'clock last night, when a small freighter crossed about a mile ahead of us- we're seeing more ships out here than I expected. The autopilot had stopped working and I was at the helm steering manually when I first saw the lights off the starboard beam. I watched for about five minutes and saw a red running light, meaning they were going the same direction we were and on what appeared to be a converging course. The radar wasn't on (again!), so I asked her to turn it on. She didn't know how, so I told her. The radar showed the ship to be about two miles out. As we converged I had her watch the radar as I steered and watched visually. It appeared that they would pass in front of us but I altered course ten degrees to starboard to make sure. When I did that, Naomi said, "I believe we have the right-of-way."

I replied, "Yes, we do, in fact have the right-of-way; however we can't assume first, that he is awake and paying attention enough to know that we are even here; or second, since it is dark, that he has any clue that we are a sailboat and therefore have the right-of-way; or third, if he does, that he gives a crap. We have found that big ships generally don't alter course for small boats."

The autopilot, by the way, is the latest thing to go wrong on the boat. When you engage it, it works for a minute or two and then gives a message "stopped-drive". Ray and Sonny have so far been unable to find a solution so we are steering manually. That is not a big deal; just an inconvenience.

This afternoon I was trolling while we were going slowly to make water. I got a strike but the rod bent only a couple of times, and no more. When I reeled in I found that the fish had eaten through a heavy monofilament leader. I had caught a couple of fish on that lure so the leader was probably frayed; in fact, the part that I pulled in had a couple of frayed spots. In any case, that was my last good lure- now I will have to improvise.

About the second night out of Mobile we were all sitting around talking when the conversation drifted onto the subject of religious beliefs, and Sonny was emphatic in stating that he doesn't believe that there is a God. Ever since that, the boat has had one problem after another! *Coincidence?*

Wednesday, December 11 - 4:40 P.M.- Here's today's fuck-up: (Seems we get a new one every day) Sonny said that Jane got the phone bill and the satellite phone calls are *not* $1.00 a minute, as we were told, but $3.00 a minute! First we were told $1.50, then $1.00, and now $3.00. This seems like something that could have been determined before we sailed! I hate to say it but I'm having a hard time avoiding the conclusion that these people are stupid!

When Mark and I came on watch at 6:00 this morning both Parkers were lying down, one on either side of the cockpit. Both were awake but nobody was steering, monitoring instruments, checking the horizon, etc. The wind was on the port beam at 12-13 knots and the sails were balanced with the main and jib sheets *very* loose. The boat was sailing a straight course, but was bobbing along at 2.5-3 knots. Sonny left it that way and went to bed. I incrementally sheeted in both sails, doing it gradually to maintain balance, and soon had us sailing at a speed of over five knots. I am convinced that he was doing that so neither of them would have to do anything on watch!

73

At the end of our morning watch we were 1,499 miles from Easter Island. This morning was the best sailing we have had yet; trade wind sailing with east-southeast winds that built to 16-18knots and bright sunshine to go with it. I thought all that was worth a picture so I asked Ray to take one; then everybody thought that was a good idea so he, Mark, and Richard all had pictures taken at the helm. Sonny and Naomi were asleep- he on the floor of the salon and she on the starboard seat of the dining table.

Ray has discovered that the hydraulic pump on the autopilot has died so we will be steering manually until we get a replacement, probably in Puerto Montt. That is no problem from my perspective, as I like to steer.

We have slowed down to make water again. Coincidentally, this was on Sonny and Naomi's afternoon watch. The jib is rolled up and we are bobbing along at 2-3 knots.

Thursday, December 12 - 10:30 A.M.- 141 miles! That's how far we came in 24 hours, and that's even with four hours at 2.5-3 knots while we made water. Otherwise, we would have topped 150. We are near 8 degrees south and 96 degrees west, 1,350 miles from Easter Island. Winds are just south of due east, ranging from 10-22 knots and swells of 3-10 feet- trade wind sailing at it's best. Ray, Richard, Mark and I all have the presence of mind to fully understand, enjoy, and appreciate where we are and what we are doing while it is happening. As far as we can tell, neither Sonny nor Naomi shows any signs of having fun.

Yesterday's weather was sunny all day and last night was clear, with a beautiful, bright half moon and lots of stars that looked close enough to touch.

Today it is cloudy and cool again. The sea temperature is now 72 degrees and I wore my fleece pullover on morning watch. Sonny and Naomi seem close to freezing- wear lots of clothes; two big coats each, shoes and socks, and still complain of being cold. I wonder what they will do when it *really* gets cold.

Friday, December 13 - 10:30 A.M.- THE FISH: Yesterday afternoon around 2:30 I caught a *really* big dolphin! We had slowed to make water and I was trolling off the starboard side with a lure that I had improvised. I took two of my largest hooks and ran the point of the first through the eye of the second to make a trailer hook rig. Then I ran the eye of the first through an orange rubber skirt that I had bought for $2.00 in Puerto Ayora, and hooked it to a snap swivel with a half-ounce egg sinker sliding on the leader just ahead of it. I saw the rod bend with the strike and by the time I picked it up from the holder the fish was about 40 yards out and trying to run off to the port side. I managed to turn him and he started to swim in the same direction we were going while still trying to head off to port. I took in some line and first saw him when he was about 20 yards off the port side and even with the stern. I could see that it was a big fish but still didn't know what it was. By then, Richard, Ray and Mark were all on the stern watching. Naomi was sitting at the helm, not steering, but reading a book and Sonny was below doing something. I asked somebody to get a camera and Mark went and got his.

The fish was trying to pass the boat and I couldn't follow him around because of the structure on the stern for the dinghy davits and wind generator so I leaned out and used enough pressure to lead him toward the boat. When he was about 10 yards off I saw the pug-dog face and unbelievable iridescent blue and yellow colors of a big bull dolphin, with his magnificent dorsal fin running almost to his eyes. The sun was shining brightly, maximizing the reflection of the colors. I asked Mark to take a picture of the fish in the water in case I didn't land him, and he did.

I slowly managed the fish across the stern, at which time he made another run, thrashing beautifully about 15 yards out, now off the starboard side. None of us had ever seen a dolphin in the water like this and the guys were amazed at the beauty of this fish. After that run he was tired and I brought him alongside. He was a good four feet long and too heavy to lift with the rod. I used the rod to lift his head and Richard got the gaff under his gills and lifted him out of the water; however Richard was leaning out and didn't have the strength or leverage to lift him over the lifelines. Before Richard could re-position himself the fish flopped a couple of times and escaped the gaff; then when he hit the water my snap swivel broke, and he was gone! I have lost big fish before but oddly enough, this time I didn't feel a sense of loss, but almost a sense of relief.

I later talked with the guys about it and though any one of us would have gladly killed and eaten that fish, every one of us was privately, and later openly glad he got away. *He was such an unbelievably magnificent fish!* So you see, I consider myself as having caught that fish and God as having released him. That was probably my greatest fishing experience ever. Through all this I don't think Naomi even looked up from her book, and Sonny stayed below.

5:00 P.M.- When we slowed to make water this afternoon Richard checked the tank and found that we used more than we made yesterday.

Sonny started bitching about where the water was being used and said for about the 20th time how he can take a shower with half a gallon of water. I was tired of hearing it so I said, "Not all of us are as efficient as you Sonny, but we do the best we can. We know how you can take a shower in half a gallon, but some of us just aren't that good." I then walked to my bunk, sat down, and started writing.

He knew that I was pissed, and he walked down and said apologetically "Don't get mad at me Charley. I'm just trying to figure out where the water is going."

In the interest of minimizing water use I wash with a washcloth one day and shower the next and when I do shower I don't think I use as much as a gallon. Richard says he does the same. I'm not sure about the others.

We're still having great sailing conditions, and covered 126 miles in 24 hours this time. Weather is still cool and mostly cloudy, with some sun in the afternoon. Naomi is still not well, not eating anything substantial, but no more aarfing.

I am getting some water on the left side of the top shelf of my hanging locker. Only two towels got wet so far. I am moving things around, putting things up there that can survive moisture, like tooth paste, sunscreen, etc. I think the water is coming in around a stanchion, and will try to caulk it.

Saturday, December 14 - 4:40 P.M.- We did an accidental jibe this afternoon. Sonny and Naomi were on watch and nobody was steering. In itself, it was not a big deal as we had rolled up the jib and were going slow as we made water. The wind was only about 12 knots, and no damage was done. The issues are, first, the way they stand watch with nobody at the helm or paying attention to what's going on even though we are steering manually. That sort of thing can get you into trouble! Second, of equal or greater concern is that Sonny doesn't seem "to have his head in the game". He shows little interest and no enthusiasm, and just doesn't seem to have a grasp of things. Sometimes he acts like he doesn't know what the hell he is doing, and doesn't care. Then there's that continuing cough of his! He sounds like Doc Holiday in those old Wyatt Earp movies - hacks like he is dying! Ray is worried and talking about finding a way to bail out at Puerto Montt. Then there is the mystery of why Naomi is here!

I unpacked my bag of winter clothes today and put them on shelves, in Ziploc bags to keep out the moisture. We have had periods of light and variable winds mixed with good winds, so made only 116 miles the last 24 hours. Good sunshine today!

Sunday, December 15 - 4:40 P.M.- Less than 1,000 miles to Easter Island! We were at 997 at the end of my watch. We should reach the halfway point- 960 miles - later today. We are getting a little light rain and variable winds, sometimes making good progress and sometimes very little. Naomi is feeling better now- actually talks a little, and cooked a dinner of sloppy joes and roast potatoes tonight.

Sonny pissed me off again this morning. I asked to use the satellite phone and he said no. He said I could wait until we slowed to make water; the theory being that there will be no spray at that time to get the phone wet. I have only used the phone three times, all in a sheltered corner of the cockpit, and I explained this to him, but to no avail. He is concerned because he found corrosion on the battery contact. I pointed out that we are on a boat, and that sort of thing happens in this environment but he didn't listen. I told him "This is just too hard", and to forget it.

I am enjoying my new role as Watch Captain and Mark is a very good watch partner. He and I alternate hours at the helm and take turns making tea or coffee. He is comfortable steering, has good presence of mind, and the best watchful eye on the boat. I trim the sails as I see fit, alter course to accommodate wind shifts, and monitor the radar and instruments.

Today was also shower day and since we are about half way, I am changing my sheets and towels. Everything is clean and fresh, including me.

Monday, December 16 - 11:25 A.M.- This morning when Mark and I went on watch Sonny and Naomi were bundled up like Eskimos. The temperature was probably in the upper 60's. Mark and I were barefoot and I had on shorts. They commented that we were going to be cold, but we never were. Naomi said that she had on three pairs of pants! I asked, "What are you guys going to do when we get down where it's *really* cold?"

She said, "I will put on my long underwear".

I always heard that *Floridians* could freeze to death at room temperature, but these people take the cake! They act like they are miserably cold and if they are that cold *here* I'm not sure they can make it around Cape Horn. The wind does feel cool, but a t-shirt and sweat shirt keep me plenty warm.

We are into our third day of unreliable winds, here in the middle of the "trade wind belt"! Sometimes the wind blows fine, and then it will drop to five knots or so and shift around from all directions. We have actually had to motor for a few hours, but are sailing again now.

Tuesday, December 17 - 4:45 P.M.- Last night's sunset was nothing short of spectacular; the best one of the trip so far. The sun dropped below the horizon at 7:09 P.M. and the show continued for over an hour with lots of colors, dominated by orange ranging from burnt orange to peach, and on to pale yellow, with shades of blue, some gray, and a hint of green. There were quite a few small clouds along the horizon and just above it. They took many shapes, and you could let your imagination run wild.

Today is the prettiest day yet. The sunrise was behind some clouds but ever since, it has been magnificent. Last night in the first hour of our watch the winds settled at 10-14 knots over the port beam and stayed there until half an hour ago when they died, and we started motoring. I decided to put up the mizzen on the morning watch, so we did.

Last night's watch was also beautiful, as the moon separated itself from the clouds and did a solo show against the backdrop of a black sky that seemed to have a blueish hint because the moon was so bright.

I have fished a little more, but no more strikes so far. Yesterday I was fishing off the stern when Sonny and Naomi were on watch. When the wind died and he decided to motor, I heard him explaining to her how to start the engine! Ray said that he heard Sonny giving her basic instructions in how to steer; to get the rudder straight, see where the boat wants to go, and steer against that. I think all her previous steering experience has been with an autopilot. We all continue to be curious as to the real reason she is here. She is nice enough; even cooked again last night, but she doesn't know shit about sailing. Also, she never goes to the cockpit without Sonny; just sleeps or reads, lying on the dining settee where she has made her bed. The only time she goes topside is when they are on watch. You would have to guess that she will get really tired of that in the next four months!

Oh yes, the phone issue has been resolved! Sonny has wrapped it in plastic with a hole cut for the microphone, so now we are allowed to use it. I was successful in calling Maureen this morning.

Wednesday, December 18 - 11:15 A.M.- 630 miles to Easter Island! At home, if you think of sailing 630 miles it seems overwhelming, but out here we look at that number on the GPS and say, "Well hell, we're almost there!" We have come nearly 1,300 miles from The Galapagos. The weather has turned absolutely gorgeous and the wind is in the 14-16 knot range, right over the port beam. We covered 70 miles in 12 hours ending at 10:00 A.M. today and it is continuing. Last night the sunset was excellent again, though not quite as good as the night before. This morning we saw a really nice sunrise, too- the first one since The Galapagos, as we have had clouds every morning before.

Richard nearly fell overboard again last night. We wash dishes with seawater and rinse them with fresh. To do that we use a bucket with a line tied to the bail to scoop up seawater. In the evening, Richard usually volunteers to wash dishes, and he scoops up the seawater. When I or any of the others scoop water we brace our feet on the toe rail, sit with our butts on the outer edge of the cockpit keeping the center of gravity low, lean forward and scoop the water. That gives us leverage to lift and to hold on as the bucket catches and fills with water while we are moving at five or six knots. If a wave tilts the boat suddenly, or it lurches for some reason, again, we are braced and have the edge of the cockpit, the bimini frame, and a stanchion to hold on to. For some unknown reason, Richard is unable or unwilling to do it this way. Instead, he moves a few feet aft of the cockpit, stands straight up with his thighs against the lifelines, and leans over with nothing to brace himself or hold on to. That way he also has no leverage and has only his arms to lift with, and he is not all that strong (remember the fish?). Several times he has nearly gone over, twice catching himself by grabbing the jib sheet, which just happened to be tight at the time. I have also seen him fall down on the deck twice. He does this on my watch, but out of concern that he would get pissed off if I said anything,

I asked Ray to coach him on this day before yesterday. Ray talked to him and last night at first he was sitting as I described, but then I looked over and he was standing, bent over the lifelines with his ass in the air. Sure enough, a wave tilted the boat and again, he nearly went over. After he went below Ray looked at me, shaking his head and said "I guess my talk with Richard about safety didn't get through". I should add that he does this as it is getting dark, and without a life jacket or tether. I am about convinced that we are going to have to turn around one of these nights and go back to fish his ass out.

3:40 P.M.- I have another Naomi story! I was just back on the stern doing my exercise workout and I noticed Naomi at the helm reading a book with one foot lightly on the wheel. Sonny was over on the port side also reading a book with neither of them paying any attention to sailing the boat. On the two previous watches the wind was great at about 14-18 knots and the sailing was great, but required a lot of effort to stay on our course, which is 200 degrees. As I was finishing my workout I noticed that there was no wind in the jib. The main was blocking it because we were sailing straight down wind, in danger of another accidental jibe, and the preventer was not tied down. As I approached the cockpit I noticed that our heading was 230 degrees. I said, "Are we getting a little off course here?"

She said, "The wind's heading us and I can't get any closer than 215 degrees".

I said, "The wind is directly behind us. If you turned left, to our course of 200, it would come over the port quarter". That kind of ignorance is amazing; especially for somebody who is supposed to be one of our captains!

The sailing and the weather have been fantastic the last two days, with the sunsets, and the sunrise today and the sea is that unbelievably beautiful deep blue! I keep looking at all that and realizing that I, Charley Hester, am really sailing from The Galapagos to Easter Island and I wait to wake up, thinking that this must be a dream because it's too good to be true!

Sonny's cough seems to be getting much better. He still hacks a bit, but not as often or as severe.

Thursday, December 19 - 4:55 P.M.- 499 miles to go at the end of our morning watch! With a little luck and favorable winds we will arrive on Monday, the 23rd. Yes, we will be glad to get there but when I think of sailing from The Galapagos to Easter Island; how exotic and adventuresome that sounds, and how beautiful, and what a great run it has been, and that I am very unlikely to ever do it again, yes, I will be a little sad to see it end. Mark feels the same way. I hate to keep harping on this but I keep thinking about it all, and how very lucky I am. For most people, they would think that if they're *really* lucky, they *might* get to The Galapagos some time in their life but to actually *sail from* The Galapagos *to* Easter Island- that's just unheard of!

An update: Mr. Watermaker is being much more cooperative these days. It will make water at speeds of up to five knots as long as we aren't heeled too far to starboard. We ran it ten hours yesterday and now have 80 gallons in the tank. As I put it, we are "practically awash in water".

Another update: When Richard scooped water last night he did it the safe and intelligent way- sitting as I described yesterday. I don't

80

know whether Ray talked with him again, or he got a good scare the night before, or what but I hope he continues to do it that way.

Friday, December 20 - 4:30 P.M.- This afternoon has turned out beautiful after a squally morning. The wind even shifted, allowing us to sail the course we want. It now looks like we might arrive at Easter Island during the day Monday.

A squall was about to blow in just as Mark and I went on watch this morning. Sonny had been watching it visually but hadn't even turned on the radar. I turned it on and commented that the squall might pass behind us. Sonny said, "Nah, we're not going to outrun it". He was talking about taking down the main as the winds started to build but I convinced him that we could accomplish the same thing by rolling up half the jib, which we could do without stopping, and which was quicker, easier, and safer; especially under adverse conditions. We did that and in fact, most of the squall did pass behind us. We had winds up to 27 knots and a little rain for about 45 minutes. Later on our watch the radar showed another squall approaching. We avoided that one by rolling up about two thirds of the jib and easing the main sheet, thereby slowing down to let it pass in front of us. As I said before, I am enjoying this watch captain stuff.

A third squall hit us directly right after Ray and Richard went on watch but it wasn't too bad, and I went below and took a nap. This was the first significant rain we have seen since Panama.

Mark and I have observed that Sonny and Naomi sleep 11 or 12 hours a day. They go to sleep as soon as their watch ends at 6:00 A.M. and don't get up before noon. In the evening they go to sleep right after dinner- no later than 7:30, and sleep until they go on watch at 2:00 A.M. When they are awake, they read books- little or no social interaction with the rest of us. They are nice enough, but they stay together like they were joined at the hip and only go topside when they are on watch. Also, Naomi sleeps mostly on the dining table settee on the starboard side, which means that her ass is on top of, or in front of several of the food storage bins for 12+ hours a day. When she isn't sleeping she lays down there and reads so our access to that food is limited! Sonny has started sleeping in the bow more and last night when they went to bed they both went to the bow. After an hour or so, she came out and assumed her position on the settee. I find all this verrrryy strange, and so do the others.

The water maker continues to perform well - 95 gallons in the tank so now we are back to showers every day!

We saw our last other vessel about our fifth day out, and we have seen no airplanes so it has now been eight days since we have seen any evidence that there is another human alive on the planet! Pretty amazing!

10:20 P.M.- At watch change tonight Ray called to our attention that tonight is full moon, brings the solstice, and we will cross the Tropic of Capricorn. I don't know what, but there must be some significance to all that happening at once. Spooky feeling in the air!

Saturday, December 21 - 5:45 P.M.- This morning's watch provided what was probably the best sailing yet. Winds and seas were on our port quarter, winds consistently 18-22 knots and seas in the 6-10 foot range. A cloud passed over with no rain, but brought winds up to 28 knots for about ten minutes. While surfing down a wave we briefly hit a speed of ten knots! We covered 26 miles on our four-hour watch.

Yesterday Ray and Naomi were having a conversation about provisioning and something was mentioned about how much Sonny likes eggs- said he could eat them for every meal- and Naomi said "Not since I've been here". The she added, "That's why I'm here".

About 3:35 this afternoon I went up to do exercises and Mark was just coming in from getting some sun. It was very warm, probably 85 degrees. The wind was about 12-14 knots and not a hot wind, but certainly not cold. There was Sonny at the helm in long pants, and his foul weather coat on with the hood up over his head. Naomi was lying down on the side with shoes, socks, sweat pants and a fleece jacket on. I continue to be amazed at their lack of tolerance for the cold and wonder how they will survive around Cape Horn.

The "man overboard pole" is attached by a bracket to the main mast backstay on the starboard side, just aft of the cockpit. The pin that holds it in the bracket kept falling out so it is tied to the bracket with a piece of small line. The pole is about 15 feet long with a flag on top. The bottom four feet are weighted and a float is just above the weighted section. Another small line runs aft from the pole about eight feet, to a strobe light that is mounted on a bracket attached to a stanchion. The strobe has a weighted top and the light on bottom. If it hits the water the weight inverts it and the strobe starts flashing. That same small line runs on another three feet to a horseshoe buoy mounted on the starboard side of the stern pulpit. The horseshoe buoy is loose in its bracket, so to prevent an accidental deployment the small line is tied to a cleat on the stern. Tied to that same cleat, *over* the small line, is the preventer for the mizzen! In theory, if somebody falls overboard you pull the pin and the pole falls over, taking with it the strobe and horseshoe buoy. In our case, you would have to cut the line holding the pole to the bracket; then go aft and uncleat the mizzen preventer, and *then* uncleat the small line, releasing the horseshoe buoy! By then the boat would be *way* too far from the person in the water for the horseshoe buoy to be of any use. If the boat was moving at five or six knots, even the pole and strobe would be 100-200 yards away, which is significant in any kind of seas. Also, there is a knife that rides in a drink holder on the binnacle, for use in cutting said line. When we got to Panama it had started to rust so Sonny stowed it below, and it didn't come back up top until we raised the issue in The Galapagos. Also, there is an air horn riding in the drink holder, to be used to call everybody on deck if somebody falls overboard. It too had started to rust, and was taken below in Panama; brought back up in The Galapagos. *ALSO*, there is a button on the GPS that you push to mark the exact coordinate if somebody falls overboard. We thought it was the button labeled "mark" until recently when I mentioned it to Ray. He told me that it is *not* the button labeled "mark", but the one labeled "mob" for "man overboard". Now we know! There has *never* been *any* discussion of a procedure to follow if somebody goes over; no discussion of who is to be the "spotter", who is to steer the boat, whether we start the engine, drop the sails, do a figure eight recovery, or *what*. What we know, we have sort of figured out for ourselves. There is also a "life sling" mounted on the port side of the stern pulpit but there has been absolutely *no* discussion of how and when to deploy and use it in recovering a person overboard. I think the message is that if you find yourself falling overboard you should bend way over, and kiss your ass good-bye!

This same scenario is also true regarding deployment of the eight-person life raft, which rides on the main cabin roof, just forward of the main mast. In The Galapagos, Richard, Ray, Mark and I read the instructions, found out how to release the cable holding it to it's bracket, found the shackle to be inoperable due to corrosion, lubricated it; then also found that a tether line needed to be attached to a cable on the raft. The tether line has two purposes; to keep the raft from drifting away prematurely, and when pulled, it causes the raft to inflate. We found a line and attached it; then secured the line to the boat. Sonny showed no interest in, nor took any part in all this. Also, he never told us anything about what to do in case of a fire. Fire extinguishers are around, but nothing has been said about any kind of procedure.

Call me picky, but it seems to me that the establishment, communication, and enforcement of safety practices should be one of the Captain's foremost responsibilities and concerns. Sonny's *only* mention of safety was the first night out of Mobile when he said, "Avoid collisions at all costs" and "Don't piss over the side. Every time they find somebody who fell overboard, his dick is out where he was pissing over the side. Take time to go to the head." That was it! I don't know whether his problem is ignorance, apathy, or both but you would think he would be more concerned about that sort of thing, especially with his daughter on board!

6:30 P.M.- Note- I was just back on the stern doing my exercises and noticed that the small line on the horseshoe buoy is no longer cleated. Ray took it loose and tied it to the stern pulpit with a slip knot - not ideal, but an improvement.

Sunday, December 22 - 10:35 A.M.- 100 miles to go! We are all looking forward to a few days in port and are excited about seeing Easter Island but as I said before, I'm sorry to see this passage end; it has been so fantastic. Mark said it wouldn't bother him if we had another week to go. This morning is bright and sunny with 12-16 knot winds still on the port quarter. The weather has been really good and winds favorable this entire passage. It looks like we will make the 1,919-mile passage in less than 16 days, averaging a speed of five knots.

10:20 P.M.- When I wake up tomorrow morning I will look out and see Easter Island! Place of mystery, and legends, and Chariots of the Gods! A place of dreams and imagination. I haven't felt this kind of anticipatory excitement since I was on a ferry approaching Bora Bora. Tonight the weather is absolutely gorgeous- clear, and the moon isn't up yet so the stars really put on a show. The sunset itself wasn't spectacular but the aftermath was, with lots of reflected oranges, pinks, and almost reds with shades of blue in the sky with hints of yellow and green. We have encountered doldrums-like winds today, light and variable coming from all over the compass. We finally gave up and started motoring around 7:00 P.M. It is amazing how much warmer the air is here than it was 500-1,000 miles closer to the equator. I got some sun today while trolling off the stern - no fish though. The sea temperature has warmed from 71 to 75 degrees. Sonny is being so nice these days that I almost feel bad about being so pissed off at him earlier.

Night Watch

The night watch is a special time
When you can let yourself unwind,
And thoughts run freely through your mind,
On night watch.

You come on deck and check the breeze;
You look for stars and feel the seas.
It all seems good, and you are pleased,
On night watch.

You slip into the helmsman's chair;
The moon is bright, the sky is fair,
And you are thankful that you're there
On night watch.

With radar at your fingertips,
You're careful as you look for ships,
And think about your lover's lips,
On night watch.

Of friends and lovers who have gone;
So many good times that you've known,
And how it feels to be alone,
On night watch.

You stay alert for rain or wind;
Remember places that you've been;
And think how much she loved you then,
On night watch.

You look around and all is well;
You feel the rhythm of the swells;
You know the sea has tales to tell,
On night watch.

But now your watch is ending soon.
You look toward the setting moon,
And think of where you'll be in June,
On night watch.

Fly-fishing in Montana rain,
Or driving out across the plains;
You'll wish that you were once again
On night watch.

9 – EASTER ISLAND

Monday, December 23 - 11:20 A.M.- Easter Island! It's hard to believe I am really here! At daybreak we approached from the northeast, and could see the island off the port side. It has low volcanic mountains up to about 1,500 feet, and a few trees, though not very many. Along the shore on the north side is an obvious volcano crater. We motored around to the west side and down to the only town, Hanga Roa. The wind, 10 knots or so, is from the north (unusual here) and large swells are breaking along the shore rendering the two anchorages here barely tenable. The one off the town looked dangerous and uncomfortable so we were looking for the second one, using the GPS, and the chart. We started into an area that appeared to have nothing but rocks and breaking swells. Sonny and Ray were not in agreement as to exactly where we were and the book of sailing instructions said you need a local pilot to get into the second anchorage. I had asked whether we should turn on the radio in case somebody was trying to contact us, but they were in a rather tense discussion at the time, and my question was ignored. We seemed to be heading into trouble when two Chilean Navy guys showed up in a 20-foot open boat powered by an outboard. They signaled us back out of there and led us back to the anchorage off the town where they had us anchor outside the breakers in 51 feet of water. They spoke little or no English and Sonny had Naomi try to communicate with them in Spanish but she seems to know less than I do. Anyway, to avoid confusion I stayed in the background and listened, offering help when I could. Now we are sitting here waiting for the port captain to come out to the boat and clear us in.

As we approached the town, we began to see some of the statues to the north along the shore. There is one group of five together; then further north of that are two others standing alone about 200 yards apart. Then we saw a few more closer to town. I can't wait to get ashore and see them up close. We are hoping that the port captain can direct us to a better anchorage, as it looks from here like a dinghy ride ashore would be a real adventure. We were told that there is no room in the second anchorage, so we will see. The navy guys were really nice and I took their picture.

It is amazing how much warmer it is here than it was 1,000-2,000 miles north in the equatorial tropics! The sea temperature has warmed from 71 degrees to 75. I have not felt this kind of anticipatory excitement about a place since I visited Bora Bora in 1988. I hope we can find an easy way to get ashore.

Tuesday, December 24 - 2:50 P.M.- There is so much to write! Yesterday the port captain showed up about noon, complete with an entourage. There were a total of eight guys in the same boat the navy guys were in earlier, six of whom came aboard, and four of whom went below. They didn't search anything but had a thorough, well-defined process which they followed to the letter- wanted a lot of information about the boat- it's systems, the dinghy, the outboard, radio, boat engine, EPIRB, etc. in addition to the immigration information. They took about an hour to do their work. The second anchorage is very small and indeed, has no room, so we stayed in the anchorage outside the breaking surf off Hanga Roa, about a quarter mile offshore.

At about 2:00 P.M. it was decided that Ray, Mark, Richard and I would go ashore and come back by 7:00, at which time Sonny and Naomi would go. Given the exposed anchorages and changeable weather here, one of their rules is that somebody has to be on board at all times in case you need to move the boat on short notice. There is a third anchorage on the other side of the island off the oil terminal, several miles from town. Ray and Mark went first to reconnoiter and find the best route through the surf to get behind the small breakwater that protects the fisherman's harbor. They have a small fleet of a dozen or so fishing and dive boats, much like the boat that the navy uses. We watched as they picked their way around and through the protruding rocks and breaking seas. It was exciting and spectacular to watch the aquamarine color of the waves as they built up and then crashed on the rocks, sending spray high into the air. We saw Ray and Mark head in between breakers, and a minute or two later, walking up the beach. They said later that they were only hit slightly by one wave. Ray came back and Richard and I went with him, experiencing a fun ride and landing without any problem.

We tried going to the bank and found that it had closed at 1:00 P.M.. We then went to the phone company where they each made calls, but I couldn't figure out how to use my A.T.& T. card. After that, we went to the Internet café where Ray and Richard checked e-mail while Mark and I went next door for a beer. Mark loaned me money until I can cash traveler's checks, as I only had $15 in cash. There, we met Raul, the owner, who told us about his Christmas Eve Polynesian dinner featuring roast pig, lamb, and fish- we are planning to go. Later we explored a little, walking to look at the second anchorage and some statues along the road. Ray and Richard then went back to the Internet café while Mark and I went to a place called Avarei Pua, down by the harbor and had another beer. Still later, Ray and Richard joined us there for dinner. Our waitress was a very nice local Polynesian lady named Erica, who wore a traditional sarong, and a garland of flowers in her hair.

At about 6:15 we started back to the boat so Sonny and Naomi could go ashore. About half way out, at the edge of the breakers, the outboard died. Ray got it started right away but as I may have mentioned before, Ray is a little excitable and put it in gear when it was revved up, breaking the shear pin. At that point there was nothing to do but paddle, so we tried that; however none of these guys knows how to paddle- to dig in your paddle, synchronize your strokes, etc., so we didn't make much progress under those conditions. The paddling was so poor that we were almost turned around and were actually facing at an angle, back toward the beach when a big wave hit us just as it was starting to break. No surfer ever caught a wave better than we caught that one and it gave us a thrill ride for a couple hundred yards, leaving us behind when it was about 50 feet from the beach! The dinghy didn't flip, but was full of water and we were rather wet and sandy, but no harm was done. We were all laughing like maniacs and the people on the beach, tourists and locals alike, seemed to really enjoy the show! We all had on our life jackets and Richard's got wet enough to activate the automatic inflator. He looked really comical, walking around with that thing sticking out like giant boobs! I was wearing my backpack with a plastic bag wrapped around it, and everything inside- wallet, camera, passport, etc.- was inside individual Ziploc bags so nothing got wet. Mark, Richard and I sat on the beach among our audience while Ray walked over to the navy station. They took him to the boat to get more shear pins. We were wet and sandy, and while he was gone we started to get cold after the sunset, so we decided to spend the night ashore instead of making another run at the surf in the dark. Ray was a little reluctant since he has little money, but I told him I would pay for his share of the room. We went back to Avarei Pua because I thought maybe Erica could help us, and she did. When I explained our situation to her, she immediately got on the phone and called people she knew until she found a room for us; then called a taxi to take us there. Ray went back to the navy station and explained our plans to them. They sent a pick-up truck to get our dinghy and outboard, and stored them overnight for us. The place that Erica found for us was at Guest House Cecelia. Cecelia was waiting for us when we arrived, and showed us a room with three single beds and a private bath, and a second, small single room with a bath two doors down. Richard took the single. Cecelia then came back and took our clothes, giving us each a t-shirt and a towel to wrap around our bottom. She also brought us cups and a pot of coffee, which we drank while sitting around a table out in the breezeway. An English couple, both doctors and on their honeymoon, were in the next room. It turned out that Mark had met them earlier on the beach so they stopped to talk with us as they were going out. I wondered if they had any idea they were talking to four guys who were sitting there without any pants!

Cecelia's is a bed and breakfast place, and this morning she had us go to the dining room wearing those same outfits. It felt very strange but since it was her idea, we did it. After breakfast, our clothes were ready. The whole thing cost us $25. U.S. each! When we were leaving she had her husband take her picture with us.

We decided to make dinghy runs to the boat with Ray taking one of us at a time. I went last, and while I was waiting I went back to the telephone company and asked the lady in Spanish if she knew a number to access A.T. & T.. She gave me the number and it worked, so now I can call using my A.T. & T. card!

The west wind continued, so at mid-day we moved around to the south side of the island to the anchorage off the oil terminal. It is protected from the west wind, but is a three- mile walk to town. Sonny, Naomi and Mark are in town now. When Ray and I were pulling up the anchor to move, it caught twice, coming loose each time with a jolt, giving us about 10 feet of line each time. I guessed that it had been fouled on coral, and I was right! When it came up there was a 10- foot section where one of the three strands had chafed and worn all the way through. If we had stayed there it would surely have worn completely through and the boat could very well have drifted into the breaking surf and onto the rocks before we knew what happened! The net result is that on the CQR anchor we now have 250 feet of line where before we had 300 feet.

Since we have no answers, we continue to wonder about Sonny's condition and why Naomi is here. Given the way he seems to think slowly, move slowly, and do everything slowly I have begun to wonder if he might be in the early stages of Alzheimer's? We're thinking that we may have to ask him to tell us the real reason she is here before we leave Puerto Montt and head for Cape Horn.

Wednesday, December 25 - 9:45 P.M.- Merry Christmas from Easter Island, or Isla de Pasqua in Spanish, or Rapa Nui to the local Polynesian people. It was a rock and roll Christmas morning! During the night the wind shifted to the southeast and by morning it was blowing 15-20 knots, causing swells of three to four feet. It was *not* a good night for sleeping! At mid-morning we pulled anchor and headed back around to Hanga Roa Bay, where we were before. This time we put down the Bruce anchor with an all-chain rode, and the anchorage was very comfortable.

We had Christmas Eve dinner at Raul's last night; at least Ray, Mark, Richard and I did. Sonny and Naomi had dinner at another place down the beach, and then went back to the boat so Ray could leave and join us. To get there we took the dinghy to the landing at the Rada Vinapu Oil Terminal; a slippery ladder that led vertically about five feet up to a platform, that led to the rock and dirt road. It was about a 3½-mile walk up and over the hill to town. The dinner was outstanding, with lamb, pork, two kinds of fish, salad, and two drinks for 15,000 pesos, or about $22. U.S.

During dinner a light rain began to fall so we took a taxi back to the top of the hill above the landing at the oil terminal. With the rain, the road was too muddy for the taxi to go down to the bottom of the hill. Ray called Sonny on the hand-held VHF radio, to come and get us. Walking down the hill in the rain, with only one small flashlight was an adventure. There are no lights at the landing and Sonny had a hard time finding us in the dark. He overshot to his right and nearly went onto some rocks, creating a few tense moments but he finally found us. We were successful in getting down the ladder, into the dinghy, and back to the boat safely in the rain. We got back to the boat at midnight, local time. An interesting note is that geographically, we are in the Mountain Time zone but they observe the same time as mainland Chile, which is Eastern.

Oh yes, when Sonny and Naomi were in town they bought each of us a small Christmas gift- mine is an Easter Island key ring. It was hanging from the light over my bunk, along with a "Merry Christmas" note. I thought it was a very nice gesture.

This afternoon Ray and I went ashore and just walked around town, exploring. Several people stopped and talked with us briefly.

90

I continue to be impressed with how clean and well kept the town is, and how nice and friendly the people are. There is a magic in the air here, much like I felt on Bora Bora. It's not just me- everybody talked about the magic in the air here. We ran into Raul, and are going with him tomorrow to tour the island -all day for $25. U.S. per person All in all, it is an understatement to say that this has been a Christmas that I will never forget!

Thursday, December 26 - 8:55 P.M.- What an absolutely fantastic day this was! Ray, Mark, Richard and I went on a tour of the island with Raul. What a bargain, at $25 U.S. for a jeep tour that lasted seven hours and included a ceviche dinner afterward! The tour included so many places and things that just blew us away!

We started near the southwest corner of the island, where we visited the Orongo Volcano and the adjacent village that dates back to the year 900 A.D., or perhaps earlier. The small dwellings, made of flat stones and earth, are still intact. Raul explained some of the more important customs and rituals of the tribe that lived there. From there we traveled east along the southern shore to an "Ahu", or altar, under which was a burial site and upon which several "Moais", or statues had stood until they were wrecked by a tsunami in 1962. These particular Moais were never restored. Raul also showed us the route over which the Moais were moved from Raraku, the mountain where they were carved, to the Ahu, roughly 20 miles or so, when you allow for going around instead of over large hills in between. We then visited Raraku, which is actually an extinct volcano, and walked around the site where the carving was done. We were overwhelmed as we stood at the base and looked up the side of the mountain where more than 100 Moais are scattered here and there with no apparent rhyme or reason. Some were upright, some tilted, and some on their faces; many were finished and many others partially finished; some were huge- maybe 20 feet tall and others not so huge; some "long ears" and some "short ears", some with adornments indicating a person of importance- kings and such; some with different head shapes or facial features. We were absolutely awestruck! Mingled with all this were some cows, just wandering around eating grass. There is an intense feeling of magic, and mystery in the air all around the island, but especially in this place. I can't adequately describe the feeling, but I have never felt anything comparable anywhere else that I have been. Another weird unexplained point is that it seems like hundreds, or maybe thousands of people were working on all this and one day they just quit, and nobody seems to know why. I still have to try and absorb it all but right now I think this place and everything there is the single most impressive thing I have ever experienced.

From there we went to a nearby Ahu with 15 Moais lined up facing inland. Raul showed us a small feature that is carved into the back of each Moai. It was believed that this feature absorbed energy from the sea, from other distant lands, or the Gods, and then it was distributed through the faces to the people the Moais were facing. We then visited two small caves above a small beach on the north side of the island; then to Anakena Beach, on the northwest shore where we stopped for a 15-minute swim. There is an Ahu there, just up from the beach, with 7 Moais lined up and facing inland. The beach is on a small bay with crystal-clear water and perfect bodysurfing waves rolling in. Ray, Raul, and I went swimming and it was weird to be there in the water and look up and see those statues! After we bought beers from a lady with a stand on the beach, we went to another Ahu with 7 Moais lined up facing out to sea. Only a very few of the statues here face out to sea. After that, we went to another volcano/quarry where the red stone used for hair-topknots on some of the Moais, was carved. Even those pieces weighed two to three tons, and those had to be moved even farther.

After that, we went to the "old people's cave" where many of the old people of the tribes went to die. Raul said that only three years ago, six old Polynesian women went in there and even though an extensive search was conducted, no trace of them was ever found. We only went about 200 yards into the cave but could see that it went a lot further. Our last stop was the "Virgins Cave", which was inappropriately named. In the course of some of the tribal rituals those found *not* to be virgins were taken to this cave to live. The opening is about four feet across and goes almost straight down, but quickly angles off toward the sea and after crouching for about 50 feet we could mostly stand up. It goes about 200 yards, and branches into two passages that lead another 30 yards or so, each to an opening that is a window in a cliff about 100 feet above the crashing waves of the sea. After this, it was back to Raul's for ceviche, then back to the boat.

Raul is a very interesting guy. He is a partner in a marketing/promotions/public relations/sports agency in New York. His office was in the World Trade Center but on September 11, 2001 he was in Washington on business. Twenty-five of his friends and co-workers were killed and he was an emotional mess. One of his clients was the government of Easter Island, and he had become friends with the mayor of Hanga Roa. The mayor invited him to come here and work in the mayor's office for a while. He liked it here and became fascinated with the island, it's people, history and culture. He has since opened his small restaurant, an Internet café, a tour business, and is in the process of opening a "Domino's Pizza" here. He is 40, has a degree in Civil Engineering, and was a professional tennis player until age 22, when his career ended with a blown-out knee. He said that he once reached the third round at Wimbledon. He is Swiss, and his wife Gabriella, is from Yugoslavia. They have a two-year-old son, Jacques, and Gabriella is five months pregnant. He works hard, and is one of those people that you would never guess to be wealthy.

One more thing- I had heard before but forgotten that the Easter Island Airport has one of the five longest runways in the world, because it is an emergency-landing site for the Space Shuttle. They handle five flights a week here- it is a stop between Santiago, Chile and Tahiti.

Friday, December 27 - 6:45 P.M.- Yesterday afternoon Mark and I ran into Cecelia and during the conversation we asked her about doing laundry. She said sure, just bring it in but she didn't give us a price. We had heard that other places were asking $5.00 U.S. per kilo, or about $20-25 for a bag of laundry. We had even talked about doing it ourselves in the bathtub on the boat, but since she had been so nice and reasonable before, we thought she might offer a better deal and decided to give it a try. This morning Richard and I went ashore at ten o'clock and took our laundry. Cecelia wasn't there when we arrived so we left it with the lady that works with her, who asked us to check back in an hour. We walked over to the cemetery, and then along the shore to the Ahu with seven statues north of town, taking some pictures at both places. When we went back, Cecelia had already started doing our laundry and when we asked the price we were delighted when she said "$10 each"!

Afterward we wandered around town, to the post office, the Internet café, and did some t-shirt shopping. We had lunch at a place called Taveka, a block off the beach on Principal Street. I had a great seafood salad and two beers for less than $7. Our server was dressed and demonstrated the mannerisms of a woman, but had a lot of masculine features. These included the appearance of shaving every day, large hairy hands, and a fairly deep voice. Also, the blouse, or top, left a small strip of stomach exposed and there was significant hair on the stomach. She had nice, long black hair that looked very feminine. Her skirt was floor length so I didn't get a look at the legs.

I didn't sense that this person was gay, but perhaps a cross dresser, or maybe even someone that is both genders? In any case, she was an interesting character and a very good server.

Ray brought the dinghy in to pick us up at 4:15 and we made it back through the surf without a significant incident- just went airborne over the top of one wave. After I got back to the boat I went snorkeling. We are in about 40 feet of water, right on a nice coral reef that we are seriously damaging with our anchor chain but I don't know what we could do differently. They really need to put out some moorings here!

Sonny and Naomi went with Raul on a tour today and even Sonny was impressed. He didn't even have one negative thing to say!

Friday, December 27- Supplemental Notes - 10:40 P.M.- For so many years Easter Island was such a mystical, magical place in my imagination; a place of unattainable dreams, that I would never have a chance to go. Now it is still unbelievable that I am really here and came by sailing ship upon which I am a Watch Captain, and that this place of legend and unsolvable mysteries and unexplained energy has so far exceeded my lofty expectations as to make them seem trivial.

Saturday, December 28 - 8:55 A.M.- I continue to find myself in a leadership role. The first day here the plan was for us to come back to the boat and have Sonny and Naomi go ashore for dinner and return to the boat after dark. Even after our incident in the surf, after Ray got a replacement shear pin he planned to make another run through the surf even though it would have been dark. I'm the one who said "I'm not going to try that again after dark; it's too dangerous so I'm staying ashore." Now, nobody even considers making the run after dark. Also with the tour, I'm the one who got the information and price, and said "That's a good deal; I'm going." Ray thought at first that it was too expensive, Richard almost backed out several times, and Sonny and Naomi were apprehensive but ultimately everybody went and now they rave about how great it was. If I had not "made it happen", nobody would have gone. I guess I take an aggressive approach to things, and I do make things happen.

I guess no place is perfect, and Easter Island is no exception, at least from the mariner's perspective. The difficulty in getting to and from shore puts a damper on things, like enjoying a nice dinner or a few drinks ashore in the evening, enjoying the local music; things like that. It cuts down on how much money you spend, though!

94

9:00 P.M.- Another great day on Easter Island! This afternoon Raul and Guillermo, who works for Raul, came out to the boat and taught us how to fish with hand lines. The hand lines consist of a piece of PVC pipe about four inches long and four inches in diameter with a wooden handle inside, on one end. The line with a small hook and sinker was wrapped around the PVC. For bait we used raw chicken. We took a chicken leg and would bite off a small piece and put it on the hook. Then we would unwind some of the line, throw it out a little, let it sink to the bottom, pull it up a couple of feet, and wait for a bite. We caught four fish (I caught two) in about an hour. They were small parrotfish that Raul was going to use to make fish soup.

I have become increasingly concerned about the damage our anchor and chain are doing to the reef. Since Raul is a friend of the mayor, I decided to tell him about it and suggest that moorings be placed out here. It is obvious that every boat that anchors here damages the reef. When Raul was on the boat he borrowed my mask, fins and snorkel to see for himself, and was appalled at what he saw. They don't get many boats here, so three or four moorings would probably be enough. Raul seems genuinely interested so I think something will be done.

I went ashore about 11:00 A.M. and went to the post office, Internet café, etc. I had lunch at Raul's- tuna fingers, and it was great! Afterward I had a beer with Mark at Avarei Pua and had our picture taken with Erica; then went to Cecelia's and picked up my laundry. Most businesses in town closed at 1:00 P.M.

One more thing: Raul told Ray and me separately and privately that he thinks Sonny has a serious health problem. He said that Sonny had a really hard time on the tour- had a hard time breathing, heart was pounding, and seemed disoriented a couple of times. He doesn't think Sonny is up to a trip around Cape Horn. Now we have to decide what, if anything, to do with that information.

Sunday, December 29 - 11:05 P.M.- We discovered a new problem this morning. The sea was glassy and clear so I decided to show Ray where our anchor chain was tearing up the reef. When he saw it, he and I decided to take in some of the excess chain to try and mitigate further damage. We took in about 50 feet and then discovered, as I had expected from my snorkeling experience, that the chain had not only worked its way into a crevice, but also had wound around and under a coral ledge, and we were stuck. When we anchored I had thought that we were putting out way more scope than was needed, but I didn't say anything. My mistake! In any case, since I am the only experienced diver in the crew it appeared that it would fall my lot to go down with SCUBA gear and try to get it loose. Sonny and I went ashore to rent gear, but went first to Raul's because we thought that he might have some gear that we could borrow. He didn't have any but volunteered to go and rent some for us because as a local, he could get a better deal. He found out that you can't rent SCUBA gear here to do work unless you have a Chilean commercial diver's card. My card is only good for sport diving, and if we used it to rent gear that we used to do work, the captain of the boat would be subject to a large fine. The owner of Orcas Dive Shop agreed through Raul to do the job for $50 after first asking $150. As it turned out, I wouldn't have been successful anyway because he had to direct us how to maneuver the boat and also had to use an air bag to lift the chain and anchor!

After the anchor and chain were freed Ray took Raul, Mark and me ashore. Mark and I went to Taveka where we sat on the porch and had a couple of beers, and then a late lunch or early dinner. Mine was a fish steak with a nice sauce and onions and peppers on top, with mashed potatoes. It was excellent, and cost 2,500 pesos, or about $3.75. After we finished, we walked around town for a while before going to Avarei Pua where we had a couple more beers. Ray joined us there, and we had great conversations with Erica, a couple from Dallas who have lived in Santiago for five years, and another couple from Boulder, Colorado. It was a really nice afternoon, and the people here continue to be so very nice!

Sonny and Naomi went ashore this morning to go to church at the Catholic Church, not for any religious reasons, but to hear the music. One of Sonny's favorite memories from his circumnavigation 30 years ago is the sound of island church music, and he wanted to hear it again. They even discussed bringing the video camera but decided that might be frowned upon. The last I heard was that they were discussing bringing in a tape recorder hidden in a bag. I'm not sure what God might think of all that! Tomorrow or Tuesday I am planning to go with Raul back to Raraku, the quarry, and just spend some time there.

Monday, December 30 - 7:00 P.M.- Erica asked me yesterday to bring her one of my t-shirts from some place that I have been; that she would like to trade t-shirts, giving me one from Rapa Nui. I understand that exchanging small gifts is a Polynesian custom, indicating respect and friendship. I don't recall details but I seem to remember a story from the Bible about such transactions and the moral was to give the other person your best, so I gave her my shirt from Homer, Alaska. She gave me a really pretty Rapa Nui shirt with a statue on the front that she had personally tie-dyed by hand. Tie-dye is not my favorite, but the shirt is beautiful and brings a lot of meaning with it. She also gave shirts to Ray, Mark, and Richard, and some small gifts to Sonny and Naomi. She is quite a lady.

After that I walked around Hanga Roa, basking in the atmosphere of this place; had lunch at Taveka again, bought a couple of t-shirts, etc. I am planning to go with Raul to Raraku tomorrow morning. The couple from Boulder are going on a tour with him and he is not charging me to go with them to Raraku. I referred them to him, so I feel good about that. Ray, Richard, Mark and I are also planning to have New Year's Eve's dinner at Raul's restaurant and watch the fireworks show from there. We will probably stay ashore instead of trying to dinghy back to the boat in the dark.

Being that it is the end of the year, or maybe for other reasons, I have felt down the last day or so, and have been doing some reflecting and introspection. One thing I have realized is that life is out there waiting for anybody who wants it, but it generally doesn't drop by and sit down in your lap. You have to go and get it. The difference between me and most people is that they are not willing to do whatever it takes to go and get it. There is usually a big gap between what a person CAN do and what they WILL do.

I am trying to fight off the feeling that after Easter Island, everything that remains on this trip will be anticlimactic. I am also trying to fight off the feeling that after this trip the rest of my life will be anticlimactic! I hope those feelings are not true. If you think about it, if they *are* true, my life will have peaked within the last week, right here on Easter Island; probably the 26th, when I took the jeep tour and went to Raraku. I always prefer to think that the best is yet to come!

Tuesday, December 31 - 6:55 P.M.- What a day of emotions this has been! I don't know where to start writing about it so I will just start at the beginning. All day yesterday the wind blew from the northwest. Then right after dark it shifted and blew from the northeast, but the swells still came from the northwest, right onto our beam. That caused the boat to roll back and forth all night and Sonny didn't get any sleep. Mark and I were having tea in the cockpit about 7:00 A.M. when Sonny stuck his head up the companionway and said, "I'm tired of this fucking anchorage. We're leaving." He made some reference to unsettled weather, but there were only a couple of rainsqualls off

97

to the west, and that was it. It was no worse than a lot of other days. Yesterday during the day I heard him say, "I've seen what I wanted to see here. I'm ready to go." He knew that we had reservations at Raul's for New Year's Eve tonight, to have dinner and watch the fireworks over the bay. He also knew that I had plans to go with Raul back to Raraku this morning, but he didn't give a shit! He was being the arbitrary, inconsiderate, selfish prick that he is! He had *said* that we were leaving the second of January, and we had made our plans based on his word. Anyway, he called the Navy on the radio and arranged for them to come and clear us out at 1:00 P.M.

I finally got ashore at 9:30 and had two hours to get things done. I knew that Raul would be gone with his tour before I got ashore since I was to meet him at 8:45-9:00, so I wrote him a note of apology and thanks for all his help and kindness and gave it to Gabriella. I was able to explain to her in Spanish what was happening. I had a very warm, almost emotional good-bye with her and Guillermo- great people! I also went to Avarei Pua Restaurant where Erica works, knowing that she doesn't come to work until 4:00 P.M. I talked with the guy who works the day shift and explained in Spanish to him, and he too seemed sad to see us go. I asked him to tell Erica good-bye. There has been not a buzz, but some conversation around Hanga Roa about a German boat with a couple aboard, that spent some time here before sailing in November for Cape Horn and the Falklands. They were last heard from on December 13 and since a search found their EPIRB but not the boat, they are presumed to be lost at sea. I think the people here are a little concerned about us.

Ray took Naomi to the boat in the dinghy this morning, with some groceries. He took the opportunity to ask her straightforward about Sonny's health. She said that he has a clean bill of health from his doctor and that she is just here for the adventure. That's her story, and she's sticking to it!

Once we were cleared and ready to go, we had a hell of a time getting the anchor up. As I said before, we had way too much chain out and it is heavy gauge chain; then the Bruce anchor weighs 75 pounds. We thought for a while that we were fouled in the coral again, but it was primarily just the weight. We finally tied a rope to the anchor chain, ran it through a block and back to a big winch next to the cockpit. I cranked it in, 10 feet at a time, cranking until the rope got to the block; then cleating it and tying it again near the bow. With Ray steering, we used the engine to maneuver the boat and make the cranking easier. Shortly afterward we sailed around the southwest point of the island

and set a course of 117 degrees, or east-southeast, for Puerto Montt, a passage of 1,948 miles. Mark and I have the 2:00-6:00 watch.

I can't begin to describe the emotions I feel about this island, and about leaving it. I can't stop looking at it as it fades in the distance. The profile to the left, from the southwest point, is that of a sperm whale and to the right you can imagine a huge Moai lying on it's back, facing up. This one also has a mountain on the far right with a clump of trees on the very top- looks like this Moai has a potbelly, complete with a belly button. This seems interesting since Easter Island is sometimes called the "navel of the world". It is such a magical, mysterious, captivating place and I feel so very privileged to have experienced it. The people were so friendly, kind, and helpful; it was overwhelming! I will never forget the surfers and boogie-boarders in Hanga Roa Bay; the little kids, some naked, playing in the fisherman's harbor along the tiny beach; people riding horses down Principal Street through the middle of town; the proprietor/server at Taveka Restaurant; -I could go on and on! I'm really thankful that I had this opportunity. If somebody started playing sentimental island music right now, I think I would cry!

10 – BACK FROM BEYOND

Wednesday, January 1 - 6:25 P.M.- Happy New Year! I slept through it at sea. After a blustery, squally, rainy early morning things cleared up by ten o'clock and we had a beautiful day at sea. The wind has been east-northeast at 14-22 knots and seas have ranged 6-12 feet, with 8-10 most common. We have been sailing a course of 120-125 degrees most of the day due to wind direction, when we really need to sail 105. We are sailing under jib and mizzen; never having put up the main due to concerns about the squalls this morning.

When making reference to the Emergency Position Indicator Radio Beacon, or "EPIRB", both Sonny and Ray persist in calling it "the E-Burp". I don't know why, but they do. Since Ray is a friend, I called it to his attention, asking how he got "E-Burp" and he seemed almost insulted, giving me no real answer. I won't mention it again, but it is one of those little things that bugs the hell out of me. Kind of like the long hair that Richard has sticking out of his nose right now!

Lots of stars were out on night watch last night but we still haven't spotted the "Southern Cross" I have the whole crew looking for it now.

Thursday, January 2 - Near Latitude 31 degrees south; Longitude 107 west; 1,712 miles to go. 6:25 P.M.- Last night on night watch the milky way looked so close that you felt almost like if you stood up on tiptoe, you could reach up and touch it. There was no moon, and the stars were so bright some of them looked like little lights. The wind was consistent, still from the east-northeast at 16-20 knots which forced us to steer a course of 125-130; not exactly what we wanted, but reasonably close.

The barometer is high and steady, the sky is clear, and except for the wind direction sailing is great. After we had lollygagged around all day under jib and mizzen, wallowing in eight foot swells and making an average speed of four knots I decided to take it on myself to put up the main about 4:15 P.M. I did mention it to Ray and he said to use my own judgment, so I did. Our speed immediately increased to five

100

and a half to six knots, and the ride is much smoother. I find that I have pretty good sailing instincts- probably as good as Ray or Sonny, although their experience is certainly much greater.

Richard is a bit pissed off with me. It seems that we have a difference of opinion regarding a sliding hatch, like a companionway hatch, above the aft cabin where he and Mark sleep, and just behind where I sleep. The hatch does not latch, but slides freely. Richard is concerned about a following sea breaking over the stern, knocking it open, and flooding the aft cabin. He wants to nail it shut, bolt it shut, or tie it shut, so that it is permanently closed. I said "no" to that idea because I see that hatch as a critical point of egress in the event of a fire, or the boat sinking bow first (like if you hit an ice floe!). I don't want to be trapped down this passageway in the stern with no way out. I spoke with Ray and suggested that we find a way to latch it from the inside, so we can open it if the need should arise. He seemed to agree and said we should be able to do that while we are in Puerto Montt. I hope that will make Richard happy.

Friday, January 3 Latitude 33 Degrees, 1 minute south; Longitude 106 degrees, 27 minutes west - 6:30 P.M.-What a nice watch we just had! We had a clear sky, friendly winds of 14-16 knots, and gorgeous swells, some in the 12-15 foot range. The waves were only three to five feet, but these long, graceful swells come by and you don't even notice how big they are as the boat glides over the top and down through the troughs. They are magnificent as they roll away to the west with the afternoon sun shimmering on their backs. They are reminiscent of rolling hills in eastern Montana, or some other western states. I suppose that if you don't feel a connection with the sea this would seem monotonous or even boring, but if you do feel such a connection it seems always constant, yet always changing and is as pretty as anything you ever saw.

The wind direction is still east-southeast and the best course we can steer is 140-150 degrees, well off our rhumb line course of 105. The result is that even though we are sailing at speeds of five to six knots, we are only making about three knots toward our destination. Mark and I only made ten miles progress toward out destination on our watch.

The breeze is cool, and last night was cold enough that I wore sweat pants on night watch; finally giving up my shorts. I used a light blanket when I went to sleep after night watch, and was still cool.

101

Saturday, January 4   Lat.- 33 degrees, 58 minutes south; Lon.-106 degrees west; 1,591 miles to go - 6:10 P.M.- We have had light winds all day- sometimes down to seven or eight knots; also still from the east-northeast most of the day so we are still sailing south of the course we want. We averaged 113 miles toward our destination the first two days but only 81 the last two. Since we were going so slowly anyway, I decided that we should slow a little more, to less than three knots, and try the water maker to be sure it works. We had 70 gallons left this morning and when you are two weeks from land you don't want to let it get too low, and then discover that your water maker doesn't work! Sonny had not thought of this. Ray had thought of it but wouldn't suggest anything because he and Sonny had another little spat the other day and he was being pissy. Since it is an issue that could become serious, I just told Sonny that I was going to do it, and why. He agreed, we tried it, and it worked so we made 12 gallons on our afternoon watch. While we were doing that, the wind shifted more to the northeast, so now we are sailing very close to the course we want. The wind also picked up to 10-12 knots.

The weather was overcast and cool this morning, and I even put on jeans and shoes. Last night I wore sweat pants on night watch and use my light blanket when I sleep. I have deployed both of the safety pins that Molly gave me to keep me safe; one inside the right pocket of my foul weather jacket and the other inside the pocket of my anorak. I wear one or the other most of the time when I am on watch these days, especially on night watch. We got the idea from our friend Clark in Montana, who does a lot of dangerous things, and carries a safety pin in his pocket to keep him safe.

When we reached The Galapagos after eight and a half days at sea we had eight bags of garbage lashed to the stern, some of it smelling pretty rank by then. We had all agreed to throw overboard everything except plastic and aluminum but we didn't have room for two trash containers in the galley or salon. Nobody was willing to go through and separate it, so we just bagged everything and lashed it to the stern. Facing three passages of two to three weeks, it became obvious to me that this wouldn't do so I volunteered to solve the garbage problem. Each morning I take the garbage basket to the leeward rail, along with a bucket. I go through and put all the plastic, cellophane, and Styrofoam in the bucket. I fill glass containers with water, so they will sink, and drop them overboard.

I punch holes in aluminum cans so they will sink, and also drop them overboard. I tear paper and cardboard into small pieces and toss them overboard, along with food scraps. I then take the bucket back to the stern where an unused ice chest is lashed down. I then cut plastic bottles and jars into small, easily storable pieces and put them in a plastic garbage bag inside the ice chest. If a jar or bottle is too thick to cut, I stuff it full of cellophane, Styrofoam and small pieces. When we got to Easter Island after a passage of 16 days we had less than one full bag in the ice chest. Problem solved!

I finally tried trolling again this afternoon, but no luck. I am using my makeshift lures since we left Easter Island in such a hurry that I forgot to buy any. I hope to do better when we are closer to land; however I caught the dolphin when we were nearly 500 miles from the nearest land.

Sunday, January 5 Lat.- 35 degrees, 50 minutes south; Lon.- 104 degrees, 5 minutes west; 1,450 miles to go - 6:20 P.M.- About 4:45 this afternoon Mark was at the helm and I was lying down on the port side enjoying the sun when I heard Mark say "Wow, what's that?" I quickly went to the starboard side where he was looking, and saw this huge white mass, a few feet under water. We immediately realized that it had to be a whale. After a few seconds it changed positions and we could see a darker mass. By then Richard and Ray were on deck, and then it surfaced, no more than 20 feet from the boat and blew water out of its air hole. We saw that it was a killer whale, probably about 35-40 feet long. It went back down and swam along with us for maybe another 15 seconds, then dived, and was gone. How exciting! Mark has been looking for whales since we left Mobile and it was really neat that he was the one to spot it, and up so close, too.

The sea temperature has dropped to 67 degrees. It was 75 at Easter Island; dropped to 71 the second day out, hovered a couple of days, and dropped another four degrees in the last two days.

This afternoon's watch was our best so far of this passage- made 23 miles toward our destination. The wind shifted and is blowing from the north at 11-15 knots, so we can sail the course we want, which is now 93 degrees, or almost due east. It is bright and sunny, and the breeze is cool. The swells are about 6-10 feet, not quite as smooth as the last couple of days, but still beautiful. Mark calls them "moving hills" and that is about the best description I have heard. They move with a rhythm and grace that is unmatched and unmatchable.

I was very frustrated this morning over our lack of progress. We have continued to have light winds and when we do have wind- anything over, and sometimes less than 20 knots- Sonny starts taking down sails. For some reason he seems to find reasons not to sail under full sails, and then we were slowed on the 6-10 A.M. watch to make water. When Sonny and Naomi went on watch at 10:00 he said, "I guess we'll just keep making water" when the wind was 9-12 knots. The main had been taken down last night and was still down. I was pissed, and went to the stern to fume and fish. Then at 10:15 I looked up and he was taking the ties off the main! I quickly jumped up and went to help. We put the main up, and conditions have been improving all day giving us a great day of sailing.

Tonight Naomi made a nice dinner of canned chicken breasts with stovetop stuffing and corn biscuits. She is trying to be helpful. She and Sonny are sleeping less on this passage too, and are trying to be more sociable.

Monday, January 6 1,341 miles to go - 6:45 P.M.- This morning was cold and overcast; enough so that I wore jeans and shoes, but around 10:00 the sun came out and by noon it was actually hot. Winds have remained light, in the 6-9 knot range so we have used the opportunity to make water most of the day. We were down to 40 gallons, so that turned out to be a good thing. I trolled throughout the afternoon watch, but no action. I am still using makeshift lures and we are over 600 miles from the nearest land. Hopefully I will do better.

We are averaging 100 miles a day. If that continues we will reach Puerto Montt about the 20th. The "miles to go" is actually the distance to Ancud, at the mouth of the Gulf of Ancud. From there we will have to make our way through the channels another 80 miles to Puerto Montt. Some of those channels have tidal flows that reach up to nine knots! That should be interesting.

The latest thing to break is the handle to the refrigerator door. Sonny took it off, mixed some epoxy and glued it back- no big deal; just something else that broke.

Tuesday, January 7 Lat.- 36 degrees, 40 minutes south; Lon.- 100 degrees, 48 minutes west. 1,281 miles to go. - 10:05 A.M.- We are motoring this morning. Light winds prevailed all day and all night, and overall we are averaging a speed of about four knots for this passage.

Another problem: The voltage regulator that we bought in Panama isn't working right so the batteries still tend to overcharge when we run the engine. Last night we motored from 9:00 P.M. until 2:00 A.M. but then had to stop because the batteries overcharged. We sailed in winds of six to nine knots during our watch and averaged about three knots. At 9:00 A.M. we started the motor again. Sonny says he doesn't think Brad installed the new voltage regulator right. In any case, this appears to have become a three-week passage. This afternoon at 3:30 makes one week, and we will have covered just under 700 miles.

6:15 P.M.- The winds picked up around 11:00 A.M. so we stopped motoring and sailed the rest of the day. The winds stayed at 11-15 knots, but are directly behind us, so we can't sail the course we want. Our speed averaged between four and five knots during our afternoon watch. The weather was clear and almost hot again. Mark and I got some sun, but still no luck fishing.

Wednesday, January 8: Lat.- 37 degrees south; Lon.- 98 degrees, 30 minutes west; 1,167 miles to go.

6:20 P.M.- 77 miles in the last 24 hours! Light winds continue, blowing from directly behind us. The consolation is that the weather is absolutely beautiful; sunny with 8-12 knot westerly winds. On the afternoon watch we enjoyed watching swells up to 10-12 feet roll in from the starboard quarter and lift us as they passed underneath- really pretty!

Last night Sonny decided to try sailing straight down wind instead of zigzagging, and the results were predictable, being that we don't have a spinnaker and don't use the whisker pole. Sails flopped around rattling lines, blocks and winches, making an awful noise. From below it sounded like a four-hour train wreck was happening up there! Needless to say, nobody got any sleep and I was in a pissy mood when I went on watch at 2:00 A.M. Oh yes, in the middle of all that, Sonny decided that it might help if he took down the main- it was blocking wind from the jib- so he did it by himself without asking for any help. This was not only very difficult, but dangerous, especially at night and especially with Naomi at the helm. Ray looked up there and Sonny was in front of the dodger by the mainmast, pulling down and tying off the sail, wearing his life jacket, but not clipped on. I don't know if he was trying to prove something to us, to Naomi, to himself, or what but that was *not* a smart thing to do. I have started clipping on when I am at the helm at night, even in good conditions; first, to get into the habit, and second, because we have concluded that if you fall overboard at night your chances of being rescued by this group are poor, at best. As I have mentioned before, there has never been any discussion of what to do in a "man overboard" situation except briefly among Ray, Richard, Mark and me and even then, nothing was decided. Sonny has shown no interest whatsoever, even when the subject was brought up in The Galapagos.

This is *really me* here, sailing from Easter Island to Puerto Montt,

Chile! I still can't believe that it isn't a dream! How I wish I was sharing it with Maureen! I miss my best friend.

Thursday, January 9: Lat.- 37 degrees, 31 minutes south; Lon.- 97 degrees, 38 minutes west; 1,124 miles to go. - 9:00 A.M.- Sailing conditions are unchanged- beautiful weather and light winds right behind us. Actually, the wind has shifted about 10-15 degrees toward the north so we are sailing the course we want, just not very fast. Mark and I covered 16 miles on our night watch, which is a slight improvement, but still slow. Ray continues to work on his bread making and we continue to enjoy the results. Good for us that he likes to cook!

This is our ninth day out and the only other signs of life we have seen have been a few birds, one flying fish that flew into the boat next to Mark one night, and the whale. Usually we see lots of flying fish during the day but none on this passage so far, and still no luck trolling, either. I have started trolling throughout our afternoon watch since the weather has been so good and we have been going so slow.

8:00 P.M.- I caught a really nice tuna near the end of our afternoon watch! I was at the helm just before 6:00 when I looked back and saw that the rod was bent. It gave me a decent fight and for once, I had the drag set right. It could take a little line, but only with difficulty. Ray handled the gaff, and we got it on board- he is stronger than Richard, and understands leverage. I estimated the weight at 20-25 pounds, based on a comparison to the combined weight of my two hand weights, which is 16 pounds. I filleted it on the stern since we don't have a knife suitable to cut it into steaks, with the bone that big. We then took it to the galley and butchered it. Ray started the process, but then had to go on watch so I did most of it- a new experience for me. It took a total of about an hour to de-bone and cut it up, and it filled four large Ziploc bags. Even Sonny and Naomi showed interest. Naomi took some video footage and Richard got my camera and took a picture. He took it looking right into the sun, but maybe it will come out O.K. I caught the fish on one of my makeshift lures, too! Oh yes, just as I got the fish to the boat, the handle broke off the reel. I just locked down the drag at that point, pulled the fish around and lifted it enough that Ray could get the gaff into the gills. I will see if I can fix the handle tomorrow. I get *very* excited when I catch a fish, and especially if the fish is big!

Sailing conditions have improved slightly, and we are now

averaging four and a half knots on the course that we want. Still slow going. In fact, just this morning Ray, Richard, Mark and I were talking about running out of food that we like before we get to Puerto Montt. The fish will help. Today is a little cooler but still great weather with bright sunshine and swells that have built up to 10-12 feet in some cases.

I had a good conversation with Ray this morning about several subjects- his finding spirituality through A.A., his impression of the book "The River Why" and the spirituality there, etc. One other subject was his relationship with Sonny, which is not good. He even talked about leaving the boat in Puerto Montt if he should find work on another boat there- very unlikely. He voiced an opinion that I have thought but not vocalized: that in all probability, Sonny is the least intelligent person on the boat.

Friday, January 10: Lat.- 38 degrees, 20 minutes south; Lon.- 94 degrees, 19 minutes west; 958 miles to go.6:50 P.M.- Ray cooked fish, wild rice, and corn for dinner tonight and it was fantastic! This morning Mark fixed the reel. He drilled out the broken part and made a new spindle for the handle. I tested it and it works fine.

When Mark and I went on watch at 2:00 A.M. Sonny and Naomi told us about a "big storm" that had approached from behind and passed us on the port side, giving us a few sprinkles of rain. They had watched it visually, but not on the radar, to find out how large or intense it was or which way it was going. I turned on the radar and watched it, about eight miles away, as the squall faded in the distance and dissipated. Sonny still says he doesn't know how to turn on the radar even though Ray has shown both him and Naomi. He *really* is techno-phobic! In this case, the radar was actually on, but was set to "stand-by" to conserve power. All it took was to push one button to turn it on and tune it.

On our afternoon watch Mark and I covered 26 miles, by far the best of this passage. Winds picked up around noon and blew 17-26 knots throughout our watch. Seas ranged 6-12 feet, following, just off the port quarter as we sailed under jib and mizzen. Steering was difficult but I think I handled it very well and it was great fun- requires all your concentration. I can read signals from the compass, the wheel, and the rhythm of the boat with the seas, and know what is going to happen about a second in advance, which enables me to steer proactively instead of reacting after things happen. That way I can counter what happens *as* it happens but with only a second or less notice, if you're not concentrating you lose the advantage of the signals. I find that I have a very good instinct for this, maybe better than anybody else on the boat. Ray says he can steer proactively if he can see the seas coming, but can't use the compass, wheel, and rhythm the way I do. I'm not sure about Sonny- maybe he can but none of the others can. Ray has also been concerned about the hydraulic steering and it's slowness to respond but after this afternoon, I don't think I am concerned. I found that you have to steer aggressively, to make sure it knows what you want it to do, and it will respond. Then you gain an understanding of what it will do when you take an action. You learn what to expect.

Today was mostly sunny again, but cooler. The water temperature is down to 64 degrees. By the way, we passed the halfway point (974 miles) on afternoon watch.

Saturday, January 11: Lat.- 38 degrees, 59 minutes south; Lon.- 91 degrees, 7 minute west; 804 miles to go. - 6:20 P.M.- After an ugly morning that was cold and cloudy, the weather improved to fairly decent and the wind stayed in the 20-28 knot range. The wind started building yesterday in the late morning and has peaked at 32 knots, still from the west-northwest, and we are averaging a speed of about six and a half knots, straight toward our destination. We covered 156 miles in 24 hours! Last night they took down the mizzen right after 6:00 (the main was already down) and we still maintained our speed on just the jib.

The following seas are amazing to watch as they approach, looking like moving mountains-really 10-15 feet- and then pass under the boat. Sometimes we surf down them and I saw 12.3 knots on the speed log once, though we usually only go eight or nine knots when we surf. We also realize that surfing down the waves can be dangerous if you go too fast in the wrong conditions. In any case, this is excellent training for Cape Horn, where we will likely have larger following seas, probably in stronger winds.

The sea temperature has dropped to 61 degrees and the air gets progressively colder. I am thinking of switching to my big blanket tonight, though the light blanket has worked fine so far.

I have concluded that Sonny is better at steering in these seas than I am. He steers just as good a course, if not better, and he makes it look easy. I have to work at it. His relationship with Ray is *very* strained and tenuous. Ray was talking again today to me, about leaving the boat in Puerto Montt. That is still unlikely, but they definitely need to put their differences aside until after this voyage!

Sunday, January 12: Lat.- 39 degrees, 19 minutes south; Lon.- 88 degrees, 14 minutes west; 670 miles to go. - 6:35 P.M.- I still can't believe the cavalier attitudes about clipping on tethers in the cockpit, even in 20-30 knot winds and 10-15 foot seas with water temperature at 61 degrees! Mark, Ray and I clip on now any time we are at the helm, and sometimes when we are just sitting in the cockpit but Richard seems to be resisting for some reason, and this afternoon when I went on watch Naomi was at the helm without even her life jacket. Richard may be resisting because I was the first one to start and he has trouble following my lead any more. I don't know if it is because I was made Watch Captain, or he feels a need to compete with me, or what. He almost didn't go on the jeep tour on Easter Island, probably because I took the lead in setting it up and I was the first to say, "I'm going". He is an odd little duck! Ray said the other day "It's good that Richard is on watch with me. He probably gets on my nerves less than he would yours or Mark's". He is still being very quiet- almost sulky- and Ray said that it's not just with me, but in general. You get the impression from Richard that before you are allowed to assume residence in Old Lyme, you have to submit to the mayor's office, the precise measurements of the stick that's up your ass. You not only must *have* a stick, but it has to be precisely the correct size!

West-northwest winds continue in the 18-25 knot range and we continue to average a speed of about six knots. Last night's watch was cold, with a few sprinkles of rain and this morning was cold and ugly. I wore my foul weather pants and jacket the last two nights; the first time I have worn the pants. They kept the companionway closed all day because the following wind was cold and blew right in, but this afternoon the sun came out and it was pretty nice. The following seas have built up some and are still amazing to watch. I swear I saw one this afternoon that was 20 feet from top to bottom! I wish I could capture it on film

I am experiencing a bit of irregularity on this passage- very unusual for me! I think maybe the change in watch schedule threw me off. I am definitely off my morning constitutional- skip some days entirely; go with difficulty other days. The day before yesterday I went twice and thought I was getting back to normal, but then skipped yesterday, and nothing so far today. I'm sure it will eventually fix itself! I wouldn't normally think twice about that sort of thing, but when you're out here, a week or more from landfall, you think about things like intestinal blockages, and wonder what the consequences

109

would be. When I am on watch, it feels good to stick my hand in my pocket and feel my safety pins!

Monday, January 13: Lat.-39 degrees, 38 minutes south; Lon.- 85 degrees, 36 minutes west; 547 miles to go. - 6:45 P.M.- Another crappy morning and nice afternoon. Mark and I had a little light rain during night watch. It started out dry but the rain came at 3:45 so I went below and put on my foul weather suit. It really was nothing more than a heavy mist, but enough to get you wet and since the wind was behind us, it blew into the entire cockpit. One more weather item- we had fog this morning for the first time. When daylight came we only could see for a half mile or less. I was at the helm when I noticed it, and I asked Mark to check the radar regularly to look for ships. We check it every half hour or so for weather anyway, but every 15 minutes for ships in the fog. We have the range set for 16 miles and since freighters commonly move at speeds of 20-25 knots, one could approach before you knew it if you weren't paying attention. We haven't seen another vessel since we left Easter Island but you can't assume that there are none in the area. The wind dropped off this morning, too, around 7:30. They tried sailing on a starboard tack for a while, since the wind had shifted to the southwest but by 10:00 it had died completely so we motored for a while. Around 2:45 P.M. it started picking up again so we stopped the engine and sailed. By 3:30 it was back to 16-18 knots from the west-northwest, just like before.

Richard still resists the idea of clipping on at the helm, even in the fog. The seas are still in the 6-10 foot range and with the fog, your already slim chances of being rescued if you went overboard are diminished further. I think Sonny, as the captain, is remiss in not making it mandatory to clip on, at least for the next two passages. The sea temperature is now 60 degrees.

Ray cooked another great fish dinner tonight. He used a different recipe with cheese and a light white sauce, small pasta shells, and corn. He is amazing, and much appreciated.

Tuesday, January 14: Lat.- 39 degrees, 50 minutes south; Lon.- 84 degrees, 4 minutes west; 476 miles to go - 9:05 A.M.- The barometer has dropped below 30 this morning, falling steadily for the last 24 hours, and sure enough, the weather is deteriorating. Winds are 25-30knots and it is raining cats and dogs. Fortunately for me, the rain didn't start until after the end of my night watch. Seas are running about 8-15 feet and following seas, especially large ones like this, produce a pronounced sideways back-and-forth rolling of the boat. Last night about ten o'clock a tray full of tools, nuts, bolts, etc. fell off the workbench, which is over the lower end of my bunk. It all hit the floor beside my bunk with a God-awful clatter as I slept soundly, scaring the *hell* out of me! The tray belongs inside a toolbox, which should have been latched. Someone, Sonny or Ray, had left it unsecured, thinking that gravity would keep it in place. I was really pissed off, and voiced my displeasure. That kind of carelessness could create a real problem down around Cape Horn.

A second safety issue has to do with the little companionway doors. They have a hasp-type latch that is supposed to keep them closed and there is a hole where you can put a lock if you want to lock the boat. Well, like a lot of other things on this boat, the latch doesn't work right and in these rolling seas, the rocking back-and-forth caused the doors to fall open and bang against the bulkhead. Sonny solved that problem by closing the latch and putting a metal pin in the hole for the lock! That means that those doors can only be opened from outside, in the cockpit! That seems to me sort of like locking a fire exit. Yes, the sliding hatch opens, but if there should be an incident like a knockdown or rollover and the sliding hatch jammed, those below could be trapped. I told Sonny that I had a problem with that and he said "If you can think of something better, we'll do it". I guess he thought about it some more because he just now came to me and suggested using a piece of cardboard for a pin- that way it could easily be kicked or pushed out if necessary.

A third safety issue, this one no direct concern of mine, is that when we went on watch at 2:00 A.M. the wind and seas were as previously described and there was Naomi sitting at the helm, not clipped on to the boat. I have not seen for myself, but I don't think Sonny clips on either. Why am I telling you all this? To give you more pieces of the picture of a man who appears to have no regard whatsoever for safety! On either side of the helmsman's chair is a little alleyway under the frame of the bimini, over the winch and over the lifelines into the water, which is a cold 60 degrees, and he allows his daughter to sit there in the middle of a cloudy, pitch black night with the boat severely rolling back-and-forth, without being clipped on. Mark and I have discussed this alleyway several times, noting how easy it would be to lose your balance and roll right over the side. It is easy to clip on, too, as there is a U-bolt down near the deck on either side of the helm, for the sole purpose of clipping on tethers.

When you mention safety to Sonny he professes to think it is important, but his actions say otherwise. Since he has lied about other things (like the captain issue), I don't know whether he lies about this, or is just too stupid to see the safety concerns! To make matters worse, I mentioned some of this to Ray and though he acknowledged the validity of my concerns, he said, "I have to admit that I'm not the most safety conscious guy either"! You have to look out for your own safety here because you sure can't count on either of those two guys doing it!

Wednesday, January 15: Lat.- 40 degrees, 55 minutes south; Lon.- 79 degrees, 59 minutes west; 278 miles to go. - 6:45 P.M.- So this is the "roaring forties"! The wind has been howling and the seas building all day. At 2:00 P.M. Sonny estimated the swells at 15-20 feet. During my afternoon watch it continued and everybody seems to agree that they are 20-25 feet now! We covered 26 miles on our afternoon watch and winds ranged a consistent 26-34 knots. Steering is an adventure in these conditions but you get into the rhythm and it isn't that difficult. When Mark is at the helm I usually lie on the lee side of the cockpit (clipped on!), and watch the following swells approach- it is truly awesome. If you didn't know better you would think, "That huge mountain of water coming at me is surely going to consume me and this piddledy-ass little boat, leaving no trace, or even any indication that we were ever here".

This morning at 5:45 Mark and I saw another whale. I was at the helm and out of the corner of my eye I saw a swirl in the water about 50 feet off the starboard quarter. I looked, and said, "There's a critter", then "It's a whale", as it swam right at us, diving under the boat as it approached. We looked for it to surface on the other side, but it never did. We saw it only for about ten seconds and didn't see what kind or how big it was. It was brown in color, and looked *big*, as you would expect a whale to look.

The fresh water pump malfunctioned briefly this morning. It wouldn't shut off by itself. We looked for leaks but didn't find any. It appears that there was an air lock so we were only without water for a couple of hours.

Last night one of the batteries wasn't charging properly so they ran the generator twice while I was trying to sleep before night watch. The engine room is directly across the passageway from my bunk. Then Sonny and Ray were working on the alternator at the workbench, just over the foot of my bunk, and were talking while they worked. I snarled at them a little, as this was the second night in a row that my

112

sleep was seriously interrupted. I later apologized to each of them for waking up grumpy, and each said that he understood, and apologized for keeping me awake. When you think about it all it's amazing that we all get along as well as we have.

Last night I wore my ski cap that I bought for $5.00 in Bozeman last summer, and I also wore my rubber boots for the first time. Both are very comfortable and effective. I still have not used thermal underwear, turtlenecks, wool socks or my Land's End jacket, but have used everything else. I had to save something back because as Mark put it, "I don't want to get down around Cape Horn and run out of ammunition". I was trying to wait until after Puerto Montt to use *any* of the cold weather stuff, but it gets cold here, so I am getting it all out. The foul weather suit works great, and so do the boots. It rained a little on night watch last night and I barely noticed. Only your hands and face are exposed and there is no way for water to run inside. Oh yes, I haven't used my gloves yet either.

Thursday, January 16: Lat. 41 degrees, 33 minutes south; Lon.-77 degrees, 4 minutes west - 7:05 P.M.- Winds continue to howl and swells have been running 20-25 feet all day, with some that I would bet reached 30 feet. I took a couple of pictures on afternoon watch but things tend to flatten out on film, so I probably wasted the pictures. These seas continue to give the boat that pronounced side-to-side roll and last night the wind shifted from west-northwest to west-southwest, putting the seas on the starboard quarter and making steering even more of an adventure. Winds peaked on our night watch at 36 knots and Sonny had us roll up half the jib. I didn't think that was necessary since the main and mizzen were already furled, but he was spooked by the winds. All it accomplished was to slow us down about a knot, which caused the boat to wallow in the swells making steering a pain in the ass and sleep next to impossible for those below.

Even Richard has started clipping on at the helm now. I made a speech to the effect that if you don't clip on you are not only risking your own life, but if you go over and we have to attempt search and rescue in these conditions you are risking the boat and everybody on board. Even Naomi was clipped on at 2:00 A.M., but at 2:00 P.M. she was at the helm and didn't even have her life jacket *on*! At the same time Sonny was out of the cockpit by the mizzenmast doing something with the jerry jugs lashed there, and was not clipped on! The man had told me a half hour earlier that these are the biggest swells he has ever seen, and he sailed around the world!

113

New development: The last few days, with the seas that I have described, both Sonny and Naomi have moved to the salon for sleeping; Sonny on the port side settee and Naomi back where she used to sleep, on the dining settee on the starboard side. What that means is that there is no place to sit to have your meals, with weather making the cockpit inhospitable. Also, with them sleeping, you don't feel like you can talk in that area either. I ate my cereal while sitting on my bunk this morning.

The last two days we have started seeing these really large birds that we believe to be albatross. They have wingspans that look to be seven or eight feet, chunky bodies, and hooked beaks. When flying they remind me of B-52 bombers.

I got through to Maureen on the satellite phone this morning- good to talk with her after 16 days, even though it was only for about three minutes. We should see land tomorrow, and hopefully spend the night at anchor off the town of Ancud!

Today is the 16th day since we left Easter Island and we have seen neither hide nor hair of another human being- no ships; nothing but the two whales. It's hard to believe that with all the people on this planet you could go 16 days and over 1,700 miles without seeing even a hint of another person!

Friday, January 17 - 6:35 P.M.- Land-Ho! When we went on watch at 2:00 P.M. I looked to the southeast and saw some puffy, white clouds built up like those you see over mountains. I looked closer and sure enough, there were two mountain peaks - land for the first time this year! We were 36 miles out at the time. Naomi was at the helm, and she hadn't seen them. This is exciting stuff- my first ever look at mainland South America, and to see it from a sailboat coming in from Easter Island, nearly 2,000 miles away! I am very thankful for the opportunity to do this. We plan to anchor tonight, probably behind the lighthouse at Ancud, around 9:30-10:00 P.M. No night watch tonight! Tomorrow we will head on to Puerto Montt.

Ray cooked another outstanding fish dinner last night, the third from that fish, and there is one more bag in the freezer. Each bag has fed the entire crew with enough left over for a couple of lunches the next day. That was a *big* fish! I trolled this afternoon, but had no strikes. The wind died down last night on our night watch and never came back up. We started the engine at 4:30 A.M. and are still motoring.

8:05 P.M.- I just went topside. We have the Ancud lighthouse in sight off the starboard bow. You can see a cruise ship lighted up in the distance. They run cruises around Cape Horn, between here and Buenos Aires. The sea temperature has dropped from 59 degrees to 53 as we leave Golfo Coronados and enter Chacao Channel. I intended to stay up for anchoring, but I am tired and it's cold topside so I'm going to bed.

Saturday, January 18 - 7:10 A.M.- We are motor-sailing east, up Canal Chacao (Chacao Channel)- we are in Chile! We dropped anchor at 9:30 last night off a village called Puerto Ingles, east of the Faro Corona (Corona Lighthouse) near Ancud. We made the 1,948-mile passage in 17 days, 6 hours. As is so often the case, the most prominent building in Puerto Ingles was a little church; this one made of stone, with a red roof and an elaborate little cemetery out front. To the north we saw some cows walk down to and along the beach a couple hundred yards, mooing all the way until they joined some friends up another hillside.

It's just as well that I didn't stay up for the anchoring last night because Sonny decided that we would do anchor watches, even though Ray had told us here would be no watches. It wasn't too bad, because you only need one person on anchor watch. Mark went up at 2:00 A.M. and I went up at 4:00. I only found out about the anchor watches when I heard somebody moving around at 2:00, and it was Sonny waking Mark up to tell him. I went up to explain to Sonny that Ray had told us there would be no watches, and his curt reply was "You asked the wrong person". I said, "He is a ship's officer". Sonny said, "He didn't talk to me".

As is frequently the case with him, it's not so much *what* he says, but *how* he says it. He tries hard to be nice sometimes but I just don't think it is his nature. I think he is an example of what Jimmy Buffett said about assholes: "They're born that way, and they usually don't change".

I don't know whether Naomi got up and shared anchor watch with Sonny or not but she has yet to make an appearance this morning. A new country, a new *continent*, land after 17 days at sea- exciting stuff to me, but she shows no interest; just like our arrival at Easter Island where she lay there on the settee in the salon doing her nails as we sailed just off the north shore on our approach!

Sunday, January 19 - 4:25 A.M.- We are anchored in a tiny bay at a place called Puerto Pilocura. I am on anchor watch, enjoying the dawning of a new day. The mouth of the bay is at the west end and we are at the east end. There are commercial fish pens at the mouth of the bay to the west, and lots of really neat, colorful little fishing boats. Some are grounded on the beach at half tide and some are anchored, one right next to us. We are anchored off an island that rises some 30 or 40 feet above the water, with maybe a dozen houses scattered around, some cultivated fields, a few cows, and roosters that are crowing right now. The sky is about half cloudy leaving some hope for a nice sunrise. First light came just before 3:30 and good light by 4:00. With one-person anchor watches I didn't have to come on until 4:00, though I showed up and had tea with Mark at 3:30. He went down to bed just after 4:00.

Yesterday we motor-sailed to the east and then motored north-northeast, as the wind came up from the north and we rolled up the jib. Naomi finally made her appearance just before she and Sonny went on watch at 10:00- glad she could contain her enthusiasm! This is the person who told Ray she was making this trip for the adventure.

Just before noon Mark was sitting in at the helm when the wind piped up into the 20-30 knot range, 20 or 30 degrees off our bow. We were trying to get around a buoy to avoid some shallows when the wind and chop built to where we were making zero headway and too much leeway to get to the buoy. Richard took over steering at one o'clock and we put up the mizzen to help with the steering and leeway, but still had no forward movement, and this with a 65 horsepower diesel! We finally came about and headed west-northwest to get position, and finally made it to the buoy. It was very frustrating to motor into wind and a three to four foot chop and get nowhere! As we approached the buoy winds built into the 30-35 knot range. I took over steering just as we rounded the buoy, at two o'clock. By then we had decided that we couldn't go northeast toward Puerto Montt, so Ray and Sonny looked in the cruising guide and found this anchorage a few miles to the southeast. A driving rain began just as I started to steer, and the wind continued to build, peaking at 43 knots. The entrance to the bay is narrow, and further complicated by the fish pens so Sonny decided to steer us in while I helped Ray and Mark take down the mizzen. We then anchored in 12 feet of water at 3:15 P.M.

We again set anchor watches, and this time it was a good thing. Mark and I had been on watch so we took the first anchor watch as the storm continued. At 5:15 P.M. it was blowing and raining like hell when it became obvious that the anchor was dragging. It was a blessing, really, because the tide had been going out and by then the water depth was only six feet. If we had stayed there we would have been sitting on the bottom, as the tide continued going out for another hour. In the driving rain Ray started the engine and I pulled the anchor with Mark's help. When it came up we found that it had been dragging because we had set it in kelp. About a bale of kelp came up with the anchor! We moved to water that was then 16 feet deep and anchored again. This time, I set it, snubbing it down as the wind- still 25 knots or so- blew us off. It seems that I am the only one here who knows about snubbing the anchor down as you set it. In any case, this time it held. The tidal range here seems to be 10-15 feet. By the way, I see why some people eat kelp, as it was green, and looked a lot like lettuce.

The storm finally ended around six-thirty and Ray cooked the last of the fish with rice, corn, and canned diced tomatoes. It was excellent again! Sonny and Naomi didn't have any. He chose a hot dog and some of the corn and tomatoes, and she had some kind of soy and tofu crap. Their loss!

We are planning to leave about 6:00 A.M. and head for Puerto Montt, about 30 miles away. This entire area of islands is very interesting. Some of them have short roads but many have no roads at all. Their primary transportation is by boat. They are fishing and farming people, and there are a few villages and towns. One island, Chiloe, is huge; maybe 100 miles long and 10-30 miles wide, and separates the Pacific Ocean from the Gulf of Ancud. The town of Ancud, with a population of 25,000, is on the north end of Chiloe. I think we are planning to go down the Gulf of Ancud when we leave, to the south end of Chiloe and into the ocean there.

117

11 – PUERTO MONTT

Monday, January 20 - 7:35 P.M.- Yesterday turned out to be a very good day. We pulled anchor just after 6:00 A.M. and motored the remaining distance to Puerto Montt, passing through a lot of beautiful, hilly islands with a patchwork of pastures and cultivated fields with a few houses, an occasional village, and one fair-sized town. The hills are up to maybe 300 feet and everything is very green and at times shrouded in mist. It was what I imagine Ireland to look like. Up almost every little bay were fish pens- not especially pleasing to the eye but you admire the way they have developed their aquaculture. We motored into light northerly winds and had a bit of light rain. I trolled most of the way but had no success. We saw glimpses of snow-capped mountains just inland from here including one that is a spectacular volcano but the clouds have kept us from getting a good look.

We arrived here about noon and got a slip at Marina del Sur, three miles west of downtown, and two miles west of Angelmo, the market and port section of Puerto Montt. Ray, Mark, Richard and I walked to Angelmo at 2:30 to explore and to eat a late lunch. I had salmon for 3,000 pesos ($4.30 U.S.) and it was outstanding. Also, Ray and I split 20 oysters, also for $4.30. They were small, but good. After lunch we all went exploring and shopping for a while, getting separated in the process. Mark and I went for a beer, had several, and got back to the boat at ten o'clock with a good buzz- mild hangover today. In the market we discovered that local handmade items, especially wool items, are really cheap.

This morning I did one load of my laundry and found that is one thing that is *not* cheap here. It cost $3.60 for wash and $3.60 for the dryer! At least they furnish the soap! They only have one washer and one dryer here at the marina so it is a pain in the ass to do laundry.

Sonny is having the roller furling rebuilt here. We had a little trouble with it in The Galapagos, as it popped out of the drum but we put it back in and it has worked O.K. Sonny and Ray decided to have it looked at here since it is a critical piece of equipment, and sure enough, it was shot.

This afternoon Mark and I took a taxi into Puerto Montt. Taxis *are* cheap here, as it is only 300 pesos, or about 45 cents per person to ride downtown. I cashed some traveler's checks, tried to call Maureen, and then ate lunch. I had Pailla Marine, with lots of salmon, scallops, abalone, potatoes, onions, and tomatoes. It was outstanding! We then pretty well walked all over the downtown area, along the waterfront, and out to Angelmo where we went to the fish market and some of the shops and stalls that sell wool items and other handcrafts. I bought Molly a nice wool sweater for $7.00. I was successful in calling Maureen from that area, and had a really enjoyable conversation. We also ate dinner there. I had abalone and it was excellent!

Puerto Montt is a very impressive small city of just over 100,000 people, set between the waterfront and mountains, built up some steep hillsides. It is clean, modern, seems to function well, and you have a feeling of safety when you walk around. Everything seems to be in good repair. We had a couple more glimpses of the snow-capped mountains and volcano, but they are still mostly obscured by clouds. People say it is unseasonably cold right now.

Ray was in a pissy mood this morning, but seemed better later on. Sonny and Naomi went provision shopping today and Sonny hurt his back while carrying a box. He is in pain, and just took some of Naomi's Midol. He gives out a "Goddammit" every time he moves. Right now, he seems to be going out of his way to be nice to me though.

Tuesday, January 21 - 10:10 A.M.- My laundry is done; at least for the moment. I got up at 6:00 and when I went for my shower I took my second load and washed it. I had more than a load of dark clothes so I left out a few items, like shorts, that I won't need for a while. The dryer runs for an hour and ten minutes so everything even got dry. I have a couple of small grease spots on a pair of jeans and a stain on a t-shirt that didn't come out. Oh well, those things happen!

Some of us are planning to take a bus to Ancud and back tomorrow. I got the idea Monday as Mark and I walked past the bus station and saw one with "Ancud" in the windshield. We went in and checked schedules and prices, and decided that would be a good day's outing. The trip is about 65 miles each way and takes just over two hours, including the 30-minute ferry ride across the Chacao Channel between the towns of Paragua and Chacao. The cost is less than $6.00 for the round trip. Also, Ray found a place that offers whitewater rafting trips so we may try that, too. The weather looks a little better today so I will take some pictures.

9:50 P.M.- Today was really nice. I did take some pictures, though not as many as I should have. I went into town by myself about 11:00 and enjoyed having a little private time. I ate lunch at the Angelmo market and had an excellent meal of fried eel for about $4.50 U.S. The eel was like a white meat fish, with a spine that started out triangular and then tapered.

After lunch I went to an Internet Café to do e-mail, then met Mark and Richard at 2:00. I had an e-mail from my friend Dave, who said that he might have some consulting work for me when I get back. I wrote back and asked him whether it would be in-office or Internet work, so I can plan accordingly if it works out. We'll see. Mark and I had a beer and Richard had ice cream with chocolate syrup. Ice cream with chocolate syrup was not on the menu, and here's Richard, telling the waitress in English, what he wants, using lots of hand motions and wondering why she didn't understand. I was able to help a little, but I didn't know how to say *vanilla* or *syrup* in Spanish. Mark and I were looking at each other; laughing so hard we nearly fell out of our chairs. Richard persists in doing that sort of thing- asking questions about menu items, or asking to substitute items, when they have no idea what he is saying.

After that, Richard left to go and take some pictures while Mark and I went shopping and exploring, and to the post office to mail cards. We found a fly-fishing shop, but it was closed for lunch. They had a brochure describing guide trips for $250 for a full day of fishing, and it sounded very interesting. Two years ago I would have spent the money and done it, but not now.

We met Richard at Angelmo at 5:30 and had dinner. I didn't know what I was ordering but I knew it would be good, and it was. It turned out to be a crabmeat casserole with lots of cheese, and it was outstanding, for only $6.00. When we got back to the marina we were walking past the bar when Sonny called us inside and bought us a beer! He is really going out of his way to be nice these days. It seems almost like he realized what an asshole he has been, and is trying to make up for it. We'll see if it lasts!

The roller furling is re-built and re-installed now. Tomorrow a guy will be trying to fix the autopilot. That one means nothing to me, as I prefer to steer manually anyway.

Wednesday, January 22 - 9:35 P.M.- Today Mark, Richard, and I took the bus to Ancud. We anchored within sight of Ancud the night we arrived from Easter Island and thought it looked nice, scattered along a beach, up a hillside and along the top of a cliff. It is a pretty, fishing town of 28,000 people located on the north shore of Chiloe Island. We left Puerto Montt on the 8:15 A.M. bus and arrived in Ancud around 10:30. First, we found a little café and had pastry and *café con leche* (Mark had *café negro*). Then we walked along the waterfront to the fisherman's harbor. The people there were working vigorously-some rigging baitfish on hooks and others preparing crab bait. Crab fishing is serious business in Ancud. They bring salmon 18-24 inches long, from the farms, filet them keeping the filets to sell, and use the carcasses for crab bait. It was very interesting to watch all that.

Next, we walked up the hill to *Fuerte San Antonio*, an old Spanish fort that used to guard the channel. After that, we had a great seafood lunch at a place with an upstairs dining room that offered a panoramic view of the harbor and the bay. Later we went to an interesting museum that had handcraft artists working and selling their creations on the grounds. One was an interesting old man who carves wooden ships and likes to talk. He showed us pictures of a lot of ships he has carved, including relatively modern battleships. I took a picture of him and of some old ladies knitting wool items. Finally, we walked around, exploring the rest of the town before taking the 4:40 bus to Puerto Montt.

We got back to Puerto Montt just before 7:00 and had dinner at Rosita's in the Angelmo market. Mark and I ordered, while Richard kept asking questions and not understanding the answers. He agonized for a time, and then said, "I don't think I'll have anything", even though he had just said he was hungry.

I wanted to hit him! He just sat there, and I said, "Richard, you're a pain in the ass!" He sat a little longer, and finally ordered mussels with a salad, which he then raved about! I had a fish soup that was one of the best I ever had.

When we got back to the boat we found that they installed jack lines today; one from the main mast to a bow cleat and one form the mizzen to the stern. The only problem is that you can't get to either one to clip on your tether without first leaving the cockpit. To me, that seems to partially defeat the purpose of jack lines. I mentioned this to Ray but he didn't agree. Ray also told me that Sonny is not willing to replace the frayed jib sheets. He said that the fraying doesn't affect the strength of the core, so we are going around Cape Horn with duct tape on our jib sheets! I also found out that our departure has been delayed until Monday because we have to wait for a part for the autopilot. I am enjoying it here, but I'm ready to get on with it. Also, the added days in port make it difficult to manage my ready cash, and I have a finite amount of money with me. Even here on the mainland, most places don't accept credit cards, at least so far. I'm sure it will all work out.

I forgot to mention that Mark insisted on buying me three fishing lures today. He had mentioned it before, because he said he really enjoyed eating the fish that I caught, and seeing me catch them. Today I found some in Ancud that I thought might be good, and he insisted on paying for them. I thought that was *really* nice of him. The other night when we were drinking beer, he also thanked me for taking the lead in finding activities for us, planning, making the opportunities available, and making things happen. That made me feel good! Today both he and Richard thanked me for coming up with this trip to Ancud and making it happen.

Thursday, January 23 - 8:30 P.M.- I forgot to mention another issue. Yesterday morning I went topside and saw Mark stuffing Styrofoam into four small vents on the starboard side between the cockpit and lifelines. I asked him about it and he said Sonny asked him to do it. It seems that Sonny is concerned that if we sustain a knockdown on that side, water would come in through those vents and flood the engine room. The vents are there to provide air to the main and generator engines. I asked Ray about it last night and he said he agreed with Sonny. I asked if he thought maybe the designer of the boat put those vents there for a reason? He said yes, but if the engines didn't run right we would open the engine room door that opens into the head, to let air in. The other engine room door opens directly across from my bunk and since the carbon monoxide incident, I will not have that one open while I am trying to sleep. I still see this issue as a problem. It seems to me that when it is cold outside we will have the cabin closed up as tightly as we can. That being the case, the cabin will contain a finite amount of oxygen and with one or two diesel engines operating and consuming oxygen, people sleeping in the cabin could wake up dead due to oxygen depletion! We will see!

When we got back to the boat last night we found a note from Naomi, that she and Sonny had gone into town for dinner. We thought, "That's nice; they are finally getting out and enjoying the seafood here, in one of these nice restaurants". *Wrong!* They were dining instead, under the golden arches of McDonald's! I heard Sonny say that he went all-out and had two desserts!

Weather wise, today was the nicest day we have had here. It was fairly warm, with no rain and we even got a good look at one of the

122

volcanoes above the city. I did "stuff" by myself around town and enjoyed the day- mailed post cards, went to the fly-shop, and arranged to go rafting with Ray on Sunday. I had lunch at a place called Café Real in the downtown area- had seafood ceviche, chicken vegetable soup with *lots* of chicken, a melon slice and a beer, for $3.15. During the period from 11:30 A.M. until 2:30 P.M. there were three bands playing outside in the downtown area, two in the pedestrian plaza in front of a shopping mall, and a very good jazz band on the corner outside a restaurant called Sherlock's. I had an Escudo beer at a sidewalk table at Sherlock's and listened to the jazz for half an hour. All the members of the jazz band were young guys, too, with a bass, a guitar, a saxophone, and drums. I met Mark and Ray at 2:30 and we wandered around for a while before Ray left, looking for strip clubs. Mark and I went to the bus station and checked on busses to the town of Frutillar, which is on Lake Llanquihue, (Yankee-way) 30 miles north of here. Bus tickets are about $1.40 and busses leave every half hour so we plan to go there tomorrow. We then had dinner at the same place we ate the afternoon we arrived. It wasn't as good this time as they got our orders mixed up, and my salmon was overcooked a little - not bad, but not as good. This was our first meal here that I would describe as less than outstanding.

Friday, January 24 - 9:05 P.M.- Our departure from here has been delayed now until Wednesday, as we continue to wait for a part for the autopilot. It is supposed to arrive Tuesday. I get frustrated with these continuing delays. I like it here, but I really need to get home by May 1, I want to make the entire trip, and I don't want to spend money on an airplane ticket to fly home from somewhere. Most of us don't consider the autopilot a critical item and don't think we should have waited. Also, when we had the autopilot Sonny and Naomi used it and didn't pay attention when they were on watch. That could be dangerous where we are going next.

Other than that, today was a great day. Mark, Richard and I took the bus trip to Frutillar, and it was very enjoyable. The weather was cloudy and misty so we didn't get to see the volcanoes across the lake, but otherwise, it exceeded our expectations. The area was settled in the 1850's by German immigrants, who were invited and given land by the Chilean government. Frutillar is divided into two sections: Frutillar *Bajo*, down the hill along the lakefront, and Frutillar *Alta*, up the hill and along the highway. The latter is a typical little Chilean town. The former is largely a German-Chilean community,

123

with gingerbread houses, and German names on streets, hotels, schools, public buildings, and restaurants. The most impressive thing was the beautiful flowers everywhere! Every yard was an elaborate flower garden! There were lots of roses, fuschias, daisies, nasturtiams, and many others that I don't know the names of, in an abundance of different colors. There is a nice black sand beach, and the water in the lake looked very clear. We went to the museum of German colonization which included a house of that period, complete with a music room, a mill with a working water wheel, a blacksmith's shop and residence, and a large, elaborate flower garden. There is a concert facility on the lakefront, and they have live concerts weekly for 35 weeks a year. It is an extremely charming well-kept little town.

We looked for German food at lunchtime, and had trouble finding it despite the German restaurant names but finally succeeded at the Club Aleman, or German Club. I had a filet mignon with a mushroom and onion sauce that was one of the best steaks I have ever had- great flavor, tender, and cooked perfectly for my taste. It cost 5,500 pesos, or $7.85. Richard gave us another performance with his ordering. The menu was in German, with Spanish translations. He pointed to an item "Ensalada Palmera" and asked me what it was. I said "heart of palm salad". I heard him order it, but paid no attention as I was deciding on my own order. When the waiter brought our beers, he brought Richard a small plate covered with heart of palm, and one curly slice of tomato peel, shaped like a flower, for decoration. Mark and I started drinking our beers and Richard just sat there staring at his plate with a stunned look on his face. I couldn't figure out why he wasn't eating the salad, so I asked, "Richard, what else did you order?" He said, "This is it! I thought there would be more to it than this!" I said, "It's not too late to order something else".

He said "No; I prefer to eat light sometimes. This will be fine". Shortly after lunch he was hungry, and looking for snacks!

The ride to and from Frutillar was nice, too. We were on a four-lane toll highway, "Ruta 5", which I later learned is the southern end of the Pan American Highway. We passed through pretty hill country with fields of crops and improved pasture bordered by fences or windrows of trees. The ride took about 45 minutes each way. On the return trip we stopped in Puerto Varas, another pretty little lakefront town where Ray and I are planning to go whitewater rafting tomorrow.

Saturday, January 25 - 9:20 P.M.- What a fine day! The weather was almost hot, the sky was clear, and the volcanoes came out and put on a show! This was by far the nicest day we have had here and the whitewater rafting was fantastic, too!

Ray and I left the boat at 7:20 A.M., caught a bus to Angelmo, and then another to Puerto Varas. We showed up at the rafting company's office at 8:45. At that time the clouds were over the volcanoes, though everything else was clear. We had a great, 30-mile van ride around part of Lake Llanquihue and into the Andes, between two volcanoes to Rio Petrohue. When we started, you could see maybe half way up, but the tops of the volcanoes were still shrouded in clouds. The river is big; about 50 yards across, and strong, clear, and a beautiful aqua color that I have seen in the ocean and mountain lakes but never before in a river. This was a first-class operation, including safety equipment and orientation. Our guide, Hermann, spoke enough English to assure communication. Also in our raft were two brothers and the wife of one of the brothers. The rapids were class three, with a couple of fours. The outstanding feature was lots of very big waves, some of which came over the raft. It was a really great run! About 30 minutes after we started, we looked upstream and there, framed by the river and trees on either side, was the perfect, snowcapped cone of Orsino Volcano! It was a sight to behold, and of course we didn't have our cameras! The drive to and from the river was filled with exceptionally nice lake and mountain scenery and we walked down to a lakefront park for a while just to look at the volcanoes across the lake.

We got back to Puerto Montt around 4:30 or so. Ray came back to the boat while I called Maureen and then stayed in the market at Angelmo for a dinner of really good salmon cooked in butter. After dinner I was walking along the waterfront when I ran into Sonny and Naomi. He was very apologetic about the delay; said he understood my situation; that we are only a few days behind schedule and he thinks we can still get back by the first week in May; that he, Naomi, and Ray also need to get back by then. He also apologized for being unable to find V-8 or tomato juice here! He was so nice I almost felt bad for getting so pissed at him. He and Naomi were actually headed into Angelmo market to have a seafood dinner! Not only that, but they had heard about our trip to Frutillar and are planning to go there tomorrow! Wonders never cease!

I really enjoyed walking along the waterfront on a Saturday evening and watching the people- families, friends, little kids, couples- all seemingly enjoying just being there and socializing. Some were taking boat rides along the harbor. Everyone looked like they were relaxed and content. We have all been impressed with this country and it's people. They really seem to have their act together. I commented to Ray today that people here see a lot less uptight than people in the U.S. They are kind and courteous. I don't recall seeing any of the locals that seemed pissed off or agitated since I have been here, and I haven't felt the least bit insecure walking around, day or night. Tonight I caught a bus to come back to the boat, and recognized the driver from last night. I was the only passenger and he apparently was headed home for the night. He wasn't coming all the way to the marina, but turned 200-300 yards down the hill. He let me off there, and wouldn't let me pay him. He did the same for Mark, Richard, and me last night!

Sunday/Monday, January 26/27 - 1:05 A.M.- Tampa Bay won the Super Bowl-Whooda thunkit?! That makes you believe that anything is possible! Mark and I went into town in the afternoon to do e-mail, go to the post office, and wander around in the rain. Then we went to the "O.K. Corral" to check it out and make sure the game would be on television, that the beer was cold enough, and so forth. After a couple of beers we went to the Café Real for dinner, after which we met Ray back at the O.K. Corral. Sonny and Naomi joined us to watch the game after they returned from their trip to Frutillar. We had a good time watching the game, and Mark and I were a little drunk by the time it was over. Naomi seems to be coming out of her shell a bit. She has talked more the last couple of days than she has on the entire trip so far. Sonny too, is being very nice and sociable the last few days. Richard, on the other hand, did not join us. He left early this morning by himself and as Ray stated it, "very secretive". Ray said that just as he was leaving to join us, Richard came back but was not interested in the Super Bowl, and chose to stay in for the night by himself. He said he had been to Puerto Varas for the day.

Monday, January 27 - 9:15 A.M.- No real hangover this morning, for which I am thankful! I can tell that I drank some beer last night but all in all, I feel pretty good. Watching the Super Bowl at the O.K. Corral in Puerto Montt, Chile was pretty cool. This morning started out with rain, but it seems to be clearing up now.

7:15 P.M.- Today turned out to be a beautiful day. I wore a t-shirt and long-sleeve shirt, and was overdressed. Ray and Sonny did some work around the boat today, adjusting the rigging for the jib halyard at the top of the mast. Sonny went up the mast twice in the bo's'n chair, and showed surprising agility; more than I thought he had. I did my laundry early this afternoon, so now that is all set for the next passage.

I didn't want to wait until the last minute. Then I went into town to the post office, and had a good phone conversation with Maureen. I took a long walk along the waterfront, and had a nice fish (Congria) dinner at Rosita's.

I am happy to report that my "irregularity" is no longer an issue. Everything seems to be back to normal.

Tuesday, January 28 - 7:30 P.M.- The part for the autopilot still hasn't arrived. Now, supposedly, it is to arrive tomorrow. Sonny is clearing us out through customs and immigration, and says we are leaving Thursday morning, with or without the part. We will see.

This morning I put together some fishing equipment for our "ditch bag", to be taken in the life raft if we should have to abandon ship. I put in hooks, line, weights, and a few lures. It is in a container, stowed in the cockpit. The bag also contains bottles of water, flares, granola bars, a portable VHF radio, and so forth.

Mark and I went exploring again today, taking a long walk east along the waterfront where we found a very nice shopping mall that we didn't know was there; then up a hill to another area of town. We continue to be impressed with Puerto Montt, and with Chile. We had an early dinner in the market and came back to the boat around 6:00.

I finished reading "Snow Falling on Cedars" today. It is a very good book, and I recommend it. I also had a nice telephone conversation with Maureen.

I just watched Ray eat French toast for dinner and I am still amazed at the way he eats. The only limitation on the size of the bites he cuts is that of what he can cram into his mouth. I wouldn't be surprised to learn one day that he had choked to death on a bite of food. And this is a guy who is very big into food and cooking; used to work as a designer of kitchens; family is reportedly full of very good cooks, yet he wolfs down his food like a man on the doorstep of starvation! And get this: Sonny eats the same way! It's none of my business, but I really don't enjoy seeing people eat like that.

Wednesday, January 29 - 8:35 A.M.- The place where we ate last night is called "El Apa". It is owned and operated by an older gentleman in his 60's or 70's, who is unable to speak, but manages to communicate very well. El Apa is out over the water and next to it is an outside stairway leading 15 or 20 feet down to the water. Harbor tour boats sometimes drop people off there, and kids with hand lines fish from the stairs. It's nice to watch all that as you eat. Once before when we ate there we tried to leave a tip, and the owner, who was also our waiter, wouldn't let us. Last night he gave us each a ballpoint pen, a little thing, but something we will remember.

We have found the drivers here to be very courteous. They are respectful and considerate of one another, and especially of pedestrians in crosswalks. If you are in a crosswalk, traffic will stop and pedestrians in turn are considerate in that they tend to cross in little groups, and step right along. Somehow, all this doesn't seem to impede traffic flow. Also, at many intersections, including some busy ones, there are no traffic lights or even stop signs; yet people drive like they are four-way stops, again making allowances for pedestrians. Through all this, you rarely hear a horn blow and we haven't seen so much as a fender bender. Not downtown, but out toward Angelmo you will occasionally see a guy standing in a two-wheel cart pulled by a horse, trotting along with the traffic flow and this is sometimes on a four-lane street. I have seen three or four different ones.

Corn is in season now and in the middle of the busy downtown area you will see from time to time, somebody with a wheelbarrow full of ears of corn, selling them on a street corner, or even in the middle of a block. A couple of times we have seen a juggler at a traffic light on the four-lane waterfront boulevard, between lanes of traffic. Once he was on a unicycle, but yesterday he was on foot. Also yesterday afternoon we were walking along the waterfront east of the Angelmo market among the people sitting along the seawall socializing, and here comes a guy leading a big, brown, longhaired alpaca right down the sidewalk! Then, a guy sitting with his family jumped up, ran over, and gave the alpaca a big kiss as it walked by!

I finally found the right sweater to buy for Maureen. I have been looking since we got here, waiting for one to jump up and say, "buy me", and finally it happened. I like it, and I think she will. I bought it from a lady in a little shop just east of the market. She was very nice, and made sure I understood that she had made the sweater herself, by hand. She said that it is made of llama wool.

Another thing we have not seen here is bums, or "homeless people". A few young backpackers can be seen lying around on the grass here and there but it's obvious that they are passing through, and not homeless. You see the occasional beggar, but they are people with some sort of obvious problem, like missing limbs, for example. You don't see bums lying around in doorways or on the street hassling people for money.

Last night I wrote down two of my poems for Mark. He had asked me twice, so I figured he was serious. Early in the voyage, the night

128

Sonny recited "The Cremation of Sam McGhee", I recited "Coming Home From the Sea" and he liked it. Then one night he made a comment about how it is so nice on night watch and I told him I had written a poem about it. He asked me to recite it, and I did. He liked that one, too, so I wrote them both down and gave them to him. I was *very* flattered that he was interested in them.

12 – CAPE HORN

Thursday, January 30 - 11:00 A.M.- Well, we're on our way to Cape Horn, and there are lots of emotions flying around. This is our Super Bowl and we have just kicked-off; our Mount Everest, and we have just left base camp! Other than riding in an automobile, this is probably the most dangerous thing most of us will ever do. Richard served a combat tour in Vietnam, so he is an exception. I don't think there is much fear among us, but maybe a little apprehension and anxiety along with the excitement, exhilaration, happiness, and anticipation. There may be others floating around, but those are the ones that come to mind.

We cast off from our slip at Marina del Sur at 9:20 A.M., bound for the Falkland Islands, after a morning that was a bit of an adventure. As it turned out, Sonny didn't successfully clear us out day before yesterday as he had thought, and he got the word through the marina manager that the Navy- he keeps saying the "Armada" even though he says everything else in English- was coming at 7:30 this morning to complete the process. He kept saying that he would be surprised if they got here by 9:00, speaking with disdain, implying ineptitude or unreliability on their part. Well, at 6:10 I heard someone knock on the hull. Sonny asked, "Are you the Armada?" and I heard an answer but couldn't make out what was said. A man in civilian clothes came aboard, and since everything was happening earlier than expected I quickly got dressed to go and take a last hot shower ashore. Some quick paper work was done and as I walked to the shower, the man was walking ahead of me. When I got back to the boat a discussion was going on as to whether the guy was from customs or from the "Armada". He had done paper work and yet Sonny had no idea. I said "Sonny, when you asked if he was from the Armada, what did he say?" Sonny thought for a few seconds and said, "I don't know, Charley". We were still wondering just after seven o'clock when another guy, this one in a Navy uniform, showed up. He had to leave to go and get a document that we needed, which he brought back at 8:30. Meanwhile, Naomi had gone into town to convert their remaining 20,000 pesos to dollars, so we had to wait a little longer for her to get back. Anyway, now we are finally under way.

The part for the autopilot finally showed up about nine o'clock last night, and is installed and working. The weather this morning was a cool 64 degrees, after several balmy days. We bought a thermometer here, so now we can know just how cold it really is.

6:20 P.M.- We decided not to go down the inside of Isla Chiloe after all, but to go back out the way we came in by way of the Chacao Channel so we are motoring toward Ancud. Everybody was anxious to get on with this passage and this seemed the quickest way to get out and on our way. The tide really rips through Chacao Channel and we were lucky enough to catch it going out. Our speed averaged about eight knots and peaked over nine even though this afternoon we were motoring straight into a wind of 18-20 knots. We will pass Ancud about 7:30 P.M., having covered the 81 miles in just over ten hours.

Our latest boat problem is that the refrigerator may be dead. About 4:15 P.M. I smelled something burning. We thought it was only a burnt-out belt, but Ray says the wheel on the compressor isn't turning freely, indicating a bearing problem. He is going to try oiling the bearings and see if that will work but he isn't optimistic. The beat goes on!

By 4:15 P.M., with clouds to the south and east, the Andes had pretty much faded out of sight. Soon the Chilean coast will be doing the same and it is kind of sad for me. When you are young and go someplace that you like, you always think that you'll go back and visit again but at some point in your life you start to think "boy, this place is really nice, but it's a pretty good bet that I'll never come here again." That's the way I feel about Chile.

We started getting small swells ten miles inside the mouth of the Chacao Channel, with wind blowing straight in against the outgoing tide, just to remind us that we are on our way. Now we are about five miles in and the swells are getting larger. I am estimating that we will reach Stanley on February 12, or with luck, maybe the 11th.

Friday, January 31 Lat.- 42 degrees, 7 minutes S.; Lon.- 74 degrees, 29 minutes W. Sea Temp.- 56 degrees; Air Temp.- 55 degrees - 10:15 A.M.- Sonny and Mark have both been seasick and Naomi is carrying around a barf bucket. Sonny has puked twice that I know of and still sounds like he is dying- "BLAAAGGHHH"- when he lets it go. We came out of Ancud into a nasty blow that has gone on for about 14 hours now. Winds have consistently been in the 20's from the western quadrant, shifting through about a 50-degree range, from 260 to

310. Seas are a bit confused because of that and are running 15 feet or so, giving us a bumpy, uncomfortable ride. It didn't take Sonny and Naomi long to come out of the bow, as they were almost literally bouncing off the ceiling! Sonny wound up sleeping on the floor and Naomi on the settee bunk on the port side. We are sailing a course of 215-225 degrees, depending on the wind, under the mizzen and jib. We are going southwest to get some water between us and land, and to clear a point of land 300 miles south of here that is at longitude 76 degrees west.

Last night we motored to the mouth of Chacao Channel, just west of Ancud, and then put up sails about 9:00 P.M. There is a point of land just south of there that sticks out to the west and with the storm starting up, and the difficult winds we had a hard time clearing it. On the 10:00-2:00 watch Sonny and Naomi tacked back and forth for two or three hours without clearing it, and finally started the engine. They were motor sailing almost due north when Mark and I came on watch at 2:00 A.M. At watch change we tacked, and stopped the engine. Sonny said to try and sail a course of 240 degrees, but that was not to be. The wind at that time was 20-22 knots and shifty. He said not to drop below a course of 230; then went below and went to bed. Mark steered the first hour and the wind shifted to where he couldn't do better than 210-215 degrees most of the time. The wind also piped up to 25-28 knots. I looked at the radar and saw where the land was, and it looked like 210 would be O.K. Then I got our coordinates from the GPS, and went to the chart and plotted out position. Sure enough, 210 was O.K. but anything under that would not be. At about 2:15 A.M. I was steering as a rainsquall came in with winds that peaked at 34 knots and then headed us to where I couldn't steer anything better than 180 degrees. We had no choice but to tack in those conditions, and we did so successfully. It was pitch-black; like being in a storm in the twilight zone! We sailed north-northwest at 320-350 degrees for maybe 20 minutes and then I could do no better than due north. That told me that the wind had come back around, so we tacked again. After that we sailed about 225 degrees for a couple of hours and got past the point of land. Another rainsquall came through about 5:15 and we could steer no better than 190-200 degrees so I had Mark steer while I plotted our position again. By then we were at a point where even 170 would have been O.K. When Ray and Richard relieved us at 6:00, my bunk and sleeping bag were calling my name out loud! I slept for three hours, as I had slept little before going on watch due to all the tacking, flapping of sails, cranking of winches, rattling of blocks, and starting and stopping of the engine. Being below is like being inside a bass drum when all that is going on.

Saturday, February 1   Lat.- 43 degrees, 56 minutes S; Lon.- 75 degrees, 48 minutes W. Sea Temp.- 56 degrees. - 10:55 A.M.- It seems that I am the only one on the boat who is eating these days. Ray started feeling sick yesterday and is worse today, though he hasn't thrown up yet. Even Richard isn't eating, but he says he is nauseous from diesel fumes, not seasickness. The cap on one of the fuel tanks wasn't on straight and a little fuel slopped out. It didn't bother me but both Richard and Ray complained. Sonny, and Naomi are still sick, as is Mark. Yesterday afternoon when I went topside for the afternoon watch I arrived just in time to see Naomi hurl into her bucket.

Yesterday was the nastiest of the voyage so far. Winds ranged 22-33 knots with intermittent rain all day, and the rain was more "on" than "off". Seas ranged 10-20 feet, and not the long swells that we have seen so much, but steep and choppy on the starboard bow creating lots of spray for the person at the helm and a very uncomfortable ride for those below. Sometimes the boat seemed to be going almost straight up a wave, or straight down, or coming off the top of one and slamming down bow first. Sometimes if one caught us sideways we would skid down the side of it- not like broaching; just an uncomfortable skid that threw things around down below. Night watch was miserable, with a light but steady rain. The air temperature was 58 degrees but it seemed a lot colder. I wore wool socks, rubber boots, sweat pants, foul weather pants, a t-shirt, a turtle neck a pullover shirt, a zip-collar sweat shirt, a denim button-up shirt, my foul weather jacket, my new ski cap, and the hood of my foul weather jacket, and I was *not* overdressed! I was comfortable, but even got a little cool the last hour of the watch. The foul weather suit is worth every nickel I paid for it. Oh yes, I wore my cheap new gloves, and of course they got wet but the ski gloves get wet too, and they take forever to dry out. Only my hands and face get wet though. The foul weather suit keeps everything else dry, with no leaks or seepage anywhere.

I had leftover potatoes, a slice of Ray's homemade bread and a 7-up for dinner last night, and then slept six hours before night watch. This was great since I got little sleep the night before. This morning I slept another 2½ hours, then got up and took a sponge bath (not ready to jump in a shower yet!), put on clean underwear and t-shirt, and felt great. I had cornflakes, juice, and green tea for breakfast and then felt so good that I washed the sink full of dishes that had been there for two days. That, in itself was interesting. You can't leave things on the counter or they take flight so you wash one or two items, dry them, and put them away. That is a slow process, but is really the only way.

I guess what we are experiencing is why they call these latitudes the "roaring forties". The good thing in all this is that we are steering the course we want, 210 degrees, with an average speed of about six knots.

Sunday, February 2   Lat.- 45 degrees, 26 minutes S; Lon.- 77 degrees, 16 minutes W.

9:00 A.M.- The GPS died yesterday afternoon! After 36 hours of nastiness the weather broke and the wind diminished all day. It was still cloudy most of the time, but the rain stopped too. By 3:30 P.M. the wind had dropped under 10 knots and stayed. Sonny is afraid to fly the mainsail in unsettled weather since it is such a pain in the ass to furl, so we were under only the mizzen and jib. We were going nowhere fast so I decided to start the engine. When I started the engine the display on the GPS went blank. "Not to worry" thought I, just push the "on" button, and sure enough, it came back on; however shortly after Mark took the helm at 4:00 it went off again. He pushed the "on" button and it would flicker a little but would not come back on. Ray came on deck about then and we told him what had happened. He messed with it a little, with no success; unplugged it and cleaned the connectors, but still nothing. He then disconnected it entirely and took it below to work on it. A few minutes later he came back up and said that one of the elements was "fried", and pronounced it dead. "Not to worry" says I; "I know that we have a hand-held GPS as a back-up". "We actually have two back-ups," says Ray. "I wonder if anybody might have tested the back-ups since the beginning of the voyage", says I, "to be sure they work?" "Probably not" says Ray.

He then goes below and comes back with the two hand-held units, and sure enough, neither of them worked! One appeared to work but you couldn't read the display and the other wouldn't acquire the satellites. It seems that you need to tell it what country you are in so it knows which satellites to look for, and Chile isn't one of the options. "Maybe they don't have GPS satellite coverage down here" says Ray.

"Bullshit", says I. "GPS satellite coverage is world-wide. GPS is GLOBAL Positioning System! Not to worry," says I. "Sonny is a celestial navigator, and has his sextant on the boat."

"Bullshit", says Ray. "He doesn't have a current almanac. The only thing he can get is latitude!"

I'm NOT making this up! "Then", says I, "unless you can get one of these puppies working, we're screwed!"

I am happy to report that he did get *one* of them to work just before six o'clock so at least for now, we are O.K., but we're going around Cape Horn relying solely on one elderly, balky GPS unit for navigation.

Sonny is getting better, and is starting to eat again and Ray too is better. Ray never aarfed but was sick for a couple of days. Mark is still sick, and Naomi is in bad shape- looks like death warmed over. Neither of them is eating. Richard also is starting to eat again. I'm the only one who hasn't been sick from one thing or another. I am lucky!

The refrigerator now also has been pronounced dead- not fixable, so we will make the rest of the voyage with no refrigeration. We're trying to eat as much of the refrigerated stuff as we can while the refrigerator and freezer are still cold. I had hot dogs for dinner last night. With all the seasickness, not much has been eaten so far, but that should pick up now.

Last night the alternator died again, so now we can't charge the batteries off the main engine, but have to run the generator. That's not a big deal though, because due to voltage regulator problems the engine tended to overcharge the batteries anyway. It's just that yet another system on the boat has died. This boat is very sturdy, seaworthy, and sails pretty well but as far as the onboard systems are concerned it is a boatload of shit with a built-in list to starboard. Sonny says that he plans to sell it after this voyage, and keep his catamaran but I have to wonder if he can find another sucker dumb enough to buy it! Not my problem. If it gets us around Cape Horn and safely home, that's all I ask. I can put up with the other stuff.

Last night we spent 16 hours motor-sailing and motoring as the wind had shifted onto our nose, but by 7:30 A.M. the wind picked up and shifted back, so we are sailing a course of 210 degrees under mizzen and jib, making about five knots in 16- knot winds. The seas have mellowed out into long swells of 5-10 feet that are the "moving hills" that we enjoyed so much on the last passage. We are planning to go west of due south until we are 100 or so miles offshore, to give ourselves sea-room in case we should get caught in a gale for two or three days. When we reach 100 miles offshore we will turn due south. All that motoring meant plenty of hot water so I had a good shower this morning, after which I cooked two hamburgers for lunch.

The other day after their watch I heard Ray giving Richard a serious speech about Richard's lack of listening skills. I only heard bits and pieces so I asked Ray about it. It seems that they were unrolling the jib, and Richard just uncleated the line to the roller-furling drum and let it go; this in spite of his being told several times to keep some tension on it when it unrolls. I have made my speech on that subject in his presence at least three times, including the consequences of a backlash and what is required to remedy a backlash. Obviously, Ray has told him several times too, including how to keep the line around the cleat if you are not strong enough to hold it. Well, there was no backlash this time; however when it went out so quickly, the jib sheet started flying around out of control and whacked Richard across the face. Richard doesn't like to admit that he has very little upper body strength so maybe he tried to hold it without the cleat and couldn't, or maybe he just had not listened, and let it go on purpose. In any case, it's good that if somebody had to be whacked it was him, and not somebody else. Both Ray and Mark comment regularly about Richard's reluctance to listen and his propensity to interrupt when you try to tell him something. Within your first ten words he will interrupt, and will not shut up, even if you continue talking. Maybe he wants to show that he understands what you are saying and agrees with you, or maybe he feels a need to show that he already knows what you are trying to tell him. I don't know. He is rarely argumentative, but it's impossible to tell him anything and it is very annoying to all three of us. I don't try to have any real conversations with him, and keep them brief and light. On a couple of occasions when I really needed to tell him something I have had to say in a firm voice, "Richard, let me finish!", and then continue what I was saying.

Our air thermometer didn't last very long. Mark had secured it in a slot on the port side of the cockpit but apparently somebody left it out on the seat, and either sat or stepped on it and broke it.

It is now 10:15 A.M. and we have just turned due south! We now are 840 miles from Cape Horn, and if we are lucky we will probably round it a week from today. From there it is about 420 miles to Stanley.

Monday, February 3 - 10:15 A.M.- The barometer has dropped from 29.8 at 10:00 P.M. to 29.5 just now, and we are experiencing winds that have reached 41 knots along with hard rain- a really crappy morning. We are still on course making about six knots under only a small piece of the jib. Mark and I had a good night watch with winds ranging from 20-32 knots, way back on the starboard quarter as we sailed under the mizzen and most of the jib. We were making about 6.5-7 knots and had just a little mist but no real rain. At 6:00 A.M. I noticed that the barometer was 29.69 and it started to rain. By 7:00 the barometer was 29.6 and it was raining harder. Ray is sick and unable to stand watch so Sonny went on watch early, at 8:00. When he went up we dropped the mizzen and rolled up half of the jib, and a little later he rolled up all but maybe 25 per cent. Seas so far are in the 12-15 foot range and give us a pronounced sideways roll. I am sitting sideways on my bunk with my feet braced against the engine room bulkhead across the passageway as I write this, and have peripheral vision up and down the passageway. I just heard a loud clump and clatter, and saw Richard come flying from the galley into my field of vision on his ass with a frying pan and French toast on top of him. He whacked his head pretty good on the chart table but appears to be O.K. He had just seen Naomi have a similar experience trying to cook about 15 minutes ago, but had to try it himself. Seems that he not only won't listen, but he doesn't learn, either! "Hard-headed" would be an accurate term.

There is some good news. Sonny has managed to get the second hand-held GPS up and running, so now we have two working units- a much more comfortable feeling.

Yesterday's afternoon watch was great. It was cloudy with occasional mist but no rain, not especially cold, and wind averaging 18 knots on the starboard quarter. Seas were remarkably small, mostly 3-5 feet and not steep or choppy. Several albatross put on a show for Mark and me with their graceful aerobatics, rarely flapping their wings but just gliding on the wind, sometimes looking as if they are dipping their wingtips in the sea. Their wingspans are in the 9-10 foot range and the way they seem to hang down on the ends really does remind me of B-52 bombers. We are heading due south, 100 miles offshore with sea room to ride out a storm if necessary. Also, we are clear of the continental shelf and the big seas that build up there.

Tuesday, February 4   Lat.- 49 degrees, 44 minutes S; Lon.- 77 degrees, 55 minutes W

11:15 A.M.- Ray is still sick, and missed his third watch this morning. He is not seasick, but has fever, headache and the runs. I stayed on watch an extra hour again this morning; then Mark came back up for an hour, and Sonny came on watch two hours early. Ray was up briefly last night, but said, "I'm so weak you could knock me over with a feather". He said that he is rarely sick, and doesn't know what to do when it happens. Right now he is on his feet in the galley cooking, so maybe he is recovering. I shouldn't judge, but if I had what he has, I *think* I would be standing my watches. I used to go to work when I was a lot sicker than he has appeared to be, but that's just me. He apologized for causing a burden for the rest of us, and that was nice but I have seen Mark on watch several times when he was so sick (seasick, but sick nonetheless) that when he closed his eyes you would swear that he was dead. I have seen Sonny up there on watch heaving his guts out, and even Naomi, looking green as a lizard and aarfing into her bucket, has not missed a watch. I like Ray, but this is a guy who describes himself as a professional sailor and I think he needs to get his ass up there and stand his watches.

A few words about sail deployment: Yesterday when Mark and I went on watch at 2:00 P.M. conditions had improved steadily after the morning storm. The wind was ranging 20-30 knots, the sun was out, and seas were running 8-15 feet on the beam and quarter, giving us that nasty back-and-forth roll that is dangerous, and uncomfortable for those below. We were still running under only about a third of the jib and nothing more. We were slogging along at 3.5-4 knots, wallowing in those seas. I asked Sonny about unrolling more of the jib and he said no, explaining that he is conservative so we had a boring and uncomfortable watch. Finally, at 5:30 he let me unroll most of the jib and we immediately picked up 1.5 knots of speed. When we went on night watch at 2:00 A.M. he had the mizzen back up but had over half of the jib rolled up and was wallowing along at three knots in winds that were ranging 10-14 knots. Seas had dropped to the 6-10 foot range but were still on the beam and quarter. This time I didn't ask but just waited until he went below and then unrolled the rest of the jib except for one turn around the roller. We immediately picked up two knots of speed and got a much smoother ride. This boat weighs 35,000 pounds and has a draft of nearly six feet, making it quite capable of comfortably cutting through seas but it needs a little momentum! Sonny is also timid about flying the main; ostensibly because it is difficult and dangerous to furl, especially under adverse weather conditions, with the problem of working around the dodger and bimini. We used it for only a day or two on the last passage (I put it up on my watch.), none so far on this passage, and I don't expect it to fly any time soon. We discussed this way back when we were in the Galapagos and I said that if I were making the decisions I would put a double reef in the main, and leave it there. We have no reefing hook on the main mast, but have reefing lines and could work around the absence of a hook. With a double reef you could put up the main and leave it up in all but the most extreme conditions. You could then use the jib and mizzen, both easily deployed, furled, or reefed, to manage your sail area. I went on to explain that in heavy weather you could furl both of those and deploy the storm jib as a staysail, sailing under that and the double reefed main. I explained that the theory of this is to lower the sail area exposed, and centralize the center of effort near the center of the boat, and is consistent with everything I have ever heard or read on that subject. Ray said that he had never heard of that theory and Sonny acted like I was speaking Greek. I don't think he grasped what I was trying to tell him. In any case, they paid no attention and we are using the jib and mizzen, or in heavy conditions only a little piece of the jib.

About the matter of leaving one turn of the jib on the roller; Sonny is deathly afraid of blowing out a sail; especially the jib where it is on the roller track. He has told us all along that if the wind gets above 20 knots to roll up some of the jib. Now this isn't a little candy-assed drifter, but a big, triple-stitched, heavy 110 genoa that was fully re-stitched last summer. The reason for his fear is- *get this*- we are sailing around Cape Horn with a spare sail inventory of exactly zero! That's right; not a spare sail on the boat. By the way, we are also sailing around Cape Horn with duct tape on both jib sheets, where they were frayed down to the core. We asked Sonny about replacing them and he said "Nah, the core is the only part that matters; the rest is just outer covering".

A bit of good news, at least from my perspective. Sonny told me the day before yesterday that he has decided against stuffing the Styrofoam in the engine room vents after all. He thought about my concerns, and decided that they are valid. He has heard about people on boats dying form carbon monoxide poisoning, and doesn't want to risk that happening with us. I still don't think he grasped the concept of the risk of oxygen depletion, which would have been the case if those vents were blocked, and we had, in cold, wet weather, an enclosed area with several people sleeping and two engines running, all consuming oxygen with no ventilation for oxygen to come in. Oh well, whatever his reasoning, I am happy and relieved that he made that decision.

Wednesday, February 5 Lat.- 52 degrees, 24 minutes S; Lon.- Not noted; Sea Temp: 48 degrees - 10:50 A.M.- Ray is standing his watches again. He still doesn't feel well but he went on last night and again this morning, both times under adverse conditions. I'm not accusing him of malingering, but to me his symptoms were not enough to warrant missing three watches. In any case, I'm glad he is back on watch.

We had three hours of beautiful sunshine on yesterday's afternoon watch and then an hour of rain. Wind was on the quarter at 12-20 knots and we made a speed of five to six knots. Rain continued off and on through the night and the wind built into the upper twenties. It also turned noticeably colder; definitely the coldest we have seen so far. When Mark and I went on night watch winds were ranging 25-32 knots and we were running on just the jib, with half of it rolled up. It stopped raining about 2:30 A.M. and we had two hours of relatively clear skies. At 4:45 I looked at the radar and saw a nasty squall line coming in from the starboard side on a converging course. It hit us just as I took the helm at 5:00 and we had a cold, wet final hour of our watch. Winds peaked at 40 knots but seas didn't really build up much-stayed in the 8-12 foot range. By 6:00 skies were clearing and the radar showed nothing else coming in. The wind stayed in the mid-twenties, and it stayed *cold*.

We had alternator trouble yesterday afternoon. We were without power for a while and were concerned that we might lose power altogether. It seems that a pin holding the alternator in place had worked it's way loose, causing the alternator to hang askew and bend the bracket mounting it to the bulkhead. This in turn, caused the belt to rub. Sonny was able to crawl into the engine room and rig it, getting everything running again. He is *very* good at finding creative ways to fix things, usually under difficult conditions.

When Mark and I started to go on watch at 2:00 A.M. it was raining, and had been throughout the night. As usual, I noticed that the radar was not on. I asked Sonny if there was any reason not to turn it on, thinking of the alternator problem, but he said no, to go ahead if I wanted. As I turned it on I mentioned that since we are approaching Cape Horn, maybe we should be especially vigilant in watching for ships and he said "Whatever makes you feel comfortable, Charley". I sensed a lack of concern on his part since his reply seemed somewhat condescending so I asked him "Philosophically, since we are getting into an area known to be a busy shipping lane, do you think we need to pay special attention to watching for ships?" Without stopping to think, he said "Not really; no". This from a man who was hit by a freighter during his circumnavigation in the late sixties! You would think that he might have learned something from that, but obviously he didn't. Of more concern to me, this is the man who, with his daughter, sits up in the cockpit on watch every night from 10:00 P.M.-2:00 A.M. while the rest of us are below sleeping. Even if you could assume that the two of them are paying attention up there, which is not always the case, in bad weather you just can't see very far and those big freighters, moving at 20-25 knots could be on top of you before you knew it. Regarding the matter of paying attention, if you look up there when they are on watch in inclement weather you will usually see one of them on each side of the cockpit, huddled up under the dodger and facing aft with nobody at the helm paying attention and the autopilot steering the boat! You have to just trust God, and go to sleep!

Thursday, February 6 Lat.- 54 degrees, 7 minutes S; Lon- 75 degrees, 55 minutes W; Sea Temp.- 47 degrees - 10:50 A.M.- I spoke briefly with Maureen by satellite telephone this morning, and am really sad about the space shuttle disaster. It was great to talk with her, but depressing to get that news.

Last night one of my rubber boots got filled up with water. After a great, sunny afternoon watch a squall blew in the last 15 minutes while I was at the helm, so when I came below I was dripping wet. Since I have no place to hang my foul weather gear near my bunk, I hang it in the head and put the boots in he bathtub/shower. The shower has faucets, and is one of those hand-held jobs with an on/off button on the showerhead. Also, the tub doesn't drain, but requires that you turn on a pump to get the water out. Well, it seems that Sonny had just taken a shower and had turned off the water at the showerhead, but not the faucets. When you do that, the water slowly leaks and accumulates in the tub. One of my boots tipped over with the rolling of the boat, and got filled with water. I was really pissed, and said so. Sonny was apologetic, but the damage was done and I had a cold wet foot to anticipate on my next watch. I dealt with it by first rolling up a towel so that it fit into the boot, really cramming it in there, and leaving it there while I ate dinner. Then I took most of a roll of toilet paper and crammed that into the boot, and left it there while I slept. By 1:30 A.M. when I got ready to go on night watch, most of the moisture had been absorbed by the toilet paper so it was not nearly as bad as I had feared.

When Mark and I went on watch yesterday afternoon it was a little cold but sunny, with winds about 20 knots. When I went up Sonny and Naomi were lying on either side, as far forward as you can get under the dodger, not on a seat but forward of the cockpit, facing aft with nobody at the helm, and paying zero attention to where the boat was going. We could have sailed right into a ship, or off the edge of the earth before they knew what was happening. Also, neither of them was clipped on, yet Naomi said to me "Don't fall in the water; it's 48 degrees"! Then, at 2:00 A.M. when I went up they were in the same place, except that they were both on the starboard side, huddled together, ostensibly for body heat. Again, neither of them was clipped on, *at night*, and Sonny wasn't even wearing his life jacket. I mentioned this to Mark and he said that Sonny doesn't wear seat belts in cars, either. He made some trips from Illinois to Mobile with Sonny last summer when they were working on the boat, and the only time Sonny buckled his seat belt was when a police car was nearby. I will try not to harp on this subject any more. They just continue to amaze me!

Now that we are this far south I am wearing all my cold weather clothes when I am on watch. There is no need to hold anything in reserve at this point. Last night I wore two pairs of socks (only because of the boot moisture), rubber boots, thermal underwear bottoms, sweat pants, a t-shirt, thermal underwear top, a turtle-neck shirt, a pullover shirt, a sweatshirt, my Land's End squall jacket, ski gloves and a ski cap. Over all this I wore my foul weather suit with the hood up. I guess I could add a button-up shirt over the sweatshirt if I needed to. In any case, I was *not* overdressed. I think the air temperature at night is probably in the upper 40's but it feels really cold; especially when the wind pipes up.

It is hard to find a place to sit and eat when Sonny and Naomi are not on watch. Since we are consistently on a starboard tack these days, Naomi now sleeps on the port side settee, and there is room for no more than one ass at the dining table because the rest of the space is filled with rolled-up sleeping bags, piles of cushions, and plastic containers full of people's personal crap. Sometimes Sonny is sleeping in that one available seat and sometimes he is sleeping on cushions on the salon floor. They have given up sleeping in the bow, at least for now. It's annoying and frustrating, to say the least.

7:55 P.M.- This journal attacked me today! We're trying to eat perishables before they spoil due to lack of refrigeration so I cooked and ate two small hamburger patties with a tomato for lunch. Afterward I was lying down to let my food digest when this book leapt from a shelf above my bunk when the boat rolled, and landed on my face as I dozed off, opening a cut on the bridge of my nose. It is nothing serious but it scared the hell out of me, and took a while to stop bleeding.

Afternoon watch was one of our best yet with steady winds in the low 20's just starboard of the stern, and well-behaved following swells in the 8-15 foot range with an occasional 20 footer barging its way through. We ran on the jib with only one turn of the roller rolled up, and averaged 6.5 knots. The best part was *no rain!* We now have had two consecutive watches without rain. We are within 300 miles of

Cape Horn and if the weather holds we should pass it Saturday night or Sunday morning. We are all getting excited, and I still can't believe that I am really here doing this. I also can't believe we are doing this with *no weather information*; just trusting God and luck! We have both weather-fax and single sideband, but *get this*: nobody here knows how to use either of them! Ray has tried with some diligence and Sonny has made cursory efforts but neither of them has had any success. I continue to be amazed! If I had known before the voyage that the *captains* didn't know how to operate some of the equipment, *I* would have taken it upon myself to learn!

Friday, February 7 Lat.- 55 degrees, 29 minutes S; Lon.- 73 degrees, no minutes W 11:25 A.M.-We are getting some of the weather that Cape Horn is known for. Early last night, right after the end of our afternoon watch, the wind started to build and light rain started. On night watch we had winds consistently in the 26-34 knot range with a peak of 41, and light, soaking rain the entire four hours. This morning winds built into the 40's and the rain increased, with a peak wind so far of 48 knots. We are running under just a small piece of the jib and still making 6-6.5 knots. Following seas slam us pretty good on occasion but the boat is handling it very well. We do have one problem though. The autopilot has quit working again so we are having to steer manually in these conditions. The barometer reading has dropped to 29.0, so we may be in for a couple more days of this. I hope it might blow on through.

A problem for the crew is getting warm. It is pretty cold, everything has a tendency to get damp or wet, and the only place you can get really warm is in your sleeping bag since the boat has no heat. I did get three good hours of sleep after night watch.

The last two nights, before I went on night watch I noticed that the radar was on. I was glad to see it, but didn't say anything. Then last night when I went up at 2:00 A.M. and Sonny gave me the status briefing, he said, "We haven't seen anything; no ships or anything, but I wouldn't be surprised if we started seeing ships down in this area". This, just two nights after talking down to me and saying he saw no reason to be concerned about ships in this area! Maybe I got his attention, or maybe he just woke up to reality.

Two more things: First, not that a person overboard in this area would have a *chance* to survive anyway, but the one thing that *might* have helped is no longer available. That was the "MOB" button on the GPS that died. The hand-held units do not have this feature, and do not live in the cockpit anyway. The "MOB" button, when pressed, records the exact latitude and longitude at that instant, to be used in a search and recovery effort. Second is the air horn. We have a compressed air horn which rode in a drink holder on the binnacle, just in front of the instrument panel in the cockpit. Its purpose was to signal everybody to come topside if someone went overboard to help with the rescue efforts. Well, it was noticed that the canister was rusting, so in Puerto Montt it was taken below, where it still resides! Really, I'm *not* making this stuff up!

1:35 P.M.- I just talked with Sonny and he said they had winds in the 50's for half an hour; though it is back in the 30's now. Definitely a full-blown gale! Good news though, as the autopilot is now working again! The barometer has dipped under 29. We're still steering east-southeast but should turn east toward Cape Horn early this evening. Exciting stuff! Uncomfortable, and a little scary, but exciting.

6:35 P.M.- We have been in a gale now for about 22 hours. All three of the day watches have had winds exceeding 50 knots and incessant rain. Winds have been from the north-northwest, almost directly behind us but just slightly to the port side, and seas are 15-30 feet and confused. Some come in on the quarter, spin us around 30 degrees, and then we skid down the side of them. Twice during a skid we buried not only the starboard rail, but also the entire starboard side of the cockpit, bringing in a volume of water. The sea is majestically beautiful; still deep indigo, and not the gray you would expect. When waves break they turn an aquamarine color normally associated with tropical seas or clear, high mountain lakes. My foul weather pants allow water in where I sit in the vinyl helmsman's chair, getting my layers of underwear and my ass wet. It seems that almost everything on the boat is wet now, and when you get ready to go on watch you put on all that cold, wet stuff! After a while your body heat warms it up though, and it isn't so bad. I will look forward to getting to Stanley, Falkland Islands and getting warm and dry. My bunk and sleeping bag are warm and dry so far, but nothing else is. I keep a pair of sweat pants, a sweatshirt, and a pair of socks *in* my sleeping bag to use just for sleeping; not risking getting them wet. This is all part of the Cape Horn experience and I am enjoying it, but I also will be glad when it is behind me. Speaking of Cape Horn, if all goes well we should pass it tomorrow, and hopefully reach Stanley Tuesday night or Wednesday.

We have just now turned east, and are starting our run to Cape Horn. It is at latitude 56 degrees south, and we are at 56 degrees, 12 minutes. Our longitude is 70 degrees, 56 minutes west.

Saturday, February 8 Lat.- 56 degrees, 11 minutes S; Lon.- 67 degrees, 25 minutes W

10:45 A.M.- Last night just after 9:00 P.M. we suffered a knockdown! What apparently was a rogue wave, coming from a different direction than the others, hit us full broadside on the port beam. The weather had cleared a little to the west and Richard and Ray, on watch, were admiring the sunset behind us as we sailed east. They didn't see the wave so we don't know how big it was, but water came all the way over the boat, and in about two seconds we were over on our starboard side. I was sleeping in my bunk on the port side and it sounded like an airplane crashed into the boat two feet from my head. I knew immediately what had happened, as when I opened my eyes I was hanging in my bunk by the leeboard, looking down, and waiting to see if we were going to roll over. All my stuff that was on shelves (not much) went flying, as did all the loose stuff on the work- bench, which is over my feet at the end of my bunk. Sonny had installed a lee cloth on the work- bench and that held the big tool boxes in place (barely), but everything else flew off with a great clatter. That damned workbench always looked like Fibber Magee's closet, and crap was everywhere. When the boat started to right itself I stopped being scared, and started thinking about what to do next.

Nobody was hurt, although Richard was washed, or knocked overboard and was saved by his tether. Ray was at the helm and Richard had just returned topside from visiting the head. He had seated himself on the port side, as far forward as he could get, under the dodger alongside the companionway hatch and out of the wind before he remembered that he had not clipped his tether on when he returned. He got up and clipped on to the U-bolt by the companionway on the starboard side, and that saved his life. During the knockdown he went flying through one of the panels on the dodger and found himself hanging over the lifelines and in the water. When the boat righted itself, he pulled himself by the tether and lifelines, back into the boat, a little shaken, wet, and cold but none the worse for wear. Ray didn't reach the end of his tether, as he managed to hang on to the wheel, even as water flowed over him.

Mark was in his bunk on the starboard side of the aft cabin and just about everything back there, including Richard's mattress, wound up on top of him. He was not hurt, but couldn't move right away. It took a few minutes for him to dig his way out. Sonny and Naomi were both sleeping when the wave hit, he on the floor of the salon

145

and she on he starboard dining settee, and neither of them realized what had happened.

It didn't take more than ten seconds for the boat to come back up, and probably less but the dodger and bimini were collapsed, and I think it is fair to say that the jib is pretty much shredded. When you look at the remnants wrapped around the roller furler, several ripped pieces are flapping in the wind. The rips probably don't go in too far though, as we had been running on about 20 per cent of the jib, with the rest rolled up so the part that was rolled up may be O.K. If that is the case, the jib is probably repairable. The dodger was split and a couple of pieces of the frame are bent but it too, may be fixable. We're not sure how the jib got shredded like that. Maybe it filled up with water during the knockdown and then tore from the weight of the water when the boat righted itself, but that would seem to account for a rip instead of shredding.

Sonny went topside and helped Ray and Richard disassemble and stow the pieces of the dodger and bimini, and then roll up the remnants of the jib and hoist the staysail so we could keep moving. The staysail, or storm jib, had been hanked on in Puerto Montt, and sheets attached so that we could use it in *severe weather*, but Sonny had chosen to use a small piece of the jib instead, because the roller furling made it easier to handle. It took about an hour for us to get things at least picked up and stowed, as we got back under way. We are now sailing with an open cockpit, fully exposed to wind, rain, and cold.

An odd thing was that this happened during a temporary break in the weather, with Ray and Richard looking back at the sunset and not seeing the wave coming. Nobody saw the wave at all so we have no idea how big it was, what it looked like, or anything. Maybe the hand of God? All in all, we are very thankful that it wasn't worse, and that the boat handled it so well!

We are now about 20 miles from Cape Horn, and should pass it early this afternoon. We will pass about ten miles south of it in these conditions, and don't expect to see it. That's too bad, but I actually would have been surprised if we did get to see it. When we pass it, we can't yet turn northeast toward the Falklands because we would have huge beam seas, making it too dangerous. Instead, we will continue to run east until the weather and the seas give us a break.

Last night about 11:00 Sonny spotted a ship on our radar (imagine that!), made radio contact, and was able to get a weather report in English. Seems that we sailed into a frontal system with a line of low-pressure cells! This will all eventually pass through, but you have to wonder if we might have been able to avoid it entirely if we knew it was there- like if *somebody* on this boat knew how to use the stinking *weather fax*!

1:15 P.M.- Right now we are just about due south of Cape Horn; about 11 miles off! It is still raining, with 40-knot winds and heavy seas so it is too dangerous to go any closer. In any event, within an hour we will have passed Cape Horn- lots of emotions going on here, at least for me. As soon as weather and sea conditions permit, we will turn northeast toward the Falklands and start our long trip home. We will be on our way *home*! Right now, we will continue going east, running with the storm.

Sunday, February 9   Lat.- 55 degrees, 59 minutes S; Lon.- 65 degrees, 53 minutes W.

5:05 A.M.- We are riding at sea anchor and I am on sea-anchor watch. The person on sea-anchor watch sits at the navigation station and watches the radar for ships. Mark spotted one about 3:00 A.M. and we went topside with my binoculars and watched as it passed us about eight miles away. It appeared to be a small cruise ship, as it had lots of lights. Ray got a bit excited when we first saw it on the radar, as it appeared to be heading toward us, and there was nothing we could do to get out of their way. We tried to contact them by radio, but got no response, so he got even more excited but soon it became evident that they would pass us at a distance.

We passed about 11 miles south of Cape Horn at approximately 1:30 P.M. yesterday. The weather was really bad and it would have been too dangerous to get any closer. It was raining hard, and winds were in the 30's. Passing it was a very emotional experience, and will probably be even more so when I have time to think about it. I couldn't stop thinking "Wow, I have actually sailed around Cape Horn!" All the other fantastic places we have been and things we have seen notwithstanding, this is *the one*, most significant thing that we set out to do.

In the meantime we have been thinking about the weather. We have now been in this storm for about 55 hours. We had hoped for better weather when we got past Cape Horn but instead, it got worse. We had sailed all day under just the storm jib and using the autopilot; standing watches in the cabin by the radar, and going up every 15 minutes to take a look at wind speed and direction, sea conditions, and so forth. We couldn't turn northeast toward the Falklands, but pretty much had to run with the storm as the barometer continued to drop. During our afternoon watch winds built into the 40's, topping out at 51 knots

147

and seas built to 20-30 feet. These were not smooth swells either, but nasty, confused mountains of water that came from both the starboard quarter and port quarters and from directly astern, sometimes all at once. About 3:30 it reached the point where the autopilot would not hold course so I went up to steer manually. Steering was a real bitch but I managed to hold course. About 4:30 Sonny, Ray and Mark came up and deployed a warp, consisting of two heavy lines trailed off the stern to try to keep us headed on a straight course. I have never had any confidence in warps, and this one certainly didn't help. It didn't make steering any easier or more effective, and it slowed us down to where we took two waves over the stern, that otherwise we probably would have outrun. About 5:30 Mark had relieved me steering and I was sitting beside him on the port side when we got hit, first by a big wave on the starboard quarter that we surfed down, dipping and almost burying the bow and bringing the notion of pitch-poling to mind. Then, just as we were recovering from that and pointing slightly to port, we got slammed by a 25 footer on the port quarter that we skidded down sideways! We skidded a *long* way and tilted about 60 degrees to starboard. Mark fell out of the helmsman's chair, but held on to the wheel. I had two handgrips and a foot brace, so I didn't go anywhere, though water came all the way over me. Everybody below thought we were going over again and we very well could have but we didn't, and no harm was done. After that, Sonny and Ray decided that it was too dangerous to try and steer at night under those conditions, and to deploy the sea anchor for the night.

None of us had ever used a sea anchor before and we had some doubts about their effectiveness, but under those conditions nobody could think of a better alternative. Sonny had directed some preparation in Puerto Montt that would prove to be very important. Those included reading the instructions that came with the sea anchor, rigging a bridle and securing it on the bow, and re-packing the sea anchor, making sure that the trip line was in place and the lines of the parachute were not fouled. Then 25 feet of heavy chain was attached to the sea anchor with a swivel shackle and the chain was placed in a bucket. The sea anchor and bucket were secured in the cockpit, to be ready if deployment became necessary. After the decision was made, Sonny and Ray spent about half an hour on deck in the storm, making preparations for deployment. Ray took one end of the line forward along the port side, outside the rigging, and attached it to the bridle. The other end of the line was attached to the chain and the trip line was tied to two fenders, which were to be used as floats. The line was coiled so that it would pay out from the top, avoiding tangles. Finally, the engine was started and the storm jib was dropped and secured, completing preparations. Watch changed during the preparations and Richard was steering at that point so Mark and I went up to help with the deployment.

The actual deployment went better than any of us could have expected. After a final check to be sure the line was clear of all legs, feet, and rigging, we threw the floats, sea anchor, and chain over the port rail as Richard turned the boat to port, taking the stern to starboard and keeping the propeller away from the line. About half way through the turn Richard shifted into neutral, allowing the bow to blow off. That allowed the sea-anchor chute to open and catch, and just like that, the bow was pointed into the wind and seas. It worked great, and even though we rocked and rolled a lot we all managed to get some sleep.

The barometer has risen from 28.80 to 29.38 and winds are now from the southwest; both indicating that the storm may finally be moving on out so hopefully, later this morning we can get under way toward the Falklands!

8:55 A.M.- YES! We retrieved the sea anchor at 7:45 A.M. That process was much easier than we anticipated, as we had heard of all kinds of problems involved in retrievals. We motored carefully forward, keeping the propeller away from the line, picked up a float with a gaff hook and hauled it aboard. We pulled the trip line, collapsing the chute, then used muscle power to haul everything else aboard, and that was that. Now we are motor sailing northeast on a course of 47 degrees under storm jib and mizzen in 18-knot southwest winds and 5-7 foot seas. It is still cloudy with a light mist, but these conditions look *great* to me! More important, we have belatedly, *really* started the long trip home!

Monday, February 10 Lat.- 54 degrees, 07 minutes S; Lon.- 62 degrees, 15 minutes W.

11:50 A.M.- Life is good! We have lots of bright sunshine, a nice breeze of about 15 knots, and it isn't especially cold! The first such day we have had for quite a while. I had a hot shower this morning- my first in four days- and it felt great! Others say that it had been even longer for them, what with all we have been through. Then, Ray decided to cook ham and cheese omelets and roast potatoes for breakfast. How much better can it *get*? We might even get a few things dried out! We are hanging stuff on the lifelines and opening hatches all over the place. Almost everything is wet after the last few days, or at least damp. I still have managed to keep my bunk and sleeping clothes dry though, and that has made a *big* difference.

This morning at watch change we decided to take down the remnants of the jib, since the wind was very light at the time. We tried to unroll it so that we could slide it down the track of the roller, but it would not unroll all the way because some of the ripped pieces are counter-rolled in the other direction. We did unroll enough however, to see that it is worse than we thought; shredded beyond repair, and a total loss. This is the jib that Sonny has protected so diligently throughout the trip- "roll some of it up if the wind stays above 20 knots", etc. It seems ironic that this happened when 80 per cent of it was rolled up. It also seems ironic that he chose to keep it deployed under extreme conditions when we had the storm jib hanked on and ready. We still can't figure out how the rolled-up part got shredded.

6:40 P.M.- What a great day this has been! We had sunshine *all day*, for the first time on this passage! It is still cold- probably in the 40's- but winds have been a relatively mellow 15-25 knots, mostly on the port beam. Tonight Ray cooked pasta shells in a really good meat sauce and last night he cooked salmon. I'm glad he is feeling better and is back in the mood to cook.

Tuesday, February 11   Lat.- 53 degrees, 29 minutes S; Lon.- 60 degrees, 33 minutes W; Sea Temp.- 45 degrees - 10:45 A.M.- Sonny took down the reefed mainsail last night, because he said the wind piped up to 30 knots. By the time we went on night watch at 2:00 A.M. the wind was ranging 15-18 knots on a close reach. That is normally plenty wind to sail but with nothing but the mizzen and this pissy-assed little storm jib we went nowhere fast, but just bobbed around. For the life of me I can't figure why the man is so scared to put up sails. If we had a reef in the main and conditions got bad, it would be easy to drop the mizzen and/or the jib and sail under just the reefed main. Finally, about 4:30 A.M. we said "enough of this bullshit", and started the engine. Since then winds have dropped more, so we are still motor sailing. Spending the night bobbing around and going nowhere will delay our arrival in Stanley until tomorrow afternoon or night.

When you're on watch, the flapping of the shredded jib is incessant. You don't notice it when you're below but on deck it never stops, and is an eerie reminder of what happened, and what could have happened but didn't. We were damn lucky!

Here, I want to put in a plug for Morgan sailboats, and I say

"sailboats" and not "yachts" because I don't like the term "yachts".
I think that word implies something sort of snooty, pretentious, and
elitist and I don't think those words describe anybody on this boat
except for Richard who is, in fact, the only one who keeps referring
to Sea Wolf III as "the yacht", or "our yacht". But I digress. As for
Morgans, I have believed from everything I have heard or read, and
from personal experience that they are built as solid as rocks, and from
the perspective of seaworthiness, structural integrity, and toughness
they are among the very best. In fact, when I learned that the boat for
this trip was to be a Morgan, that was a very positive factor in my
decision to make the voyage. Sea Wolf III has certainly reinforced that
confidence in the last week, coming through it all, definitely "bloodied"
but also "unbowed", with the asses of the crew all intact.

Yesterday Sonny pissed me off again about the satellite telephone.
He had been shuffling through some papers that included a telephone
bill and made the comment that the charge for use of the phone is
$4.00 per minute. I said, "That's not what I was told in the Galapagos.
I was told that it would be $3.00, and that's what I agreed to pay."

He said, "I never said it was $3.00".

I said "Yes you did. That's what you told me personally, and that's
what I agreed to pay."

He then said, "If you're not willing to pay $4.00 then you can't use
the phone any more."

I said "Fine, I won't use the damn phone any more because you
never say the same thing twice about what it costs".

He said, "Hell, I don't know; it may be $5.00 a minute. They have so
many taxes and charges in there, I can't figure it out!"

The man is unable or unwilling to read and understand the contract.
I was successful in resisting the urge to tell him to stick the phone
up his ass. He knows that I need to get home by the first of May or
thereabout, and has seemed to understand my desire to complete the
entire trip and not fly home from somewhere. Toward that end, I think
he has been trying to manage the schedule accordingly. That isn't all
for my benefit, as he, Naomi, and Ray also need to get back around
May 1 but as long as he is trying to help work my problem I will try
hard to avoid getting into a pissing contest with him. That is also one
reason I have not confronted him about lying to us about the "captain"
situation.

The deal on captains, included in our contracts, was that he would
furnish two fully competent, knowledgeable Coast Guard licensed
captains so that there would be one on each of the three watches.

On the telephone last summer, he made reference several times to hiring the other two captains. Once he mentioned that he had hired Ray and was interviewing candidates for the other position. Then in September, he told me that his daughter Naomi would be the third captain. According to the contract, each was to have "significant miles of offshore experience", and each was to be with us for the entire trip. He knew all along that Brad, who was one of the "captains" for 2,500 miles was *not* Coast Guard licensed. He also knew that Naomi, though she has a Coast Guard license, is a *long* way from being "knowledgeable", by any stretch of the imagination. In the Galapagos, I wondered aloud once how at age 21, and having been a full time student all her life, she had compiled the year of sea time necessary to qualify for a Coast Guard license. Brad said he was pretty sure she had "fudged on the sea time" on her application and that Sonny, as a licensed captain, had verified it. This will be an issue for a future discussion with Sonny.

I don't mean to be too hard on Sonny, as he is not without redeeming characteristics. He can be quite charming and amiable when he wants to be, and he sometimes goes out of his way to be nice to me. Under sail he is the best helmsman on the boat, with a feel, instinct, and effortless-looking style that is unmatched. Also, his decision to deploy the sea anchor Saturday night was definitely the right one, and one that I would not have made. That decision may have saved our lives. Otherwise however, he is no better sailor or navigator than I am. He can get latitude and longitude coordinates from the GPS and plot a precision course, as he did in getting around Cape Horn, but so can I, and I think that I am better at sail deployment and trim than he is. Ray is far and away the best helmsman on the boat under power. I try to be fair and objective in my thinking about Sonny but every time I start to feel a little positive, he pisses me off again.

Oh, one more thing. Since we lost the dodger and bimini, he has decided that it is O.K. to stand watch below, in front of the radar screen; going topside every 15 minute or so to check on things. He and Naomi are the only ones that do that, as the rest of us still stand watch the way we always did. The only thing we do differently is that we take turns going below for a few minutes occasionally to warm up. Sonny says that since we're so far from land there is no need to sit up there all the time, but he didn't say that when we were 500-1,000 miles from the nearest land on the last two passages! He also didn't say it on this passage until we lost the dodger and bimini. In other words, this is bullshit- he and Naomi just don't want to sit their asses out there in the open cockpit, in the cold and wind with no protection!

By the way, Naomi is sick with whatever Ray had- fever of 101 last night. - 6:40 P.M.- After a cloudy morning today cleared into another beautiful, *sunny* day and the air seems a bit warmer. When we went on afternoon watch, *all* sails were up, and no reef in the main. We sailed along in 20-25 knot winds for three hours, making a speed of about seven knots. Then the wind picked up to about 30 knots and we took down the main. Not a reef, but took it down entirely.

At 3:43 P.M. I spotted land for the first time in 12 days. It is a small rocky island that is the southernmost of the Falklands, and is not inhabited. Right after that, we passed a large commercial fishing boat and a guy with a British accent called on the radio to see if we needed help. He had seen our shredded sail and open cockpit. I guess we look a little beat-up.

The last half hour of our watch, three dolphins put on a show for Mark and me. We had some waves about 8-10 feet, and sometimes when one would start to break, all three would come flying of the wave, side by side. They were really pretty- black, with white bellies.

Wednesday, February 12 Lat.- 51 degrees, 56 minutes S; Lon.- 57 degrees, 45 minutes W

9:15 A.M.- We'll be in port this afternoon! We made good time motor sailing through the afternoon and night, including our night watch, so it looks like we will make it to Stanley by mid-afternoon. I will look forward to a beer or two!

6:40 P.M.- Well, we have arrived in Stanley- sort of. We continued to make good time through the morning, and reached Stanley Harbor at 1:30 P.M., happy to be alive. By then, however, the wind had piped up and was blowing 30-40 knots, even in this extremely well protected harbor. They, being so well protected, have no breakwater and no marina. They have a government dock that we can use, but with the wind howling this way we couldn't get to it. Sonny kept going in circles for about three hours, trying to find a protected anchorage but of course in this wind no anchorage is really protected. Finally he pulled up fairly close to a cove and we dropped the anchor, but it wouldn't hold. I thought I knew why, and when we pulled it up to try again my suspicions were confirmed as a really *huge* clump of kelp came up with the anchor. After motoring around some more we found a very large cylindrical mooring buoy, about ten feet long and four feet in circumference, that is used for cruise ships and that is where we are now, waiting for the wind to die down. This is *very* frustrating, as we are *really* ready to go ashore after a long and difficult passage. Stanley is a very pretty little town that is strung out along the waterfront and up a hillside, with lots of colorful houses, with especially colorful roofs. I can't wait to explore it.

13 – THE FALKLAND ISLANDS

Thursday, February 13 - 8:00 P.M.- We finally made it! We are tied up at the government dock in Stanley, Falkland Islands, so now we have officially completed our passage around Cape Horn! When we arrived yesterday this dock was being used by launches from a cruise ship, ferrying passengers back and forth but around 8:00 P.M. the wind died down and the dock was clear so we came in and tied up, with the permission of the customs officer. By the time we finished clearing customs it was 9:30 but Mark, Ray and I decided to go out anyway. We went to the Globe Tavern, a block or two up the street, and had a fine time. Last night was a combination of disco and karaoke night and the place was lively. People here seem to have a good time. The people there were primarily British and were of all ages, although several races were represented. Toward the end of the evening we found ourselves howling along to Neil Diamond's "Sweet Caroline" with the rest of the crowd.

An interesting observation last night at the Globe was that if you were suddenly beamed here from a spaceship and didn't know where you were, you would look around and say, "Most of these people look like Brits". The customs guy did too, and also a couple in their 50's that we talked to on the dock. Regardless of Argentina's claim, this place gives every impression of being a little piece of England. The entire population is just over 2,000. Stanley is really a pretty little town with well-kept houses along the waterfront and up a hillside. The houses are very colorful, especially the roofs.

Early this morning Mark and I went for a long, exploring walk around Stanley while the others were still sleeping and it was really pretty in the morning sunlight. There are lots and lots of flowers blooming in everything from elaborate gardens to little boxes. Almost every house has bright pastel colors; the house, the trim, or the roof, and the architecture is decidedly English. They have a very impressive memorial commemorating the liberation from Argentine occupation in the 1982 war, including the names of the British dead. There is another memorial nearby, commemorating the naval battle here with

155

a German fleet in 1914. Things are a bit expensive here; most notably telephone calls. You cannot access A.T.& T. from here, but instead have to use a Cable & Wireless company phone card for long distance. My A.T.& T. Sam's Club card is useless, and the Cable & Wireless card charges $2.10 a minute! Postage is high too- $1.53 to mail a letter. Beer last night was $2.50. We have been spoiled in our previous ports of call!

We found out that there is no sail maker here, so we will be stuck with that storm jib at least through the next passage. We will try to get the voltage regulator repaired here, and get the bracket for the alternator welded. The plan now is to leave here on Monday, the 17th.

The weather was great today- cool, but sunny and dry. We got a *lot* of things dried out on the boat. We also took laundry to be done, as there are no coin-operated machines here. That will be expensive, at 2.4 British pounds per kilo, or $1.75 per pound of laundry. The lady did agree to weigh it after it is dry, as a lot of the clothes were wet when we took them in. Tonight Mark, Ray and I had dinner at the Victory Bar, a nice pub about four blocks up the hill, with decent food and cold beer. I had curry chicken. I did a *lot* of walking today and I am tired. I will go to bed early.

Friday, February 14 - 9:00 P.M.- My laundry bill was $46.50! It was 2.2 pounds sterling per kilo of laundry and I had just over 14 kilos- what a shock! But at least I have clean laundry now. I didn't feel too badly after I heard Sonny whining that his and Naomi's laundry bill came to just over $100! Everybody was *stunned!*

I had an enjoyable Valentine's Day telephone conversation with Maureen this morning, and also mailed some post cards and journal notes. It was cold and rainy all day but we still got out and about, and the forecast is better for tomorrow. I scouted around and found a tour to a place called Volunteer Point to see the King Penguin colony, so Mark, Richard and I are planning to go tomorrow. We will go with a lady named Sharon Halford of Tenacre Tours. It will cost 60 pounds, plus another six per cent for using a credit card which comes to $99 each but is an all day Land Rover tour and you get to see quite a bit of this island. It is not cheap, but then when will I have another chance to see King Penguins in the wild? I am looking forward to it.

Sonny and Ray searched the Internet and found a Hood Sails loft in Buenos Aires. We have ordered a new jib, to be picked up on our arrival there. That determined that we would go to Buenos Aires instead of Montevideo. It will cost $1,750, a really good price for a *new* sail of that type.

All the restaurants here were fully booked tonight because it is Valentine's Day. Mark and I took a long walk up the hill to Shorty's Diner for dinner. It was the only place we could get in without a reservation. I had barbeque chicken, and it was decent- not great, but pretty good.

Saturday, February 15 - 10:05 P.M.- The penguins were fantastic! Our specific interest in the trip to Volunteer Point was to see the King Penguins, but two other species, the Gentoo and Magellenic Penguins also live there, all within very close proximity. They all live on a little spit of land with a bay with a nice sand beach on one side and a surf beach on the other. The surf beach is as pretty as any you ever saw, with white, powdery sand, waves breaking that are aqua/green and clear, and dunes partially covered with grass. Each species of penguin is fascinating in their own way, keeping mostly to themselves, but occasionally wandering through groups of other species. The Magellenic are the smallest, at about two feet tall and are burrowers. They migrate to Brazil in the winter and come back here in the summer, to the same burrow. They are also the only ones who are shy, ducking into their holes if you get too close, much like crabs on the beach in Florida. The others stand around in rather large groups and show no fear whatsoever, but will walk right up to you if you stand still. The Kings get up to about three feet tall and I swear they look like a bunch of teenagers standing around, slumped at the shoulders and talking in groups. Kings make a noise like a kazoo and Gentoos make a different kind of noise that I can't describe. Magellenics are said to make a sound like a donkey, and are therefore known as "jackass penguins" but I didn't hear them make a sound. They are all just really cool and somehow, watching them gives you a good feeling. You will be walking along the beach, and up in the dunes you will see a group of three or four of them casually walking down to the water to take a swim.

We had great weather for the tour, cold but sunny with almost *no* clouds. The drive there and back was an adventure, too. We drove for an hour on mostly gravel roads, and then went "cross country" for an hour and a half. It gave real meaning to the term "off road" as we went places that I wouldn't even attempt on a tractor! We went up and down hills so steep I was sure we were going to tip over; through ravines, across creeks, through marshes- I was amazed to see what that Land Rover could do. We came to one little creek with steep banks on each side. Sharon stopped, got two steel runners out of the back; one for each wheel, and laid them across from bank to bank and then calmly drove across! I could do a television commercial for land Rover after this experience!

Sharon is a native of the Falklands, and is very knowledgeable about the area. She worked with British Intelligence during the Argentine war, and her husband was in the Royal Marines. She showed us where battles were fought, and positions occupied by the Argentines and the British during the fighting. She also showed us where there are still minefields. The Argentines put out an estimated 30,000 land mines, with poor or no records of where they are. The mines are mostly plastic, making them difficult or impossible to detect so large areas are still fenced off and unusable for anything. We still haven't seen any trees except for those planted around houses and in town.

When we got back to town Mark and I went for beers at the Victory Bar, and then Richard met us for dinner at a nice restaurant called the Brasserie. I had lamb cutlets, new potatoes, a salad, and an ice cream triple-decker for dessert. Mark and I split a bottle of wine, and everything was so good I felt that I had sinned! The whole thing cost me about $25. Sonny and Naomi would not go to the Brasserie because he said it is too pricey.

Sonny and Naomi did provisioning today in preparation, hopefully, for a Monday departure. The electrician came and fixed the voltage regulator, the welder fixed the bracket for the alternator, and we're getting the dodger and bimini sewed and the frame fixed. Progress is being made. Sonny and Naomi are taking the penguin tour tomorrow!

Sunday, February 16 - 8:45 P.M. - We moved the boat to the industrial dock two miles east of town this afternoon. A cruise ship is coming in early tomorrow and they need the dock we were occupying to land the launches bringing in the passengers. The move went very smoothly, even though a pretty stiff wind was blowing and the industrial dock is concrete, with no fenders. We almost looked like we knew what we were doing.

This morning I got up early and went for a run; my first since Panama. I ran for 28 minutes so I figure I covered just under three miles. I also did my workout with my weights. Later on I took a walk down to the 1982 war memorial and read the names of the dead on the British side. They lost 255. What good is it to have a memorial with the names of all the dead if nobody ever reads them?

After I got back Mark and I had lunch and a couple of beers at the

Globe. I had a chicken and veggie plate that was very good, especially for pub food. I also had another good telephone conversation with Maureen. Tonight Mark, Richard and I walked a half hour each way to Shorty's for dinner.

We may be delayed in our departure from here because of the weather. It seems that a low-pressure cell is forecast to pass through tomorrow, bringing rain and 25 knot northeast winds. We will see. All of us are ready to get on our way. We are of a mind that we have done what we set out to do, and all of us have started looking forward to getting home, even though we still have nearly 7,000 miles to go.

It is looking more and more like I will end up leaving the boat and flying home from somewhere- probably Barbados- especially if it turns out that I have to be in Montana to start work by May 15. Sonny is so damn disorganized that we have ended up staying longer than we planned, everywhere we have been except for Easter Island. We just can't seem to manage our time in port. This pisses me off, but I have accepted it. If I get as far as Barbados, at least I can say that I not only sailed around Cape Horn, but also circumnavigated South America.

I wake up on a morning like this and realize that I am in the Falkland Islands, on a sailboat that I helped sail here, and I am amazed. This is such neat stuff! Whatever happens from here on out, this has been a truly fantastic experience for me. I had hoped to make this a trading voyage, taking a boatload of troubles and personal dissonance and trading it for a boatload of self-respect and inner peace. So far, I have pretty well succeeded. Some of the negative stuff is still with me but most of it is gone, and I have really gained a lot of self-respect. Offhand, I don't know anybody else who would be both capable and *willing to do what it takes*, to do what I have done. I have learned that I am a pretty damned decent sailor, and I am proud of myself!

Monday, February 17 - 5:55 P.M.- The weather never got bad but we managed to piss away the day anyway. We did get what's left of the dodger and bimini back up. The split was sewed, and we have the port and center panels of the dodger but no starboard panel. The starboard panel is where Richard went flying through when he went overboard in the knockdown. One piece of the bimini frame is missing and another is rigged with a dowel. At least we will have a little protection from spray and rain. The latest thing to go wrong with the boat is the solenoid that turns the flow of propane to the stove on and off. It died and no replacement is available, so when we want to use the stove, somebody has to go back to the stern locker where the tank is and turn it on; then remember to go back and turn it off when they are done. If you leave it on, there is a danger of a gas leak and an explosion. It's just an annoyance in good weather, but a real pain in the ass and dangerous under adverse conditions.

This morning I went for another run, this time along the pathway above the beach into town and back, a distance of nearly four miles. It felt good. I also helped to properly re-pack the sea anchor, which was a good learning process. I certainly hope we don't need to use it again!

Hopefully, everything is ready for an early morning departure tomorrow. I think everybody is ready to get back to warm weather. Oh yes, Sonny keeps calling the solenoid the "cellunoid", and keeps saying how he is looking forward to going to "Bonus Airs". It's nothing to me, but little things like that bug the hell out of me sometimes- kind of like "E-Burp"!

Tuesday, February 18 - 9:00 A.M.- The customs guy came at 8:00 to clear us out, and at 8:20 we cast off from the industrial dock. By 8:30 we were passing through the "narrows" at the entrance to Stanley Harbor, heading north on a cold, wet, foggy morning.

Leaving Stanley makes me sad. It is the last really remote place we will go, and it seems like the end of a phase of the voyage; something that I know I will never experience again. Buenos Aires, Rio, Recife, Barbados- I know people who have been there, but I don't know *anybody* who has been to the Falkland Islands. I'm sure I will enjoy each of our remaining ports and sailing between them as all being a part of the adventure but it will be at a different level.

14 – THE LONG TRIP HOME

Tuesday, February 18 - 6:50 P.M.- My world is once again in motion, as we are back at sea. It was a nasty morning as we rounded Volunteer Point and headed north; damp, cloudy and cold, with a thick blanket of fog. The fog finally cleared and it never rained but the cold and clouds stayed with us all day. Winds have stayed in the 12-20 knot range; from the southeast and benign seas have ranged mostly three to six feet

Wednesday, February 19 Lat.- 50 degrees, 29 minutes south; Lon.- 57 degrees, 39 minutes west - 9:55 A.M.- Naomi is the only one seasick so far. Seas are still pretty mellow, in the three to eight foot range and winds, still in the 12-20 knot range, are almost directly behind us as we sail due north on a cold, wet day. Sailing straight down wind without a spinnaker is always a pain and in our case, without a real jib, it is worse. Then, the sail plan on this boat is such that if you let the main out too far, such as on a downwind run, it chafes against the shrouds, so that compounds the problem. You just have to zigzag 15-20 degrees either side of the wind, using a jibe to change tacks.

I went to sleep after night watch and when I woke up, about 8:15, the generator was running. That meant that we had hot water so I took the opportunity for a hot shower. By the way, when Sonny and Naomi take a "shower" they heat water in the kettle, pour it into a gallon jug, and take it into the head for their "shower". Now call me a skeptic, but that is *not* a shower, and I don't see how they can get clean that way. Mark brought this up this morning, pointing out that they do this even though the water maker is working, giving us plenty of water, and we run the generator often enough that there are plenty of chances to take a hot shower- a *real* one!

A few minutes ago Sonny and Naomi were about to go on watch. He was in the galley making tea, and asked if she wanted some. She said, "I'll come and make it. I'll use your tea bag; just leave it there". I continue to be amazed at how cheap these people are! Some time ago several of us were talking and the subject of tea came up. She said that when she was away at college she had discovered that you can use tea bags several times and I said "Sure you can if you want to drink hot water".

6:40 P.M.- I hooked an albatross this afternoon! Mark was at the helm and I was trolling off the port side. I was leaning back in the cockpit looking aft and watching the rod. I admired this huge albatross as it went gliding by, just off the stern. A second later I saw the rod begin to bend, and thought I had a fish. Then I remembered the bird and thought, "Oh shit, I've caught an albatross!" I looked back and sure enough, the albatross was flopping around on the water but just as I was wondering what to do, the line came loose. I reeled it in and discovered that the top hook on my improvised two-hook lure had broken in the bend of the first hook where the eye of the second hook had hung. I guess they had started to rust a little at that point, and had weakened. I was very thankful that it broke before I had to cut the line or reel in a huge, struggling, beautiful bird. This way I don't think the bird was seriously injured; just *really* pissed off! I sure hope that is the case, as I would never intentionally hurt one and I certainly don't want to bring bad luck to the boat!

The wind died around 2:30 P.M. so we have motor-sailed since then. It isn't quite so cold out but is still cloudy and damp, with occasional sprinkles of rain. Seas are still benign with low swells five to eight feet, so smooth that you hardly notice them.

Thursday, February 20: Lat.- 48 degrees, 52 minutes south; Lon.-58 degrees, 19 minutes west - 10:35 A.M.- I can't *stand* to watch Ray eat. I had just finished cooking some eggs when he and Richard came off watch. He cooked some peach pancakes for himself and then put the rest of the can of peach quarters on top. As they swam in maple syrup, he cut the pancakes into roughly quarters. He would then stab a peach quarter and a quarter of a pancake dripping with syrup and cram the whole thing into his mouth, chewing just enough to swallow, and then repeating the process. These were not little medallion pancakes, either, but full size; probably six to eight inches in diameter. He is a great cook but I don't see how he can enjoy the products of his efforts the way he eats. He really is a sugar freak, too. He dumps two huge, heaping, running-over spoons of sugar into a cup of coffee. He does the same with oatmeal, too, and then pours maple syrup all over the top of it. No wonder he is so hyper all the time! No wonder that he has had some significant dental problems, too. I have talked with him about this and he just shrugs and says, "That's just the way I like to eat".

The weather has turned to crap- still cloudy and misty with occasional light rain, but the wind has been blowing 25-35 knots since midnight, and it is *cold*! The wind continues to blow from the south and since we have trouble going straight downwind we are going about 20 degrees off our desired course. All this happened after yesterday afternoon being relatively warm with winds that dropped so much we motor-sailed. The barometer keeps rising though, so we are looking for clearing skies and good west winds. This morning was so cold and nasty that I slept for three hours after night watch.

I am actually looking forward to getting a haircut in Buenos Aires. My last one was in The Galapagos and what hair I have is pretty shaggy but I didn't even look into it in Stanley after learning what they charge for things like laundry, phone calls, Internet service, and postage! Naomi's seasickness seems better, and so far nobody else has become sick.

Friday, February 21: Lat.- 46 degrees, 39 minutes south; Lat.- 59 degrees, 48 minutes west - 9:30 A.M.- The sun is shining! It's amazing how much that can lift the spirits after a stretch of cold, cloudy, wet days. The air temperature is probably in the upper 50's and it feels relatively dry. People are already hanging towels out to dry. Night watch was quiet, with southwest winds in the 12-16 knot range and gentle seas. The wind died this morning so we are motor sailing. I got creative with breakfast this morning, as I cut up little pieces of Spam and threw them in with my eggs as I scrambled them- no points for presentation here, but it was pretty tasty. This was my second breakfast, as I had my usual bowl of cereal when I came off night watch. I eat a lot here on the boat but have still lost weight, as have the others. Maybe it's because we use a lot of energy just being here with the boat constantly in motion. You're holding on, or bracing yourself, or both, all the time; even when you're sitting still. You even brace yourself when you are sleeping, to keep from rolling back and forth in your bunk. I guess you burn a lot of calories when you are cold, too.

Yesterday's afternoon watch was a bird show. Albatross and petrels played the lead roles with a supporting cast of smaller birds that I can't identify, but whose aerobatics were no less impressive. I am especially enjoying the albatross while I can, knowing that soon we will pass the northern extent of their habitat and in all likelihood I will never see them again. Afternoon watch was also the best since we left Stanley as the weather began to clear and the sun finally peeked out around four o'clock. Winds were from the south, moving to south-southwest, mostly in the 25-30 knot range and seas were 6-15 foot swells that were generally well behaved.

I keep thinking of and referring to Richard as an annoying little shit but in fact, he is not that little, standing just a shade under six feet tall. It's his upper body that is little, with an emaciated look and an I.O.U. for a chest. He looks like he has never picked up anything heavier than a ball point pen and his lack of upper body strength has shown up several times, like when he lost my dolphin because he couldn't lift it over the lifelines with the gaff. He rides a bicycle a lot at home, and actually has a lot of strength in his legs. One of his annoying habits is pronouncing "cycle" in the word "bicycle" the way most people pronounce it in "motorcycle". Another was in Puerto Montt where many restrooms have long metal trough-type urinals. One day in a restaurant Richard came back from the restroom appalled that you have to urinate in a "trauw". The first annoyance was that he complained about something like that and the second was that he kept on pronouncing trough as "trauw". Mark and Ray made fun of him about it but he never did understand that the word trough is pronounced "troff" and *not* "trauw". Ray told me in Stanley that he is fed up with Richard and would like a new watch partner, but there appear to be no other options. I certainly don't want Richard for *my* watch partner and it's for sure that Sonny and Naomi aren't going to split up. Richard and Mark as a team is not an option, as neither is ready to function as a Watch Captain and besides, Mark doesn't want to be on watch with him either. It looks like Ray is stuck. Another thing about Richard is that he always appears tense, and never relaxed. Ray says his jaw muscles always appear to be taut, like his teeth are clenched, and he talks as though he can't open his mouth; also like his teeth are clenched.

Saturday, February 22: Lat. 44 degrees, 40 minutes south; Lon.- 59 degrees, 3 minutes west - 9:25 A.M.- Today's sunrise may well have been the best of the entire trip, with just enough clouds to fully reflect the bright oranges and fiery reds (sailor, take warning!). It was truly spectacular. The weather was nice but sailing poor on night watch. Winds were 12-18 knots, just west of due north and we were trying to go just east of due north. We were very close-hauled, and without a real jib this boat won't do squat when going to windward. We wound up motor-sailing for a couple of hours and bobbing along at a speed of about two knots the rest of the time.

Yesterday we had to stop motoring after an hour, as the batteries were overcharging *again*. It seems that our *third* alternator repair still didn't fix the problem. Sonny and Ray put the old alternator back on and disconnected some wires so the batteries won't charge from the engine, so the problem *should* be solved. We will just charge the batteries with the generator. Mark says he will be surprised if we don't have a total failure of the electrical system that would end the voyage prematurely. We will see.

Sonny has stopped using the radar at night, even though he has seen ships the last two nights. Also, when I went up for watch at 2:00 A.M. he was up there alone and not even wearing a life jacket, much less being clipped on. Mark said that he heard what appeared to be somebody eating in the galley at 1:15 A.M. and when he started topside at 1:45 Naomi was already curled up in her sleeping bag on the starboard settee. We don't know how long she had been below, but it just doesn't seem right. We *still* don't know why she is here and will probably never know the truth. She really has contributed nothing. Even during the deployment of the sea anchor she stayed below instead of helping. As far as we can tell, about the only thing she does is wipe Sonny's ass.

Yesterday afternoon Ray made pizza from scratch for snacks during our afternoon watch, and it was excellent! Today so far is another nice, sunny, not-too-cold day that lifts spirits and makes us think that maybe the worst of the weather is over. We are all looking forward to the end of hull condensation wetting everything, and getting out of so many clothes. Getting back into shorts and t-shirts seems very appealing!

Sunday, February 23: Lat.- 43 degrees, 27 minutes south; Lon.- 58 degrees, 37 minutes west. - 9:35 A.M.- Ray and Naomi got into a small pissing contest yesterday. Ray was reorganizing the food storage bins because he had found the food to be stored in what appeared to be a haphazard fashion, with canned tomatoes in three or four different places, canned meat in three or four different places for example. Food is stored in probably ten different places; under and behind settee cushions, in sliding panel bins, and so forth. It has been a pain in the ass to find things, or even know what was here; especially with Sonny's and Naomi's asses often sleeping on top of the bins. Ray was co-locating all of each item in the same place and Naomi didn't like it. She had stored things that way on purpose, explaining that the things in one place are for lunches, and in another they are for dinners, like she was our mommy, and had to tell us what to eat and when to eat it! She also said that if all of a popular item was stored in one place, we would eat it all right away and then not have any left for the rest of the

165

passage. As I said, we have had to look all over hell and half of Georgia to find anything, or to even know what we had available. It has been almost funny to watch whoever happened to be hungry, with their ass in the air and their head in whatever storage bin happened to be accessible, foraging for something that looked appealing. It's not like she even pretends to cook for anyone but herself and Sonny, either. Ray usually cooks, and if he doesn't we fend for ourselves. Ray's interest in cooking sometimes depends on what ingredients are available so it is especially important for him to know what is here and where it is. Ray, Richard, Mark and I eat roughly together, and she and Sonny eat together. Both of them act like they are doing us a *big* favor by buying food to provision the boat, conveniently forgetting that Mark, Richard, and I provided the *money* to *buy* the Goddamn food!

Yesterday was an absolutely beautiful day and so far today is a carbon copy, with almost no clouds, bright sunshine, and warming temperatures. The only bad thing has been that yesterday the wind dropped to about five knots most of the day and last night it picked up but is right on our nose. Since you really can't sail close to the wind without a real jib, we have now been motoring for 20 hours. Normally you could tack back and forth, beating to windward but with only the storm jib, and no *real* jib that doesn't work. We tried sailing about 50 degrees off the wind a couple of days ago and could only make two or three knots. We are not going very fast motoring into the wind either, but at least we are making about 3.5 knots in the direction we want.

Monday, February 24: Lat.- 41 degrees, 54 minutes south; Lon.- 57 degrees, 58 minutes west - 9:45 A.M.- I can't fish right now! The albatross won't leave the lure alone as we troll. The other day I didn't see what happened, and assumed that the albatross accidentally flew into the line, but early this morning Richard was trolling and hooked one that fortunately, was able to shake the hook loose. When I heard this I assumed another accident, but a few minutes ago I was trying to troll and two albatross kept trying to catch the lure and eat it! When I saw what was happening I started reeling the lure in because I *really* don't want to catch an albatross. As I reeled it in, they followed it. Then I started reeling franticly, trying to keep the lure ahead of them and one of them actually started flapping it's wings and literally *running* across the surface of the water, trying to catch it! I wouldn't have believed it if I hadn't seen it myself. Anyway, I have given up fishing for the time being, even though we are on the continental shelf and fishing should be good. Oh well, at least the lure is good enough to fool an albatross,

166

so maybe it will be good enough to fool a fish!

The wind is still right out of the north and we have been motoring for 40 hours. If this continues for another day we may have to find a place to go in and refuel. Hopefully, that won't be necessary. The weather continues to be beautiful, and a little warmer every day. I have stopped sleeping in sweat pants and gone back to my boxers and a t-shirt.

Here's another Richard story. In addition to real fruit juice, we also drink Tang, or some similar powdered juice that we mix and keep in a two-liter jug. Whoever drinks the last of it is supposed to mix a new batch. For a while now I have been finding the jug with only two or three ounces in the bottom. At first I thought nothing of it; would drink what was there and mix a new batch. After it happened several times I figured out that somebody was doing it intentionally because they didn't want to mix a new batch so I decided "this is bullshit; I'm not going to play that silly game", and have since stuck to drinking real juice. A few days ago Ray and Mark commented that Richard was the one doing it, but nobody said anything because they couldn't prove it. Then yesterday, Ray and I were sitting in the salon when we saw Richard come down from topside. He had previously left about three ounces in the jug and when he reached in and brought it out he looked shocked to see those same three ounces still there. Then the sorry shit poured about two ounces into his cup, and was starting to put the jug back when I said, "Just finish the damned thing off, Richard". He looked up like a kid found with his hand in the cookie jar, knowing he was caught! Then he poured the remaining ounce in his cup and sat there pouting as he mixed a new batch.

Richard also had the habit of coming down and cooking, like oatmeal for example, when he and Ray were on watch; leaving the dirty pot for somebody else to wash after the remnants had dried and stuck to it. We were all sitting around a few days ago, when Mark said "I think we need to have a rule that whoever uses a pot is responsible for washing it when they finish eating instead of leaving it for somebody else to wash. I'm tired of going to fix something to eat and having to scrub somebody else's dirty pot before I can cook". Ray and I jumped right in and agreed, and so far it seems to have worked. Mark made the comment to me, that he thinks that Richard considers himself to be a little bit better than everybody else.

167

Tuesday, February 25: Lat.- 40 degrees, 43 minutes south; Lon.-
57 degrees, 39 minutes west. - 8:45 A.M.- We hit a fog bank about
4:30 yesterday afternoon and are still in it as we continue to motor
north, straight into the wind. This is the first really serious fog we
have encountered and it is a little eerie, especially at night. Daytime
visibility is maybe around 200 yards and at night it seems even less.
When we went on watch at 2:00 A.M. Sonny was actually sitting there
watching the radar! He had the flare gun loaded and handy and the
air horn and spotlight in the cockpit. It seems that when he got hit
by the freighter during his circumnavigation it happened in fog, so I
guess he is sensitive in foggy conditions- uncharacteristic for him to be
conscious of a safety issue! It was unusual too, in that the fog doesn't
go very high and we could see the crescent moon during most of our
watch. We even saw a few stars now and then.

Recently Mark and I have been finding the flush/dry valve on the
toilet set on "flush". That is something you *never* do because when it is
on "flush", water can come in and if a siphoning effect got started, the
boat could fill up with seawater and sink. You *always* leave it on "dry"
when you finish. Last night I started to go to the head and the light
was on, so I waited and saw Richard come out. When I went in, the
valve was on "flush", so I reminded him. He acted like I was speaking
another language, so I carefully explained it to him. The next time I
went to the head it was on "flush" again, but later Mark went in after
Richard and it was on "dry", so maybe he listened. This sounds trivial
and petty, but it could be a very serious matter.

Early this morning near the end of our night watch we saw the light
on in the head and knew that Richard was in there getting ready for
watch, as he does every morning. Then we heard the pump come on,
that drains water from the bathtub/shower. The pump kept running
and running, and we said, "wow, Richard must have taken a hell of a
shower", and finally asked Ray, who was in the galley, to check on it.
He came back and told us that Richard had turned on the pump and
forgotten about it. Now maybe that's what happened, but when you
use the shower/tub, there is a squeegee that you use to help get all the
water out of the tub as the boat rocks and rolls, and then a sponge to
get out the water that is left. If Richard's story is true then he obviously
skipped the last two steps. It makes me wonder if he is "losing it".

As we approach Buenos Aires and it gets progressively warmer
I find myself really looking forward to getting back into shorts and
t-shirts and out of the sleeping bag. Even though it is confining and
I look forward to getting out of it, I have to say that dollar-for-dollar,

my $9.97 Wal-Mart sleeping bag has probably been the best value of anything that I brought on this trip.

We have now been motoring for 67 consecutive hours and our plan now is to go in to a little town called Mar del Plata tomorrow night and refuel. The headwind had remained around 15 knots and seas no more than three or four feet. I would love to be fishing as we approach the coast but the albatross are still around, so I don't even try.

Wednesday, February 26: Lat.- 38 degrees, 30 minutes south; Lon.- 57 degrees, 19 minutes west - 9:00 A.M.- One of the things I will miss most at the end of this voyage is night watch. This is very likely the only occasion I will ever have to sit and watch the nighttime sky for four-hour stretches, night after night. You get to see the moon, stars, and planets as they rise, set, and move across the sky as the earth rotates. You get to watch and appreciate the beauty of the silent, subtle changes as they occur; the moon as it progresses through its phases. You get to see the night birds as they follow the boat, occasionally flashing through the glow of the stern running light. At home we sometimes look up and marvel at the stars, or the Milky Way, or the moonlight shining on a lake but we stop only for a few seconds, or a few minutes at the most. Most of us never have, or take, the time to stop and watch it over a period long enough to fully appreciate the awe-inspiring splendor that is just above our heads. The night watch truly *is* a special time.

We are still motoring, 91 hours now and counting. I would never have believed it. We had a wind shift at 3:15 A.M. as the wind suddenly came from the west and dropped to about eight knots. It came on around and is now from the southeast, but has almost stopped completely. The sea is glassy, and nearly flat. At least we are making better time-about 5.5 knots- now that we aren't bucking a head wind.

6:40 P.M.- We are sailing again! After four days, 96 hours almost to the minute, we put up all three sails and stopped the engine at 2:10 P.M. The wind was just aft of the starboard beam at 14 knots, and built as high as 24. A warm, sunny afternoon turned cool, cloudy and damp. I wore shorts today for the first time in six or seven weeks, though I did put on a sweatshirt and windbreaker before afternoon watch was over. In any case, it really felt good to be back in shorts. Hopefully the weather will stay warm, and we won't have to revert back to long pants.

This afternoon as the weather closed in and visibility dropped to just over a mile, we sailed through a small fleet of Argentine fishing boats, watching them on radar before we made visual contact. We counted eight, and they all seemed to be heading for port- very interesting.

This change in the weather means that now we won't have to make a fuel stop in Mar del Plata after all, but are heading for Buenos Aires. We hope to arrive late Friday.

Thursday, February 27 - 9:30 A.M.- This time, night watch was a doozy! We had a storm within a storm. After five hours of good sailing Richard and Ray took down the mainsail at 7:00 P.M., as radar showed a large thunderstorm approaching. Sure enough, it came, and stayed with us- nothing too severe but lots of lightning and rain, with winds up to 25 knots. We were trying to go northeast to get around Cabo San Antonio and the winds came from the north, so it made for slow going and difficult conditions for those of us trying to sleep. Around midnight Sonny started the engine and tried to motor-sail, but with little success. When Mark and I went up at 2:00 A.M. we were crawling along at about one knot and were heading southeast. We couldn't go any to the west, as we were only 10 miles off the coast, which had become a lee shore. Winds were still in the mid-twenties. About 2:30 Mark was at the helm, and just as Sonny stuck his head up to see if we were O.K., the second storm hit and the wind spiked up to 40 knots before settling in the upper thirties. We were making no headway at all, and drifting to the southwest so we decided to take down the storm jib and mizzen to reduce the drift. Sonny offered to come up and help but I said we could take care of it. I said I would take down the storm jib myself but Mark wanted to help, so with the autopilot on, he followed me forward. I told him to loosen the halyard and that I would pull down the sail and secure it. By then it was raining hard, stinging my face and the boat was rolling side-to-side about 30 degrees each way. Just as I got the sail secured, Mark lost his end of the halyard and we couldn't find it. About that time, Sonny showed up and came forward, in his foul weather suit, but without even his life jacket, let alone a tether! He was standing up by the main mast fruitlessly looking for the jib halyard when I suggested that we get the mizzen down and worry about the halyard later. He agreed, so we moved aft to the mizzenmast. About that time the autopilot quit working due to the conditions, so Mark had to steer and try to keep us pointed into the wind. Sonny stood by the port side of the mizzenmast and I was on the starboard side, trying to get the halyard loose. He got a little confused between the mizzen halyard and mizzen sheet, and wanted to argue about it but we got it squared away and lowered the sail. He was standing there holding a sail tie and hugging the sail and mast. The boat was still rolling as I mentioned before. I thought he was putting on the first sail tie, and I moved halfway down the boom, gathered as much of the sail as I could, and tied on a sail tie. About then he said "I can hold this if you can put on the sail tie", so I did. Then just as I moved out to the end of the boom to put on the third sail tie, somehow the mizzen sheet loosened and the boom started swinging back-and-forth, about three feet in each direction. In the middle of all this Sonny inadvertently shined the spotlight directly in my face, blinding me completely for about 30 seconds, which seemed like a very long time when you are trying to get something done in those conditions. I managed to hold on, sliding back-and-forth and managed to get the third sail tie on, securing the mizzen. Of course I had my tether clipped on to the jack line, but it was still a pretty hairy experience. I then checked and found that the mizzen sheet was cleated, so I am not sure why the boom started swinging.

Anyway, Sonny took over steering at that point and we started crawling to the southeast again- a bad course, but at least away from land. About 3:30 he gave the steering task to me. Pretty soon conditions eased a little and I was able to get us around toward the east, and a little later, back on our northeasterly course. By 5:00 winds had dropped to 10-12 knots, the rain had stopped, and in spite of a nasty chop we were making a speed of three knots on the course we want. Mark took over steering at that point and I came below for a bowl of corn flakes.

I continue to be amazed at Sonny's lack of concern for safety. If he had fallen his stupid ass overboard in those conditions there is no way we could have rescued him! We were barely holding our position with the engine, and sometimes not even that. With no momentum you have no steerage, so maneuvering for a rescue would have been literally impossible even if we could have seen him, which we couldn't have because without his *life jacket*, he would have had no light or strobe and it was pitch dark!

This morning it is still cloudy and threatening rain, but no wind so we are motoring slowly through a pretty good chop, toward Buenos Aires. We still hope to get there late tomorrow. Mark isn't feeling well today, not seasick, but just bad. We have had difficult sleeping conditions the last couple of nights and I think the lack of sleep may be getting to him. I put my sleeping bag away under my mattress, in the middle of the night. For the third night in a row I was sweating like a pig, and it felt confining and uncomfortable. It has served me well but I'm hoping I won't need it again.

171

7:25 P.M.- Ray just called me up on deck to watch a really spectacular sunset! I was already in my bunk, and went up in my boxers- it is *that* nice out, and *warm!* We are motoring again in winds of two to four knots and glassy seas, making a speed of about six knots. We still have a glimmer of hope to make Buenos Aires tomorrow night. It seems that this has turned into the passage that wouldn't end!

Friday, February 28: Lat.- 35 degrees, 36 minutes south; Lon.- 56 degrees, 37 minutes west. - 9:00 A.M.- The boat is crawling with bugs! It started three nights ago when Mark and I noticed moths flying in the glow of the stern running light when we were 70 miles offshore. We confirmed it the next morning when I caught a moth in the cockpit. A little later that morning Richard caught a grasshopper in the cockpit. I wouldn't have believed it if I hadn't seen it myself! None of us could figure out how that grasshopper got way the hell out there. That one must have won the jumping contest! The following day we started to see flies, some tiny bugs that we can't identify, and then mosquitoes. Now, we seem to have quite a few flies; some small and some large, like horseflies. I got out my Sawyer Insect Repellent for the first time, and so far I haven't been bitten but all kinds of bugs are here, and we haven't even touched land yet! I hope this isn't a sign of what we can expect in Argentina.

At daybreak we noticed that the water is getting a bit brown in color where the silty Rio de la Plata is mixing with the seawater. This is the first discolored water we have seen. Now we are in what looks like a sea of *very* muddy water. They must have had a lot of rain lately, as we are seeing shoes, plastic bottles, boards, plants and such junk floating in the water. Mark said that he went to the head for his morning constitutional and when he flushed the toilet he had trouble getting it clean. "I pumped and dried, and pumped and dried, and still the water was brown" he said. "I thought 'Man, I must have really done a bad one', and then it occurred to me that the flush pump uses sea water and I was pumping in brown river water!"

This morning's sunrise was very nice, but the pre-sunrise colors were prettier and more varied. Oddly, they faded about 6:10 and the sun didn't come up until 6:30. We are motoring northwest on a bright, sunny morning and are excited to be approaching Buenos Aires. We hope to arrive during the night tonight.

Just before 3:30 A.M. Mark saw what appeared to be a yellow light on the eastern horizon, and said "There's a ship coming up behind us". I looked at the radar and it was clear. After a few minutes we realized that it was the planet Venus, our morning star, rising out of the sea and appearing yellow because of atmospheric conditions! About twenty minutes later we looked back and the little sliver of a moon appeared to be resting on the water like a teacup. Then for the next two hours, in tandem, they put on a celestial show with Venus just above and to the left of the moon. It was a great night for star watching.

After all this time Sonny has finally discovered that I know how to plot our position on the chart using latitude and longitude coordinates, so now I am participating in taking GPS readings from the hand-held unit, plotting positions, and adjusting our course as necessary. We are plotting hourly as we approach the ship channel up the Rio de la Plata to Buenos Aires. I *told* him early on that I could navigate!

Saturday, March 1 - 10:35 A.M.- We were arrested this morning by the Argentine Coast Guard! It seems that we came in the ship channel last night without calling on the radio for clearance to do so, and they were *very* unhappy with us. To make it worse, we were in the ship channel all night, poking-ass along at a speed of two knots. Sonny had us do that to time our arrival in Buenos Aires with daybreak. They spoke almost *no* English but I heard them use the word "arrest", and they had us tie on alongside their vessel and be brought into the harbor area. After a long discussion however, they let us go and wished us a good visit to Argentina. They dropped us off just outside the Yacht Club of Argentina, who sent out a man in a boat to lead us in to a slip in their marina. All this happened about a half hour before the end of my night watch, and we arrived in the marina just before 8:00 A.M.

We were going too slowly for the autopilot to work so we spent night watch with Mark steering and looking for flashing red and green navigation lights while I navigated and helped look for those lights. We both also watched for ships, and had to get out of the way of three. The channel is only about 100 yards wide and of course the big ships like the middle. With our engine running we couldn't hear them, and you couldn't see them except for their running lights, which are red and green; same as the navigation lights. I took GPS readings and plotted our position every half hour to be sure we were where we were supposed to be. We also checked the numbers on each navigation light and channel marker that we passed and then found them on the chart to verify our position. The channel is not straight but has a couple of "dog legs", and had two branch channels leading off to the side. With all those lights against a background of city lights in the distance, and trying to avoid getting run over by a ship, staying on our course was no easy task. We did well, but it was a busy and tense four hours.

Sonny didn't know he was supposed to call in and get permission to run the channel at night, and thought for a while that he was going to get a stiff fine, or maybe even have the boat impounded but it turned out O.K. Now we are waiting while he and Naomi try to get us cleared in through customs and immigration, and they seem to be fumbling through the process. It is complicated by today being Saturday, and also carnival weekend. He still has Naomi try to translate but she knows less Spanish than I do. I just keep my mouth shut and let them do it.

Yesterday we motored and motor-sailed all day, watching as the water got muddier and muddier. They must have had a lot of rain, because this river is muddier than the Mississippi River *ever* was and has a *lot* of junk floating in it. When we got into the Yacht Club of Argentina marina, you never *saw* so much trash in the water, including lots of plastic bottles, plates, flip-flops, and so forth. The clubhouse and restaurant look very elegant and ritzy, which is such a contrast with all the trash! The downtown area, right by the marina, has lots of nice-looking high-rise modern buildings, but we haven't seen them up close yet. My first impressions of Argentina have not been good, but we will see. The weather today is mostly sunny, warm, and humid.

15 – BUENOS AIRES

Saturday, March 1 - 10:55 P.M.- I am *very* tired so this will be just a few basic, short notes. I have been awake since 1:30 A.M. except for a one-hour nap this afternoon.

Ray, Mark, Richard and I just had an *outstanding* Argentine steak dinner at a place called Xcaret's on the waterfront in the Puerto Maduro section of town, not far from the marina. Mine was an equivalent of a New York strip with a blend of four sauces, a half bottle of wine, and a dessert of pie and ice cream for eleven dollars, including the tip!

Buenos Aires is a modernistic city with lots of new high-rise buildings and an extremely impressive walkway along the waterfront with quite a few nice, mostly Italian restaurants.

Sonny bought us two rounds of beers here at the yacht club this afternoon. Heineken costs 75 cents! I am going to bed now.

Sunday, March 2 - 8:40 A.M.- I just finished a great run along the waterfront boulevard in Puerto Maduro. It goes alongside a salt marsh with lots of birds- odd to have that so near the middle of downtown in a huge city. The marsh is also a great breeding ground for mosquitoes, which are abundant. There is a nice, wide promenade by the water, and in the boulevard area between the two streets is a running track so I went outbound along the promenade and back on the track. I did my workout with my weights before the run. Now, Ray is making peach pancakes, and after I have some I am looking forward to a nice, hot shower.

Yesterday we finally cleared customs and immigration about noon. By then Mark and I were starving, so we walked down the Puerto Madura canal front and had lunch. I had a steak sandwich, he had a ham sandwich, and we each had two beers, and the *total* bill was eight dollars U.S.!

10:05 P.M.- Today was a bit of a downer day; overall, not a good one. It started out good, as I mentioned before, but then I had a somewhat negative telephone conversation with Maureen. After that, instead of going to the bullfights, as I had wanted, I tried to be a team player and went with Ray, Mark and Richard to Dorriego Plaza in barrio San Telmo. On Sundays there they have something like a flea market for antiques in the square- it looked mostly like junk to me- and they also have all kinds of street performers including everything from a guy doing a "Charlie Chaplin" imitation to musicians, to puppeteers, to card tricks, to mimes, to *lots* of tango dancers. I found the antiques to be almost *insufferably* boring but the street performers sort of made up for it. We also visited an impressive cathedral in San Telmo. It was O.K., but all things considered, I would rather have gone to the bullfights. Ray and Richard separated from Mark and me, agreeing to meet us on a specific corner at 3:00 P.M. We got there at two minutes after three, waited 45 minutes, and they didn't show. I later asked Ray and he said that he got there at 2:55, waited seven minutes, and left! I was unhappy with him, and said so. I told him we would not plan to meet that way again. One good thing: Mark found a painting that he wanted to buy for $100. U.S. but he didn't have the cash, and couldn't get the ATM to work. Since they only do this on Sunday, it was his only chance to buy it and I was there to advance him the $100. Later, he and I had a great dinner at Xcaret's while listening to a concert complete with lots of fireworks across the canal.

When we came in tonight the security lady at the yacht club gave us a note for Sonny, telling him to report to the Coast Guard, where they are giving him a citation for running the ship channel at night without permission!

Monday, March 3 - We will be here an extra day because of Richard. He wandered off on his own early this morning and has been gone all day while the rest of us went to the Brazilian Consul and applied for our visas. This is something that we couldn't do in advance, but had to do here. It takes 48 hours to get the visa after you apply (and pay your $120. U.S.). So, we will all supposedly get ours Wednesday but now Richard can't get his until Thursday after 4:00 P.M. so we can't leave until Friday. We are all somewhat annoyed at his lack of communication and consideration.

We also put our laundry in to be done, and mine will cost $4.33; less than ten percent of what it cost in the Falklands, and I am having more stuff washed here! After we finished the visa application process Mark and I walked back, exploring along the way. We went to San Martin square and several other parks along the way. W have found that once you get away from the waterfront, Buenos Aires is a relatively clean city, and very beautiful with lots of parks, plazas, and green areas with big flowering mimosa trees, oaks, and *huge* palm trees. There are very wide boulevards, and the wider streets have lane dividers in place to enhance traffic flows. A section of a street in the middle of the downtown area- Florida Avenue- has been turned into a pedestrian mall, surfaced with little tiles! That section is probably about two miles long. It is all quite impressive, and things are *cheap*! We have discovered that taxi rides are cheap here too; no more than a dollar to go most places we have gone, such as to the Brazilian Consulate.

We stopped by an Internet Café to do e-mail and while I was there I sent inquiries to Reader's Digest and "Sail" magazine regarding a description that I wrote of our experience at Cape Horn. In all likelihood, nothing will come of it, but it's worth a try.

I had a bad telephone conversation with Maureen this morning but it all worked out, and we ended our third conversation of the day on a positive note. News from Montana has been less than good, but not all bad. Hopefully it will all work out so that we will still go out there again this summer. I'm still rather discouraged though, as I hate for things to be hanging.

Tuesday, March 4 - 10:55 A.M.- Today is off to a good start. I went for a run along the salt marsh at 6:30; then came back and did my exercises. I saw some very pretty swans that were white, with black, or dark brown necks and heads. I also saw all the crap that people throw over the rail into the water, too. It is disgusting!

After breakfast and a shower Mark and I went and picked up our laundry, still amazed at the low cost here compared to the rip-off in the Falklands. Now we have clean clothes, and can put away the winter stuff. On the way I mailed some post cards and put in a roll of film to be developed. I want to get a group picture of the crew for Ray to send to the "Passage Notes" column at "Cruising World" magazine. Richard went to apply for his Goddamn visa, Sonny and Naomi went shopping for provisions, and Ray went shopping for some things for the boat. Things are happening.

10:50 P.M.- I found out that all this trash in the marina comes in with the tide, and dealing with it is a constant battle. At least it isn't thrown into the water by boat owners, but *somebody* is throwing it into the water, including the salt marsh adjacent to the marina! At least in the city, the downtown area is relatively clean.

Today was another beautiful, *hot* day- no complaint about the heat, just an observation. Mark and I had lunch in an Irish Pub up near Florida Avenue. The food prices were cheap but *relatively speaking*, the beer was outrageous at $3.00 U.S. for a pint of Heineken.

Richard is in his shell. I think he knows that Ray, Mark and I are pissed, and fed up with him. He went out with Sonny and Naomi tonight. Sonny and Naomi bought a lot of provisions today, and we all helped bring things to the boat from the entrance of the yacht club.

Wednesday, March 5 - 10:05 P.M.- Today I witnessed a bit of social unrest! I was wandering along Florida Avenue late this morning when up ahead I heard a commotion with metallic noise, chanting, and yelling. Then I started noticing a lot of cops; then cops with riot shields and flak jackets; then about thirty in full riot gear with helmets, face shields, shoulder pads, knee pads, flak jackets, night sticks, and of course guns. About every fourth one had a tear gas gun and several canisters of tear gas. The crowd started moving and I decided to follow along because I have never seen anything like that up close. I eased along on the periphery, not getting out into the crowd or between the crowd and the police. I talked to one cop who told me that the demonstration was over the economy and recent devaluations of the peso. The crowd built to about 300 people at the peak. They would stop in front of a bank, yell for a while and beat on metallic objects like frying pans, and then move on. The cops stayed just ahead of them and alongside, with the ones in heavy gear blocking entrances to the banks. I discreetly and not so discreetly, took about 15 pictures along the way. The crowd was loud, but otherwise well behaved so no heads got cracked. After the banks, they tried to go to the Argentine equivalent of the Federal Reserve but the street was barricaded at the head of the block and guarded by cops in heavy gear. Then they marched to the Presidential Palace and found that it too was barricaded. By then the crowd had dwindled to less than 100 and the demonstration began breaking up. It was all kind of exciting, but the cops kept everything under control while using appropriate restraint.

I also got my ear pierced today. Mark and Ray really wanted to have theirs pierced but wouldn't do it without me. Also, Mark and I had agreed to pay for Ray's if he wanted to do it, so we all went this afternoon. It cost 20 pesos each, just under seven dollars including the stud, and was relatively painless. We'll see how it goes. We did that for Ray as a little "thanks" for all the cooking he has done for us. Cooking is *not* part of his job, and he has cooked a *lot* of really good meals and snacks for us. We *really* appreciate it, and wanted him to know.

Early this morning Mark walked with me down by the salt marsh to see the birds. We saw about 30 of the hooded swans, including what appeared to be a family, with a male, a female, and six young ones swimming in a line. The male would sometimes swim ahead of the others, ever alert for any sign of danger. We also saw quite a few wild green parrots that looked like conures, but seemed larger. They were in the trees along the promenade, and came down to feed with the pigeons. I continue to be appalled at all the trash- mostly plastic bottles- that people throw over the rail into the salt marsh. I think the tide brings a lot of that crap into the marina, where dealing with it is a never-ending battle.

This afternoon Mark, Ray and I picked up our Brazilian visas before getting our ears pierced. They were ready on time, as promised. After all that we went to Florida Avenue to have dinner and enjoy the street performers. We saw a really good jazz band that was playing big band/swing music of Louis Armstrong, Count Basie, and Glenn Miller. They had a guitar, a drummer with a single drum, a saxophone, and a trumpet. The trumpet player also sang. They seemed to be having great fun playing, and it carried over to the crowd. We also saw a young couple in their twenties tango-dancing, and they were excellent too.

Richard is continuing to be reclusive, knowing that Ray, Mark and I are pissed at him and about fed up with him. He went out with Sonny and Naomi last night, and has started sucking up to Sonny. I think Ray gets lonely since he has fallen out with his watch partner. He came and joined Mark and me for dessert as we were finishing our dinner last night. I like Ray and understand his insecurities. I also understand his difficult relationship with Sonny.

Thursday, March 6 - 9:30 P.M.- I have to mention the beggars here. It seemed the first few days here that there wasn't enough of it going on to be worth mentioning but as the week has progressed, it seems that we are seeing more of it every day. Early on, most of it was little kids in roughly the six-to-ten age range who walked around with little accordions. They would come up to your table at an outdoor restaurant, play about a half dozen notes, put on a sad face and stick out their hand for you to give them money. Sometimes they would sit outside a store on the Florida Avenue pedestrian mall with a tin cup for money, and play a few notes as you walked past. The fact that *somebody* must have bought those little accordions, and that they all played pretty much the same half dozen notes caused me to wonder if they might be part of a scam, and I paid them little attention. The last two or three days we have been seeing greater numbers and varieties of people begging; ranging from more little kids *without* accordions, coming up

179

to you and asking for money, to people with obvious disabilities, to lots of women with babies hanging in slings, sometimes breast feeding as they walk along. These latter groups are more aggressive and more persistent, reluctant to take "no" for an answer. They can be annoying, and at the same time tear your heart out. You have to keep reminding yourself that you can't fix all the world's problems. You wonder if all those women with the babies are for real, because in the U.S. I have heard of young women, especially druggies, borrowing a friend's baby to go out panhandling but I have seen some of these sleeping on the sidewalk with their babies beside them. One thing I have noticed is that they seem to lock on to people like me, who do not appear to be locals. In my case they see me in shorts, t-shirts, flip-flops, and carrying a backpack. I have also seen some of them standing around in groups, laughing and socializing; then put on a sad face and accost a passer-by. Whatever the case, it has increased to the point where I find it really troubling.

This morning when I ran, I took some pictures of the hooded swans in the salt marsh that should turn out pretty good. I also had a really nice phone conversation with Maureen before she left to go to Mississippi for the weekend. I also finally reached Gordon Patton in Montana and he said that the new owners are definitely counting on Maureen and me to work at the Crazy Lady Outpost this summer. That was encouraging!

I checked my e-mail and had a positive reply from the editor of "Sail" magazine, asking me to send him my story of our Cape Horn passage. I had my draft with me in my notebook so I typed it in and sent it to him immediately. He acknowledged receipt and said that he would look it over and get back to me in a few days. He also asked if I have pictures, so it seems like he is seriously interested. That would be a kick in the ass, to get an article published in "Sail"!

I met Mark for lunch at Café Doria, and then we went touring on foot. I took him and showed him the Presidential Palace, and then we toured two old square-rigged sailing ships in the harbor. One was the Uruguay" and I can't recall the name of the other. Both were very interesting, with lots of history.

We still may leave tomorrow afternoon but it looks more like it will be Saturday morning. Sonny is so damned disorganized; it takes him *forever* to get things done. There seemed to be a lot of negative vibes around the boat this morning. Mark and I both noticed it. I left around 9:30 and he left at 11:00, and we both stayed away until about 9:15 P.M. We haven't sampled the abundant nightlife here, as the locals don't even *think* about going out until nearly midnight, way past our accustomed bedtime. Also, they dress to the nines when they go out, or even to work, and we don't have anything more formal than blue jeans.

Friday, March 7 - 10:55 P.M.- Tomorrow is departure day; at least that's the latest information we have. At 8:30 this morning we went to immigration to check out and were told that you have to do that within two hours of your actual departure, and you have to go to the Coast Guard after that, so we will go back tomorrow morning and take it from there. This morning Sonny was doing the talking and Naomi was "interpreting", so I'm not sure what really transpired, but that's what we were told.

My mission today was to find and buy some good fishing lures to use trolling. I was successful after considerable effort. After looking in the yellow pages of the phone book, and asking the manager of the yacht club, I had a list of places to go and look. The first one, given by the yacht club manager, I never found. The second place I went was vacant, and the third is now a locksmith shop. The fourth, on Perana Avenue, was a good resource and I found a couple of lures there. Then I discovered that there were a dozen or so fishing shops almost side-by-side! That is the way shopping is set up here, with shops for any single category of items, side-by-side, or nearly so. It is an efficient way to do things; just different form the way things are set up at home. I ultimately ended up buying a total of five lures.

I had good news in my e-mail- "Sail" is interested in publishing my article on our rounding of Cape Horn. Peter Nielsen, the editor, asked me for a re-write that would include some additional information on deployment and recovery of the sea anchor and said that if I can do what he asks, he thinks we can do business. I am *excited*! I am asking Ray for input on the preparation for deployment and recovery of the sea anchor. We will see!

This afternoon I took some pictures of the beggars on Florida Avenue, giving each of them a peso or two to pose. It is sad, but interesting, and a significant part of life here in Buenos Aires.

Tomorrow night, our last Spanish speaking country will be behind us. Portuguese will be a challenge!

16 – ON TO IPANEMA

Saturday, March 8 - 9:40 A.M.- At nine o'clock we cast off our mooring lines at the Yacht Club of Argentina and are motoring directly into a 14 knot east wind, through the muddy waters of the Rio de la Plata. I took one more picture of downtown Buenos Aires as we left. We were really ready to go, but again I got that sentimental, somewhat sad feeling of leaving a place that you have enjoyed, knowing it is very unlikely that you will ever be there again. I still don't care for large cities, but Buenos Aires exceeded my expectations.

Yesterday I rode the subway by myself for the first time *ever*! That would seem to be a non-event for most people but it was somewhat significant for me. My only previous subway experience was in New York with my last ex-wife, and doesn't include fond memories. Since then I have been something of a subway-phobe, not confident that I would get on the right train, going in the right direction, or get off at the right stop but this worked out fine. The cars were *clean*, modern, with no graffiti, and efficiently operated. I got where I was going very quickly, even got a seat, and the cost was 70 centavos, or 23 cents!

In addition to the new sail, we got the framework for the bimini replaced here, so that is in good shape. Now, only the starboard panel of the spray dodger is missing.

Here's a Naomi story. Early this morning I was sitting in the cockpit having a cup of tea when I saw her come topside carrying the garbage. I idly wondered why she was doing that, since I have responsibility for dealing with the garbage but I didn't think much about it. A couple of minutes later I realized why she was doing it when I saw her come back, carrying the empty garbage bag, to be re-used!

As we leave here the interpersonal dynamics are difficult and interesting, in a twisted sort of way. We are still pissed at and somewhat fed up with Richard, and he is still rather reclusive; however he is still trying to suck up to Sonny. Mark keeps commenting that Richard thinks he is superior to the rest of us and that observation is probably accurate. Ray is not looking forward to standing watches with Richard. Then, there is the Sonny and Naomi team. We are pretty fed up with them, too and there is little or no social interaction with them. As Mark put it, the closer we get to the end of the voyage, the lower our tolerance level. I don't know when I am going to do it but sometime before the end of the voyage I am going to ask Sonny why he lied to us about the "captain" business. All in all, there is a definite feeling prevalent that we have done the things we came out here to do and now we are on the way home, even though we still have over 5,000 miles to go.

6:40 P.M.- By the time we went on watch this afternoon the wind had shifted to the southeast and built to 18-20 knots. We were trying to make an east-southeast course of 105 degrees to get around Punta del Este, Uruguay but the wind continued building to 25 knots and the seas to the six-foot range, slowing us down to a speed of about two knots. Just after five o'clock we decided to fall off the wind to a course of 80 degrees and try sailing under the *new* jib and the mizzen. It is working so far but we will have to tack in a couple of hours and actually head *south* if the wind doesn't shift or lay down some. It's *always* something, but at least it's warm!

Sunday, March 9 Lat.- 35 degrees, 9 minutes south; Lon.- 57 degrees, 5 minutes west

9:35 A.M.- Night watch was interesting, tense, exciting, and busy! We are still trying to make our way far enough east to get around Punta del Este, so we can then head north toward Rio. This is complicated by headwinds that have remained in the 18-25 knot range all night, sometimes shifting to the southeast, and sometimes to the northeast. Then, we are going to considerable effort to stay out of the channel, to keep from pissing off the Coast Guard again and to avoid getting run over by a ship, as the channel stays busy day and night. We were *damn lucky* on the way in! Finally, there is the matter of avoiding the numerous wrecks, obstacles, and foul areas in the wide expanse of water *outside* the channel, including a light and a wreck that were on the chart, but not really there. This avoidance is made more difficult by the headwinds, which limit maneuverability, and a significant tidal current that can set you well off your intended course. During night watch Mark stayed at the helm while I took GPS readings and plotted our position every 15 minutes, altering our course as necessary. In between, we both concentrated on watching the radar and getting visual fixes on ships, markers, and obstacles. By 5:00 A.M. we were converging on the channel and the wind wouldn't let us turn away from it without tacking to a really undesirable course or starting the engine. We managed to sail right on the edge of the channel until daylight, as I really didn't want to cross the channel in the dark.

6:55 P.M.- Beating to windward against winds of 25 knots in a sea of muddy water- that's my description of today's afternoon watch. Throw in playing tag with a couple of freighters as we sailed across the ship channel and you have the whole picture. Actually, we crossed the channel five minutes ahead of the closest freighter, but that is closer than it sounds when you consider that we were under sail, and couldn't really tell how fast the freighter was moving. It is really weird to be out here, totally out of sight of any land, in a sea of brown, muddy water as far as you can see. I will be *very* happy to see blue water again.

I started on the re-write of my article for "Sail" magazine today, and I got quite a lot done. I hope to finish tomorrow or Tuesday. Then I'll have to figure out what to do about pictures.

Monday, March 10 Lat.- 35 degrees, 45 minutes south; Lon.- 56 degrees, 2 minutes west - 11:00 A.M.- Ray is in a pissy mood and I haven't been able to figure out why. He says he isn't sick, and it isn't directed toward Mark and me, yet he has smarted-off a little, even to us. I think he is fed up with the Sonny and Naomi situation and doesn't like standing watch with Richard. Their relationship is strained, to say the least. Also, he has bitched a lot about the provisions that Sonny and Naomi have bought, and he has been out of the provisioning loop since she arrived. We all make our own lunches and yesterday Mark and I were sitting on the port settee eating ours and talking to Ray, who was in his bunk above the settee. Richard was at the navigation table just a few feet away; just staring at his lunch when Ray said to me "I don't enjoy cooking any more except for you and Mark". Richard didn't say anything, but Ray saying that had to exacerbate the strain in their relationship. In any case, he didn't feel like cooking last night so I cooked two hamburgers for myself. Mark wasn't feeling well, and didn't eat.

I strained something in both shoulders yesterday, cranking winches without proper leverage. They hurt enough last night that I couldn't sleep until I took a second ibuprofen. After that I slept fine, and today they don't hurt.

6:50 P.M.- Afternoon watch was shitty; still beating into winds and seas, and this time it rained off and on for about three hours. Winds were 25-34 knots for the first three hours, making the rain sting when it hit your face. During the last hour the winds dropped to 18-23 knots and the rain stopped. We are still not making the course we want, at about 70 degrees or so, but we're getting closer. It looks like this is going to be a slow passage but at least we're out of the muddy water

With this weather, Mark and Naomi are seasick again and Sonny is on the verge. Mark hurled over the leeward rail at the start of afternoon watch, but was fine after that.

Ray is in a much better mood now. I'm not sure what happened, but I am glad. He cooked pasta with meat sauce tonight (the last of the canned meat), and it was very good.

I should make a final comment about Argentina and bugs. All the bugs that I mentioned on the way in there seemed to go away once the wind started to blow and we had no problem with bugs while we were there. There were a few mosquitoes in the marina and some of the others complained about that but I was only bitten twice. I guess my Sawyer's Insect Repellent with "DEET" did the trick, but even when I forgot to use it I still had no problem.

Tuesday, March 11 Lat.- 36 degrees, 17 minutes south; Lon.- 53 degrees, 50 minutes west - 7:20 P.M.- We have had two nice, easy, *dry* watches in a row! Around midnight last night the wind dropped into the teens, and by our 2:00 A.M. watch it was down to 12-14. It also had shifted to north-northwest so we were able to steer the northeast course that we need. Throughout the night watch the wind was marginal for sailing, at 9-13 knots and since Sonny is still very timid about flying the mainsail; especially at night, we slogged along at about 3.5 knots. If I was captain I would put a reef in the main, and leave the son-of-a-bitch up except in extreme conditions, and use the roller furling jib and the mizzen to reduce or increase sail area as appropriate. BUT, I'm *not* the captain! His timidity sure makes for *slow* passages.

Today I finished the rough draft of the re-write of the article I submitted to "Sail". I was able to work in the items they asked for after getting input from Ray and Mark. Now I just have to copy it over, cleaning it up, and then add the sidebar of what we did right, what we did wrong, and lessons learned. I want to be ready to type it and send it to them as soon as we get to Rio. I will then have to decide what pictures to send to them after I get some film processed. I am *really excited* about this!

Near the end of afternoon watch a pod of what looked to be about 20 black-and-white dolphins showed up, put on about a five minute show, and then left as quickly as they came. We are still seeing albatross, and enjoying their shows, too. The sun came out

185

occasionally but today was mostly overcast, and now a misty rain is falling. I hope it stops before our night watch.

Having no refrigeration is turning out to be a real pain in the ass, especially now that we are in a warm climate. Even the "shelf milk" goes bad within a day after it is opened so when you open a quart it is "use it or lose it".

We found out for sure today that Naomi is planning to leave the boat and fly home from Recife. It will be interesting to see how all that works out and how Sonny gets along without her to wait on him. From my perspective she has contributed nothing positive to this trip and I won't be sorry to see her go. Her being here put a real damper on the trip. It is interesting, and I think commendable, that in spite of some animosity there have been no fistfights among the crew. I mean, we have been living in a very confined environment with people we didn't know, and in some cases don't even like, for nearly five months. I think it is amazing that we have gotten along as well as we have.

Wednesday, March 12 Lat.- 34 degrees, 30 minutes south; Lon.- 51 degrees, 56 minutes west - 7:30 P.M.- We had to jibe to get out of the way of a tanker this afternoon! At 4:45, Mark was at the helm and spotted it on the horizon, just off the port bow. When I checked the radar I found that he was seven miles out, and it looked like he was going to cross our bow from port to starboard. When I took over the helm at 5:00 he was three miles out and I noticed that he was staying on the same bearing from us, indicating that we were on converging courses. I altered course five degrees to port, trying to go behind him. The wind was almost right behind us; just a few degrees over on the starboard quarter so I couldn't go to port any more without doing a jibe. If I had turned to starboard I would have been turning right in front of him, as he was on a course diagonal to ours. It almost looked like he was trying to run over us, and I could see that big red hull *very clearly*, but I'm sure he was only maintaining his course. At that point it still looked as if he would pass in front of us, but not by much so when he was a half-mile out, I decided to jibe. With only our genoa flying, it was easy and we cleared his stern with no problem. After five minutes we jibed again and continued on our course. I don't think he gave a crap *who* had the right-of-way!

Afternoon watch turned out pretty nice after a cloudy, misty morning. Sailing has been great, with 15-20 knot winds coming from back on the starboard quarter, nice, gentle swells of 10-15 feet, and even a little sunshine. We have had these sailing conditions since noon yesterday and are buzzing along at about six knots, in the direction we want to go.

I cleaned up and copied over the "Sail" article today, and let Ray and Mark read it. They both seem to think it is very good. Now I just have to add the sidebar and pictures. I read an article of this type today in an old issue of "Sail" that we have on board and I honestly think mine is better written and more interesting.

Thursday, March 13 Lat.- 33 degrees, 12 minutes south; Lon.- 50 degrees, 14 minutes west; Sea Temperature- 78 degrees

7:25 P.M.- Ray isn't cooking these days so Mark usually comes up with something for dinner, and I clean up the kitchen. He doesn't cook *great* stuff, but it's better than I could do, and I appreciate it. I think Ray doesn't want to cook for Richard and can't figure out how to cook for Mark and me without including Richard. Also, he is still disgruntled over the provisioning- nothing here that he wants to cook. As I said before, he is nice to me, but a bit of a head case.

Sailing is still great and Sonny is still timid about deploying sails. At 2:00 P.M. today he had only the jib up in 16-20 knot winds over the starboard quarter. As soon as he went below I decided to put up the mizzen and we picked up about a knot in speed. Mark and I did have a little light rain, and winds picked up to the upper twenties, with a peak of 35 knots but seas were well-behaved swells in the 8-15 foot range and the boat handled it nicely with the sail pattern we had deployed. We have had these great sailing conditions for over 48 hours now, and are making very good time. It looks now like we will reach Rio on Wednesday, March 19.

I wrote the "Hindsight" sidebar for the "Sail" article today and had Mark and Ray read it. They both think it is good. I can't *wait* to send it in! Now I have to work the issue of pictures.

We still have albatross around so I have not yet tried fishing on this passage but I am anxious to try my new lures.

Friday, March 14 Lat.- 31 degrees, 23 minutes south; Lon.- 49 degrees, 3 minutes west

6:40 P.M.- I hooked a fish this afternoon. It was small- probably not more than 18 inches to two feet, and it got away but it was fun anyway, and that's progress. It skipped out of the water three or four times, and looked like a Spanish Mackerel but I'm not sure what it was.

Ray decided to cook tonight and it was very good. It was pasta with a sauce of tomatoes, onions, and some kind of canned meat that he found. When he cooks, we appreciate and enjoy it but when he doesn't, that's O.K. He is still being very negative about nearly everything. As I have said before, underneath it all he is a very insecure guy with low self-esteem, and tries to compensate by knowing things that others don't. Half of what he says is bullshit, and he has admitted as much; yet he still does it. I have started challenging things he says, in a good-natured way and he seems to enjoy our debates, even when he turns out to be wrong. You just can't take things he says at face value. I understand why he does it so I don't even get pissed at him. I just think he is a candidate for a heart attack, a stroke, a nervous breakdown, or more likely, falling off the wagon, perhaps with disastrous results.

Now we are (over) hearing that Naomi may leave from Rio. Sonny is said to have told her that if she can find a ticket from Rio as cheap as an advance purchase from Recife, she can leave from Rio. The interpersonal dynamics will be interesting after she leaves.

We are all talking more and more about things we are going to enjoy when we get home. "The horse can smell the barn." so to speak, even though the "barn" is still over 5,000 miles away. At the same time, I am still enjoying the fantastic experience of being out here doing this, knowing it is highly unlikely that I will ever do anything comparable again.

After 72 hours of great sailing conditions we had erratic winds this afternoon. Just after noon Sonny and Naomi actually motored for a couple of hours. Mark and I had winds shifting in direction, between 80 and 120 degrees. That was a pain in the ass since we wanted a course of 55 degrees but we still averaged a speed of five knots.

Saturday, March 15 Lat.- 29 degrees, 48 minutes south; Lon.- 49 degrees, 0 minutes west

6:25 P.M.- We spent most of today sailing back and forth, going nowhere slowly. We are dragging-ass around because this morning Sonny made us take in sail and slow down. He said we were bouncing around too much! We had only the mizzen and 80 percent of the jib out (forget using the main!), and were making about six knots. Yes, it was a little bumpy but that's part of sailing. Winds continued from the northeast, where we want to go so we slogged along at two to three knots most of the day, going mostly east. Finally, on afternoon watch I was able to convince Sonny that we should tack and unroll the rest of the jib. He is so Goddamn stupid that I had to turn it into a lower math problem and lead him through it so that he could see how we could make a better course by tacking, but it finally worked. Then I helped him reach the decision to put up the main, around 4:30. In our eighth day of this passage, we *finally* put up the main for the first time! It really *is* a pain in the ass to put up and take down because of that stupid-ass "Dutchman Furling System" that has never worked, and whose lines always tangle when we raise or lower the main. I also reminded Sonny that if the wind pipes up we don't have to drop the main, but can reduce sail by rolling up part of the jib and/or taking down or reefing the mizzen. We'll see how it goes. I did get some sun on the afternoon watch.

Night watch was pleasant except for the headwinds, but they were light. We just couldn't sail very fast, or in the direction we wanted. We did get to see the moon and it appeared to be about three days from being full. We had a total of six ships show up on radar but we actually saw only two and the closest one passed us four miles out.

This trip continues to drag out. It almost seems like Sonny is trying to drag it out as long as he can even though he still says he needs to get back by early May, too. Every time I start to hope that I might get to finish the whole trip it seem like something else happens to slow us down. I guess you should never hope for anything, but just accept whatever comes your way. I am just a little pissed and frustrated.

One thing I *have* just about realized is that I have the best sailing instincts on the boat. The scenario this afternoon is a good example. At least I feel good about that, although I'm sure Sonny and Ray would not agree.

Sunday, March 16 Lat.- 29 degrees, 10 minutes south; Lon.- 48 degrees, 2 minutes west

12:20 P.M.- I have to write this down now so I won't forget. Ray and I tried to eat some stale potato chips that had been stored in a Ziploc bag for a while. They were so bad we couldn't eat them so we put them in the trash, down next to an empty egg carton, and amongst other stuff like empty cans and assorted garbage. Well, I just watched as Naomi, passing by, saw them and pulled them out of the trash, took them topside and dumped the chips overboard, and saved the bag!

Ray didn't cook last night so Mark was making some soup from a dry mix, adding some pasta and canned vegetables for substance, when we ran out of gas in the propane canister. It just sat there for a few minutes while we changed canisters and it wound up being a gummy mess; probably the worst meal of the trip. I ate it anyway, cleaned up the galley, and slept very well.

I lost a fishing lure this afternoon because my knot failed. I had clipped the tag end too close when I tied it on. You would think I would learn about that, but I keep doing it! Mark said that I got two strikes while I was in the head, but the fish didn't get hooked. We reeled it in and the lure was still there but when I reeled it in later, the lure came off. Oh well, maybe I'll learn *this* time.

We are finally once again making good progress on a good course; now less than 400 miles from Rio. It looks now like we will get there Thursday, the 20th. I am looking forward to getting answers to a few important questions while I am there.

Monday, March 17 Lat.- 27 degrees, 33 minutes south; Lon.- 46 degrees, 39 minutes west - 9:10 A.M.- I had a confrontation with Ray last night. He mouthed off at me during a tense sailing situation and everybody heard it. We had sailed great all afternoon under just the main, making a speed of six knots in winds that had built into the 18-20 knot range over the starboard quarter. Seas had built to the 8-12 foot range and become a little steep, but nothing bad. Near the end of our watch we saw a squall that was catching up to us, and Ray was watching it too. Just as he and Richard went on watch it hit with rain, and winds that peaked at 40 knots. Following seas built up a little higher, with maybe an occasional 15-footer, and became steeper and nastier, swinging us from side to side a little as they passed. This caused the autopilot to stop working, so Richard, at the helm, had to steer manually. Steering in those conditions is a little difficult but I have done it before, and it is not really a big deal. I stuck my head up about that time to see how they were doing, and Ray yelled "YOU SUCK". I asked why, and he said, "Because you didn't take down the main before this hit". I told him that I didn't take down the main because it was the only sail we had up; that I didn't think it was necessary at the time, and still didn't. I then closed the hatch and let it go for the moment. A little later, when he came down to start the generator I caught him in the passageway by my bunk. I asked if he was joking or serious when he yelled at me, and he said "About half and half".

I said, "The joking half is O.K. I don't mind a joke, but as for the serious part, don't ever talk to me that way again".

He said, "I'm one of those people who can't control their emotions, and when I'm angry I just say things".

190

I replied "Well, you had better direct your emotions at somebody besides me. Don't ever talk to me the way you talk to Sonny, because I won't take it. My experience with people like you is that they *can* control the *direction* of their emotions, and they direct them at people they know will take it. If you ever talk to me that way again you'll find me in your face before you know what's happening." Mark was in his bunk in the stern and overheard this conversation even though I had tried to make it private. He told me later that he agreed with me completely, and that Ray had been way out of line.

I believe that Ray understood because this morning he was very apologetic. We shook hands, and that was that. I told him that as far as I was concerned, it was over and I certainly hope it is because I do like Ray and enjoy talking with him. This was another case in which conditions became difficult and Ray got a bit scared- emotional and excitable, as I have mentioned before. He commented some time ago that before this trip he had never done any heavy weather sailing, and I think his lack of experience shows at times like this.

The squall blew on through as they generally do, and I still think my approach of leaving the main up is the right way to go. You can put a reef in and leave it if you want, but leave the damned thing up! Unfortunately, I don't think that's the approach we will use. I expect the main will come down this morning, and go back to being used sparingly, if at all.

To his credit, during all this Sonny made it a point to say what a good job Mark and I have done handling our watch. He said it three times, and it did make me feel better.

Night watch was nice, with winds mostly in the 20's and following swells of 8-12 feet that were low and well behaved. We are finally making good progress and are now about 300 miles from Rio. The moon put on a nice show, ducking in and out of clouds.

Tuesday, March 18 Lat.- 25 degrees, 58minutes south; Lon.- 45 degrees, 34 minutes west - 8:40 A.M.- Last night the moon really *was* full and it put on a solo show, as all the clouds stayed home and applauded! It gave a virtuoso performance, all the while reflecting off the water in that pale, delicate yellow that is impossible to adequately describe or accurately duplicate. Winds were gentle, in the 9-13 knot range and seas were low swells, no more than three or four feet. It made me remember again that Christmas dinner at the Edgewater Hotel in Sandpoint.

Vindication! Miracle of miracles! Amazing things *do* happen! Get this: The main *didn't* come down yesterday after all! Sonny decided that we would put a reef in the main, and leave it up, using the jib and mizzen to manage sail area utilization. Just what I have been recommending for the last 10,000 miles! Just after 3:00 P.M. Mark and I decided to go ahead and put the reef in even though we still had 20 knot winds and seas six to eight feet, that rolled us around some. Ray offered to help, so he steered as we did this without using the engine. First, we put up the mizzen and sheeted it in tight to act as a vane, helping us stay pointed into the wind as we reefed. Before we started, we conferred and decided who would do what. As Ray turned us into the wind, Mark went out to the main mast to pull the sail down to the reefing point as I, in the cockpit, tightened the reefing outhaul and eased the main halyard. When the sail was down to the reefing point I cleated the halyard. Since we have no reefing hook on the main mast, Mark tied a short line through the reefing grommet and around, under the gooseneck where the boom joins the mast. Then he and I tied the four reefing lines around the boom. After that, he and I hauled the sail back up, cleated the halyard, and that was that. We unrolled a third of the jib and got back on course. The boat seemed to sigh and say "thank you" as it sailed great at 6.5 knots with an easier ride, and felt balanced. Even Mark and Ray said so. Ray said "I hate to admit it, but I like your sail plan", and so, apparently, does Sonny. Ray also said this may make a *reefing convert* out of him. He has never done much reefing. I *really* feel good about all this!

Wednesday, March 19 Lat.- 24 degrees, 43 minutes south; Lon.- 44 degrees, 50 minutes west - 9:35 A.M.- We had fish for dinner last night! About 5:30 P.M. I caught a tuna that weighed six or seven pounds- just the right size for dinner, and at just the right time, since we don't have refrigeration to store anything. That was about as fresh as it gets. I caught it on a jig-type lure that I bought in Buenos Aires, that has a chrome head and yellow tail to which I had added a second, trailer hook to catch fish that strike short. The fish was hooked on the trailer hook. I was very pleased!

Yesterday morning the wind dropped to less than five knots and came around on our nose, so we have been motoring for 22 hours. Seas flattened out so we are making good progress in swells that resemble waves on a waterbed. The weather continues to be beautiful.

We had problems again with the alternator and voltage regulator overcharging the stupid-assed "jell-cell" batteries so we motored at only 1,200 rpm during afternoon watch. Ray thought he could fix the problem by disconnecting a wire, and about 6:00 P.M. he convinced Sonny to let him try. When he disconnected the wire the whole electrical system went down, and all this happened just about the time dinner was ready. The two of them worked on it for two hours, right in front of my bunk during which time it got dark. They finally discovered that the problem was *not* with the wire that he disconnected, but with a loose and corroded connection at the battery terminal. After that, everything was fine and now we can motor at our normal rpm of 1,800-2,000, and use the generator to keep the batteries charged. During all that I made my way past Sonny and Ray to the galley, and ate some fish and sauce in the dark. Mark was in his aft cabin and wound up not getting dinner, as he was asleep by the time they were finished. He was pissed that all this took place at the dinner hour, as there was no urgency to get it done. I was pissed too, but at least I got to eat dinner.

On afternoon watch yesterday we were visited by a pod of at least 40 dolphins, and they put on a show for us. They didn't jump out of the water very much, but did a lot of zipping around the boat. There were several mothers with babies and they were neat to watch as the babies made precisely, every move that Mom made. On night watch the moon put on another great solo show, as the night was very clear. Mark and I have now gone eight consecutive watches without being rained on.

It is with great anticipation that I approach Rio; not just to see and enjoy the city, but some important uncertainties should be resolved there. I should find out what the deal is with the new owner of the Crazy Lady Outpost in Montana, such as *when* I will need to be there to start work, if in fact we are to work there. That, in turn, will determine whether I will get to finish this trip or will have to fly home early. It would really mean a lot to me to get to finish the trip, but I will do whatever I have to do. I should also get resolution regarding whether my article will be published in "Sail" magazine, and hopefully, on the availability of the house we rented in Montana last summer. I could leave Rio feeling really great or really depressed. I'm excited and apprehensive at the same time, but at least I should have some answers. I have always been able to handle adversity better than uncertainty.

Tomorrow we will be in Rio! I, Charley Hester, in Rio! Yet another place that I never imagined I would go!

17 – RIO DE JANEIRO

Thursday, March 20 7:45 A.M.- At daybreak we got our first look at Brazil as it got light enough to see some low mountains off our port bow, through a light foggy haze. At that time we were 27 miles from Rio, but probably only about 15 miles from the nearest land. We motored throughout night watch into a headwind of five to eight knots, on another beautiful night. This was our tenth consecutive watch without being rained on!

I have yet another Sonny and Naomi story. First, a little background: Our Magellan hand-held GPS has a backlight like many watches, that you can turn on and see the display in the dark. Several nights ago I saw Sonny shining a flashlight on it to read the numbers. I asked why he wasn't using the backlight and he said, "It's hard on the batteries". Now we have a cabinet *full* of batteries of all kinds, including the kind used by the GPS so we have *plenty* of spares. Anyway, as Mark and I were going on watch at 2:00 A.M., I saw Naomi over on the port side of the cockpit staring at the GPS, waiting for it to track enough satellites to give a reading. I paid little attention, as Sonny had been teaching her to take readings and plot positions on the chart. A few minutes later I saw Sonny standing at the top of the companionway shining a flashlight on the GPS. Then he went below, and after a couple of minutes came back up and told Mark to change course from 070 degrees to 345, a change of 85 degrees. We had been steering 070 for several days to make sure we went far enough east. Just yesterday afternoon Ray had been concerned that we still were not far enough east. I mentioned this to Sonny, asking why we had gone so far east that we now had to turn 85 degrees toward the west. He acted like he had planned it that way, saying, "Well, you want to come in upwind of your target, and the prevailing wind is from the east".

I said "Yes, but isn't 85 degrees a pretty dramatic course change? It seems like we have been just wandering around out here."

He said, "Well yeah, a little".

He then got the GPS out and took another reading, and after a couple more minutes he came back up and told Mark "Go back to

070". I asked what happened, and he said, "The GPS was misread". Then he went below and went to bed. I'm not sure which one of them misread the GPS but I think he was appropriately embarrassed.

Friday, March 21 - 6:50 A.M.- What a screwed-up day yesterday was! Not much went right all day. It took us *forever* to get into Rio, as what should have been an early morning arrival turned out to be early afternoon. As we approached we could barely see the city due to the fog, or smog. There was no wind to speak of and the cloud just hung there. Then, there was all the trash in the water. The water isn't muddy, but it was like motoring in through a garbage dump. The setting for the city is absolutely beautiful, with the sea and the beaches in a cluster of mountains but the city itself is rather ordinary, with the buildings looking a lot alike and showing signs of age.

Then of course clearing in can never be easy. First, Sonny and Naomi went with a guy from the marina some place for half an hour, and came back with a piece of paper telling us where to go for customs, immigration, and the Navy. All of us had to go to immigration so we set off in two taxis on about a five or six mile jaunt that took us to the wrong place. From there, we walked a mile or so and finally found immigration at the cruise ship terminal. Then, they only had three forms (I got one!), so only three of us could clear in. The others have to go back this morning. It seems that they had three cruise ships come in yesterday, so they ran out of forms.

One good thing did happen. I was able to find a *casa de cambio,* or change house, where I was able to cash some traveler's checks at a good exchange rate with no fee. Afterward, Ray, Mark, Richard, and I went to a sidewalk café where Mark and I had a couple of beers; then walked around and found a place to eat. It was ordinary, and overpriced for here. They did have a good jazz band with a singer, and on the way out Richard and I stopped to listen to a song after Ray and Mark went on ahead. Then Mark got pissed off because we didn't tell them we were stopping, and they had to wait. That was out of character for Mark, as he is normally the most even-tempered of the group.

When we got back to the marina I found that I couldn't get the phones to work to access A.T.&T. and there was no place to buy phone cards, so I didn't get to call home. Also, we wound up on a mooring in the marina, the Yacht Club of Rio de Janeiro, instead of at a dock, so getting back and forth to the boat is a pain in the ass. The yacht club furnishes a launch service, but they aren't always available when you want them, making it difficult to go ashore for things like showers for example. I think we will be moving to a dock today. I should mention that the yacht club is located in a spectacular setting, right underneath the "Pao de Acucar", or Sugar-loaf Mountain.

Saturday, March 22 - 7:10 A.M.- Well, we didn't move to a dock after all. You have to do a "Mediterranean style" docking stern-to with your anchor holding the bow out, and Sonny didn't want to do that. He was afraid that the stern would bang into the concrete dock. Never mind that everybody else here does it without any problems. Anyway, that leaves us still having to deal with the problem of getting to and from shore. We inflated our dinghy, so maybe that will help. It rained cats and dogs last night so this morning the dinghy is full of water.

Yesterday was a better day than Thursday. I finally managed to make a phone call home, and that helped a lot. Maureen told me that out situation in Montana is still unsettled both in regard to our jobs, and where we are going to live. Our friend Joanne did find us a place to rent though; it's just that we would rather be where we were the last two summers, and still don't know whether that one is an option.

The phone system here is a real pain in the ass, as you can't access A.T.& T. from public phones, or even in the telephone offices. You have to buy a phone card; and not a regular phone card, but a special card called a "DDD" card. The regular cards don't work for international calls. I found all this out by trial and error, and finally finding a German lady who works here at the yacht club, and who speaks English. She didn't know, but was nice enough to ask people until she found out. The place to buy "DDD" cards is at the post offices. Each card is good for five minutes, and they cost 10 reals, or about $3.00 U.S. That is a little expensive, but not totally outrageous. The phone offices are a little cheaper but there are none here in the Botafogo section of Rio. You have to make your way to Centro, or Copacabana to find one. By the way, I didn't realize how much Spanish I knew until I got here and couldn't speak *any* Portuguese!

I also went to an Internet café, where I typed and sent the re-write of my article to "Sail". I had some negative stuff in the "Hindsight" sidebar, about what we did wrong and now I am fretting over that, hoping it didn't turn off the editor. Everything I said was true though, so I am not going to worry too much about it.

I took the subway to Copacabana in the afternoon to check out the telephone offices and to use the Internet again. I am getting to be quite the city boy, using these subways all by myself! A ride here costs 1.47 reals, or about 45 cents.

I got back to the yacht club last night about six o'clock, just before it rained. I had a cheeseburger and a couple of beers at a little grill off to the side, and sat outside under a roof, watching the rain. It made me lonesome for home.

Sunday, March 23 - 7:35 A.M.- I never thought Jesus Christ had a goatee! All the images I have ever seen showed him with a full beard, until yesterday. Ray, Mark and I went up Corcovado Mountain to the statue of Christ the Redeemer, which stands overlooking the city, with arms outstretched, from an awe-inspiring venue 2,300 feet above the sea. We took a taxi from Copacabana that took us there, up a really steep road that is an engineering marvel. We took the cog railway back down. We had some clouds roll in and obscure the view from time to time, but when they went away, there was Rio, at your feet! The statue itself is 98 feet tall and is overwhelming as you look up from his feet. Sometimes when you looked up clouds partially obscured the view, and it was almost spooky. The Pope came here and dedicated the statue in 1980. The only problem is that when you look up, you see that goatee! Somehow, that is a little disconcerting to me.

While we were in that area we also visited the "Museu de Art Naif", or Museum of Native Art, which is near the cog railway station. They have some really spectacular art there, of the kind that Maureen and I saw in Managua a few years ago. I am not knowledgeable, but I thought this was just as good, if not better and there was a greater variety with art from many different countries around the world; not just Brazil.

I also got my laundry done- a huge relief- for only $10. U.S., and I had a *big* bag full. Ray, Richard, Mark and I took a bus over to Copacabana, where Richard had seen this laundromat the day before. After we dropped off the laundry we decided to get something to eat. We started to discuss what we wanted to eat (I had no preference.) and before we could reach a decision Richard got annoyed and just walked away by himself. We didn't see him again the rest of the day. He really is a weird little shit!

Ray, Mark and I bought gold earrings yesterday. Mark and I split the cost of two pair, since they only come in pairs. We completed our deal with Ray to pay for his, to thank him for all the cooking he has done. The earrings are 18 karat gold, and cost 30 reals, or about $12. U.S.

I also bought a painting yesterday, over in Copacabana. I paid 15 reals, or about $4.50 U.S. for it. The artist is an old man- hard to tell *how* old- who was sitting on the sidewalk painting as we walked by, and had several of his paintings spread out beside him. They jumped up at me as we walked by. They are of fish, and are brightly colored, in a style that I have not seen before. The old man's arms and legs are underdeveloped and bent in a way that I can't describe. Maybe he had polio as a child, or maybe it was birth defects but I'm not sure whether he can even get up on his own. I'm pretty sure he can't walk. But he sure as hell can paint! Actually, he was doing these pictures free hand, with colored pencils. His deformities are such that some people would call them grotesque, but the man had such dignity despite his situation that I could *never* apply that term to him. He had a smile for us as he sat there in these humble surroundings and created things of beauty. He let Ray take his picture with me beside him. I sure hope my painting survives this trip!

Monday, March 24 - 7:00 A.M.- I saw a really interesting game being played on the beach at Ipanema yesterday. I don't know the name, or if it even *has* one but I will call it "soccer-volleyball". They use a soccer ball and volleyball net, and a beach volleyball court. To serve, they build a tee about eight or ten inches high out of sand, and kick the ball over the net. Just like in soccer, the players can't touch the ball with their hands, but any other body part is legal; even the chest. We saw it played by four person and two person teams, and they were good.

Yesterday was a very good day all around. It started out raining but that ended by mid-morning and though it wasn't a beautiful, *sunny* day, the weather turned out nice. Richard left early with Sonny and Naomi. Mark was tired and decided to spend the day on the boat so Ray and I took off and walked all the way to the far end of Ipanema Beach, a distance of probably five miles. On the way we stopped at the telephone office and made phone calls. I had a nice conversation with Maureen, and also checked e-mail while I was there.

After the "soccer-volleyball, we saw some serious women's two-person beach volleyball being played. It was the finals of a tournament in a fenced off area, complete with sponsors, judges, and trophies. They were very good, too, and impressive to watch. After we left the beach we wandered into a large arts and crafts market and saw some more nice paintings. Ray bought a small one for his Mom. What we *didn't* see were the famous skimpy bikinis that are legendary in Rio! We walked the length of Copacabana and Ipanema beaches, and there were *none!* The weather wasn't *great* but it was bright enough to need sunglasses and they just weren't there. Maybe it's not the right season, or maybe it's just more myth than reality!

Around 3:30 we took a bus back to Botafoga and walked up the hill to the cable car terminal. Ray has a problem with heights and a bit of claustrophobia but I convinced him to go with me on the cable car to the top of Sugar Loaf Mountain, and it was truly spectacular! You actually have to take two cable cars; one to a vantage point about a third of the way up, that has shops and lookout points, and then another one with a steeper ascent that takes you on to the top. The sun wasn't out but the ride and the views from the top were indescribable anyway, definitely a highlight of the entire trip! This was definitely one of the two things I wanted to do most in Rio, the other being the trip to the statue. Interestingly enough, Mark wouldn't go on the cable car ride, not because of any fear of heights, but because he doesn't trust anything man-made in these circumstances. I asked how he could feel that way after just sailing 10,000 miles and what we experienced at Cape Horn. His rationale was that out there, he felt that he had some control over what was happening and here, he didn't.

When we came down from Sugar Loaf it was getting dark and we were hungry so we walked into a little neighborhood called Urca, right under the mountain, that we had seen from the top. It is just around the bay from the boat, and we found a little restaurant called Garota, overlooking the water and the beach. We each had filet mignons, I had two beers, and he had two orange juices, and the total bill was 54 reals, or $16. U.S.! The food and service were outstanding.

On the way back to the yacht club we walked past this little cove with nice, clear water and no waves, and on the beach they had set up for a wedding, with flowers, food, cakes, an altar, and tables with chairs for 50-75 people. It looked really neat.

Tuesday, March 25 - 9:50 A.M.- We're ready to go. We have made all preparations to sail and are now waiting for Sonny. He took Naomi someplace to get her into a hotel to wait for her flight, which I understand is at 5:30 A.M. tomorrow. I wished her a safe trip and she thanked me but she and Sonny haven't been talking to Ray, Mark and me for the last few days- barely spoke, and sometimes didn't even speak at all. We can't figure out what sparked it and I really don't care but it is bugging the hell out of Ray, and Mark is really pissed. Neither of them even wished her a safe trip. The only person who will miss her is Sonny. For the rest of us, she has contributed nothing, and has put a sort of damper on the trip ever since she showed up. Whatever sparked this "not speaking" business, Sonny needs to come off it, as he still has to sail 5,000 miles with us. It will be very interesting to see how it develops with Naomi gone. There is potential for a real blow-up.

11:15 A.M.- I stopped to help us get under way, and to watch as we left Rio. At 10:15 we cast off our mooring at the Yacht Club of Rio de Janeiro and began our passage to Recife. Sonny seemed to come back in a good mood and is talking to me, at least so far. We have a little haze, or smog today, but nothing like Thursday when we arrived. In fact, the air has been pretty clean throughout our visit. I have to say too, that the city itself has been pretty clean, as has the water in the bay, with nothing like the trash we saw on the way in.

Yesterday was a good weather day, as Mark and I were out and about most of the day. We rode the subway to Copacabana again. I got some more film processed, added three pictures to the group I am sending to "Sail", and mailed the package to them. I still have not heard back from Peter Nielsen about my re-write of the article. Normally I would not expect to hear anything this quickly but he answered my previous e-mails right away so I am beginning to fret. After that Mark and I had lunch and then wandered around Copacabana for a while. Later Mark wanted to go to Urca and have dinner at Garota Restaurant after hearing how good it was from Ray and me, so I went back with him and it was great again.

Leaving Rio gave me that same sentimental feeling that I have experienced as I left other places that I enjoyed and probably won't visit again. I have some observations about Rio:

• It is a multi-racial city; much more so than Buenos Aires where white-skinned people are a *huge* majority and you see almost *no* black faces. You see all shades here, from very light-skinned to black.

• The geographical setting here is unsurpassed, with Corcovado and Sugar loaf dominating, and lots of other peaks in and around the city.

• Rio is like several smaller cities clustered around the bay, between the mountains and up the mountainsides, connected in some cases by tunnels. There are probably a dozen really nice, natural beaches.

• The buildings are aging and in some cases, beginning to run down. I didn't see even one construction crane here, as not much is being built.

• There seem to be fewer beggars here than in Buenos Aires, and they are not well organized.

• There seems to be more emphasis on art here, with art museums, arts and craft markets, and sidewalk artists.

- Although I didn't see many "idlers", the city doesn't seem as busy as Buenos Aires and people don't dress up nearly as much. Rio just isn't as vibrant.
- The people here seem happy, and everyone treated us *very* well in spite of the language barrier. As elsewhere in Latin America, we got lots of smiles, and "thumbs-ups". I have really enjoyed that and think I will probably use the "thumbs-up" gesture the rest of my life. It's a *lot* better than the middle finger!
- I didn't see *any* roaches here; in fact, I haven't seen a roach the entire trip!

There are still a lot of uncertainties going on with me as we approach this next passage. When I talked with Maureen I was disappointed with the news I got regarding our efforts to rent a place at Hebgen Lake in Montana for the summer. I still haven't heard from the new owner of the Crazy Lady Outpost regarding our summer jobs, nor from the Harris Corporation about the possibility of doing some consulting work for them. Somehow I think the Montana stuff and job stuff will all work out, but the uncertainty surrounding the interpersonal dynamics here and for the rest of the trip causes me a little more apprehension.

18 – AGAINST THE WIND

Tuesday, March 25 - 6:40 P.M.- On afternoon watch we motor-sailed along a truly beautiful stretch of the Brazilian coast, about five miles offshore. We passed long, pristine beaches backed by majestic mountains that fell away the closer we got to Cabo Frio. At Cabo Frio, 55 miles east of Rio, we can turn northeast toward Recife, nearly a thousand miles away. Our visit in Rio was short, but surprisingly enjoyable, and the city really was spectacular.

With Naomi gone, Sonny is planning to stand watches by himself. That being the case, I suggested that he switch to the six-to-ten shift so people would be awake most of the time when he is on watch but he intends to stay on the ten-to-two shift. That scares me a little, as I am not sure he can, or will, stay awake on his night watches. We will see. Today marked the first time since Belize that we have left a port when we planned to! Tonight we are having alternator problems again, with the engine overcharging the batteries. I thought they had resolved that by disconnecting some wires but that obviously isn't the case. I trolled all afternoon without success, and we were in what appeared to be prime fishing waters, too.

Although I enjoyed Rio, it does feel good to be back at sea, in a world that is always in motion. It seems natural now to move around, anticipating the movements of the boat and bracing or holding on without even thinking about it. There really is an appeal to it, and I can understand why some young men go to sea early in life and never come back.

Wednesday, March 26 Lat.- 22 degrees, 37 minutes south; Lon.- 41 degrees, 31 minutes west - 10:20 A.M.- We had to tack rather quickly to avoid a cruise ship last night. We first saw it at 2:30 A.M. off our port beam, and it was at an angle such that it looked like a blob of lights so we couldn't tell what it was. I got my binoculars and soon was able to make out the hull. I also noticed that we seemed to be on converging courses. Mark and I also watched on radar to determine the distance. We were hard on the wind on a starboard tack, so we couldn't turn that way and if we turned to port we would have gone right toward it. When they were two miles out they flashed a light at us and I decided that it was time to come about, as they were closing fast. As we were preparing to turn, they flashed us again. We didn't have our radio on, which precluded their contacting us that way. With no time to waste, we quickly came about, let them pass, and then jibed to get back on course. This may sound mundane, but it was a little exciting in the middle of the night. Later on we had to alter course ten degrees to avoid a fishing boat that was dragging a trawl. *Lots* of traffic around here! All through night watch we could see at least three or four other boats either visually, on radar, or both, at any given time. It seems amazing to me that with all this expanse of ocean out here, how many times we have had to alter our course to avoid collisions.

Sonny is still being cordial but rather subdued, and seemingly a little lost. When Mark and I went on night watch at 2:00 A.M. he didn't have the radar on, even in all that traffic. Yes, it was a clear night and you could pretty well see the boats but you didn't know distances, and you can't always assume that they have lights. For the *life* of me I can't understand why you wouldn't use the radar at night; *especially* when there's a lot of traffic. Richard is still keeping largely to himself.

Although our course to Recife is directly against the prevailing winds we are making good progress *so far*, motoring, sailing, and motor sailing in marginal winds that have stayed mostly on our starboard beam. Dare I hope that this passage may be quicker than I expected? Now though, Sonny and Ray are starting to be concerned about fuel since we have motored or motor-sailed most of the time. I have felt hyper and restless all day today, for no apparent reason.

Thursday, March 27 Lat.- 21 degrees, 8 minutes south; Lon.- 40 degrees, 8 minutes west - 9:25 A.M.- My innovation of adding a trailer hook to fishing lures came back to bite me in the ass yesterday afternoon. About 3:30 we were motor sailing and I was at the helm when I got a hard strike. I throttled back, and started aft as the fish took line against a fairly tight drag setting. Just before I got to the rod the line went slack and the fish was gone. It seemed like a *big* fish, too! When I reeled in the lure I found that the first hook had broken in the bend, right where the eye of the second hook had hung. I think a little rust had started there and it broke under the pressure. This has happened a couple of times before. I think the solution is to put the trailer on each time I start to fish and take it off when I stop. I will try that after Recife, as I don't have any extra hooks now.

Night watch was busy again with a lot of fishing boat traffic but we didn't have to alter course this time. We also passed an oil well platform.

When I got up at 1:30 A.M. to get ready for night watch, Sonny was in the galley making pancakes, and when I went topside at 1:50 he was washing dishes. Mind you, he is standing watch alone so that meant that nobody was in the cockpit for at least half an hour, *at night*, with lots of boat traffic around- makes me a *little* uncomfortable! Oh well, at least he had the radar on this time. He is still being cordial, but subdued. His tone of voice is always depressing- this isn't new; only worse. I swear, he could tell you that he won the lottery and make it sound like somebody just died!

Friday, March 28 Lat.- 19 degrees, 16 minutes south; Lon.- 39 degrees, 10 minutes west

9:10 A.M.- Fish for lunch yesterday! About 12:15 P.M. I caught a small tuna. It was only about two or three pounds, but there was enough for four good-sized portions. Sonny didn't want any and Mark didn't eat because he is sick (cold and sore throat), so I had seconds. Ray broiled it with wild rice, and it was very good.

Last night when I got up for night watch I noticed that the radar was not on. When I went topside Sonny was looking up at the sail. As usual, I asked him "Any boat traffic?".

After hesitating, he said "Uh, yeah, they're around". Then he looked around the horizon, and said "Hell, I don't know where they are though". Again, this guy is on night watch *alone*! I know it seems like I am picking on him but as I have said before, he just doesn't seem to have his head in the game.

We had 15-20 knot winds and sailed for four hours yesterday, but then the wind died. We have motored or motor-sailed for most of this passage so far. At least we haven't had the wind in our faces yet. Oh yes, the streak has ended. Mark and I had gone 15 consecutive watches without getting wet but this morning at 5:30 we had a pretty good rain. The scotch guard is wearing off my black anorak so my arms and back got wet. It's not cold though, so it's O.K. My foul weather jacket is heavy and hot, so I would just as soon get a little wet.

Saturday, March 29 Lat.-17 degrees, 38 minutes south; Lon.- 38 degrees, 12 minutes west

8:45 A.M.- We had enough wind yesterday to sail for 13 hours- nothing to brag about at 12-15 knots, but it was way back on the starboard quarter and we averaged a speed of 4.5 knots. The wind died around midnight and we motored through night watch. This morning we are motor sailing in light winds. At least we *still* have not encountered the headwinds we had anticipated, and are still on track for a nine-day passage if nothing goes wrong. There is still a remote chance that we could make Key West by my birthday, May 9, in which case I will get to finish the entire trip.

We had a really nice "non-sunset" last night. We never saw the sun for the clouds, but in the west there were some horizontal streaks that turned fiery red, then faded to a nice orange as the sun set; then back to a shade of red that burning charcoal gets in a grill. To the southwest there were dark clouds with small patches of rain falling through horizontal streaks of yellow and orange just above the ocean.

Sonny is still subdued. He talks a little to Richard but hardly at all to the rest of us. I am beginning to wonder whether Naomi, or Sonny, or both of them read one or more of our journals when we were off the boat. That is a possible explanation of why they stopped talking to Ray , Mark, and me.

It is interesting that as we begin to anticipate the end of the voyage I find myself thinking more and more about sex! I didn't think much about it down south when the end of the voyage seemed a lifetime away, such that I wondered if I might be "losing it" but now all that has changed!

I fished some of the morning and all afternoon, with no success. I think it is time to switch lures.

Sunday, March 30 Lat.- 15 degrees, 52 minutes south; Lon.- 36 degrees, 57 minutes west

8:35 A.M.- Last night's sunset was a sizzler, as we saw it go right into the water! The colors were not as bright as the night before, with orange the color of the day. A container ship passed west of us at sunset, and silhouetted against the orange sky- pretty neat!

This morning we are motoring in five-knot south-southwest winds. We motor-sailed through a peaceful night watch with winds averaging 9-12 knots, after motor-sailing all day yesterday. The engine is getting a workout! We chased rain all day but never caught up with any, and today is bright and sunny. We are *still* on a pace to make Recife early Thursday. The water maker is working fine these days, so we get a shower every day- lifts the spirits! Sonny and Ray are still struggling with the electrical system, and Mark and I are speculating on whether it will make it through the end of the trip.

I was in a really down mood throughout most of night watch, feeling the weight of responsibility and the anxiety of uncertainty looming when I get home but I am much better this morning. I know everything will work out fine.

Monday, March 31 Lat.- 13 degrees, 40 minutes south; Lon.- 36 degrees, 15 minutes west - 8:30 A.M.- Good news and bad news in regard to fishing! The good news is that I caught another small tuna, about two pounds, just before lunch yesterday. Sonny and Richard declined so Ray, Mark and I enjoyed nice portions. Now, the bad news: Shortly after 2:00 P.M. I was in the cockpit when I got a strike, and before I could get back to the rod the fish took all my line and broke off where it was attached to the reel. I had the drag set pretty tight, too, but obviously not tight enough. Mark was at the helm, and throttled back but before I could get back there it was all over. I have no spare line, so that rod is out of action until after Recife. Now, I am trying to troll with the spinning rod but that's not a good prospect, as it is really too light.

We sailed for a while last night, but we are still having light, south to southwest winds so we are motoring or motor-sailing most of the time. It's interesting that before we left Rio Ray said he wished we would have no wind, and motor all the way to Recife! He said that because we were expecting head winds, that *so far* have not developed. Yesterday was a beautiful, bright, sunny tropical day and we got a *lot* of sun.

Yesterday Mark asked Richard if he knew why Sonny and Naomi stopped talking to Ray, me, and himself and Richard said "Weeelll, you know, conversations on boats get overheard and so forth", so maybe they didn't read our journals after all. In any case, I haven't said anything verbally or in my journal that wasn't true, or that I wouldn't say again. If they had a problem with anything I said, that's just tough shit!

I forgot to mention that we had two whale sightings yesterday. Around noon, Sonny saw one some 30 yards off the port beam. He said it was about 30 feet long. Ray got topside just in time to see the tail before it went under, so it was a confirmed sighting. Then at 4:00 P.M. I was below making tea when Mark and Ray saw several whales 200-300 yards off the starboard quarter. When I got topside I could see them spouting through their blowholes, and some splashing. I couldn't tell whether they were whales or a pod of dolphins but they both said they saw them, and they were much bigger than dolphins so that qualifies as a confirmed sighting too.

206

Tuesday, April 1 Lat.- 11 degrees, 28 minutes south; Lon.- 35 degrees, 43 minutes west

8:45 A.M.- We have an outside chance to make Recife tomorrow night! It isn't likely, as we would have to average six knots for the next 33.5 hours, but it *is* possible. We continue to motor-sail in light southeast winds.

Ray is back in good spirits these days and is cooking dinner every night; much to our benefit. He really is creative, consistently making something out of virtually nothing and everything he has cooked has been good. Sonny is showing signs of mellowing out, at least a little. I can't help wondering if he has felt any embarrassment at all, along with his anger. I certainly think he *should* feel embarrassed!

Sunset yesterday was rather ordinary but sunrise today was very nice as it came right out of the water like a *big* yellow eye, peeping over a wall.

Trolling with the spinning rod is less than ideal, but better than nothing. I have had no strikes on it so far, and I know that anything big will just break the line. The sea temperature is 84 degrees now- 40 degrees warmer than the coldest we saw down around Cape Horn.

Last night when I got up for night watch Sonny was in the galley eating a grilled (Velveeta) cheese sandwich and drinking a cup of coffee that he had obviously been there long enough to make, and the radar wasn't on. He makes me *really* uncomfortable when he does that because ships move fast, and as I have said before, can be on top of you before you know it. When I turned on the radar I saw a ship just over 16 miles out, and in half an hour it was two miles off our starboard beam as it passed us.

Last night was the hottest yet, and I sweated like a pig! My sheet and both pillowcases were wet but they dried out while I was on night watch.

We sure miss having refrigeration- nothing cold to drink, and it really limits the menu. We eat a lot of stuff out of cans these days. It's amazing how quickly even the shelf milk spoils in 24 hours or less after it is opened. I have cereal every morning at 4:00 and if I open some one morning, it *might* still be usable the next morning or it might not. I give it the "sniff and taste" test before I pour it on my cereal. I will be ready for a *cold* beer in Recife!

Wednesday, April 2 Lat.- 8 degrees, 58 minutes south; Lon.- 34 degrees, 59 minutes west

8:45 A.M.- It looks like we might make Recife before dark today! That will be amazing, and totally surprising to make this passage in

207

less than nine days! The headwinds that we were dreading so much, never developed.

We had fish for dinner last night- *another* good surprise! I caught a small tuna- about two pounds- on the spinning rod and on a lure that I had rigged. I was amazed. I caught it just before five o'clock., too; just in time for dinner, and Ray got four servings out of it. Sonny was asleep, and doesn't eat much fish anyway. I had made the lure by running a small wire leader through a yellow squid-like skirt and attaching it to the head and hook of a small jig. I then pulled the jig up into the skirt to give it weight. It *worked,* and I was pleased.

I had just commented to Mark that the sunset last night was rather ordinary, when the whole western sky started to light up, from north to south. It wasn't solid, but huge chunks turned a *little* orange, but mostly as bright a red as you ever saw, reflected on strategically placed clouds that looked like they had been painted there with an artist's brush. It lasted about 15 minutes and was truly magnificent.

Another "Sonny on watch" story: When I started up for night watch *last* night at 1:45 A.M. Sonny was in the galley drinking a cup of coffee, and *again* the radar was not on. When I went topside it looked like we were in the middle of the Brazilian fishing fleet! I counted nine boats that I could see visually, and they were in every direction; though none were straight ahead. The only thing Sonny said was "I hope they all have lights on". Later on we had to alter course to go between two of them. It was a busy night watch, between watching the radar and watching the boats visually.

4:40 P.M.- Wonders never cease! At 4:00 P.M. we picked up a mooring at the "Iate Clube Cabanga" in Recife, completing the passage in eight days and six hours. We ran aground while trying to find the channel in here, but were able to back off without much of a problem. We are still hoping to get a slip at a dock- Sonny is ashore doing his thing right now- but none appear to be available so we will probably be stuck going back and forth in our dinghy.

We put on a show for the locals when we came into the marina. Here, you tie the mooring to your *stern,* and tie your bow to a sea wall and we looked like idiots trying to do it as the wind kept blowing us off. Two guys in an inflatable boat with an outboard came out to help us, but it was still comical. To make matters worse, there was a small piece of line in the water, and sure enough, it found it's way into our propeller. One of the guys in the inflatable got a mask and went under the boat to cut it loose.

19 – RECIFE

Thursday, April 3 - 7:15 A.M.- Well, we did get a slip, at least for three days. Some guy is out on his boat and we can use the slip until he gets back. We'll see how it goes. There is no finger pier alongside the boat; only a small platform on the sea wall. We are tied up with the bow to the sea wall, so we do acrobatics getting on and off the boat. We get off by climbing over the bowsprit and jumping to the platform, three or four feet away. Getting back on, you lean out from the platform, grab the bow pulpit, and pull yourself over. The trip both ways is significantly more difficult when the tide is high, as the bowsprit and pulpit are about three or four feet *higher* than the platform. Still, this is much better than being on a mooring!

By the time we got squared away it was getting dark so we ate dinner here at the yacht club, at a nice restaurant that is on the porch of the clubhouse, overlooking the marina. I had a steak dinner for 13 reals, or just over $4.00. Later, Ray and I took a taxi to "Old Recife" and looked unsuccessfully for an Internet café. We stopped at a couple of sidewalk cafes that had live music, and came back to the boat around ten o'clock.

Friday, April 4 - 5:25 A.M.- I am trying hard not to be depressed this morning. Yesterday generally was not a good day and things just don't seem to be coming together very well. I made a phone call home but didn't get to talk with Maureen nearly enough, and that always frustrates me when it happens. Then, she is having to deal with a lot of crap from the other condo board members, and their antics both piss me off and get me down because I am not there to help her deal with them. Also, things haven't come together well in regard to our summer plans for Montana, I still have not heard from "Sail", and I haven't heard back from my friend Dave about my prospects for doing consulting for the Harris Corporation. On top of all that, I didn't get to cash any traveler's checks because Sonny was gone all day with my passport, clearing us in, so I am short of cash for the moment. Hopefully, some of these things will improve today. I *really* get frustrated with the uncertainty, even though I know things will work out.

We did have a couple of *good* things happen though. Marco, one of the guys in the inflatable who helped us get settled in the marina, speaks fairly good English. His wife does laundry and is doing ours for 14 reals ($4.12) per person. He is also helping us get propane tanks filled, etc.

Then, we met the owner of another Morgan 46 that is two slips down from us. His boat is two years older than this one but is in much better shape. Anyway, his name is Luis and he is an international banker. He is a citizen of Uruguay and is married to a lady from Annapolis, Maryland. He is based in Washington, D.C. but is here on an extended assignment so he brought his boat here to live on. We asked him about an Internet café and he told us there is one in a shopping mall in the Boa Viagem section of Recife, several miles away. They aren't common here like they have been everywhere else. Well, he called his driver, a Senor Lima, who drove us there in Luis' Chevy Blazer, took us inside to the Internet café, and offered to wait for us! Senor Lima was truly a nice, and classy gentleman. I greatly appreciated their kindness and was glad to get on the Internet, even though I didn't have any good news.

On the way back our taxi drove along the beach for a couple of miles and they have a very nice beach with what appears to be clean, clear water. Recife seems to be a *large*, functional, working city, strung along the beach, but not really a tourist destination. People here seem pretty happy. Last night Mark, Ray and I went to "Old Recife, to the area around "Rua do Bom Jesus", (Street of Good Jesus) where we had dinner and wandered around. There is some sort of festival going on and they had a lively, free concert on a *huge* stage set up along the waterfront. They were playing *loud* salsa-type music and had five choreographed dancers, three of whom were scantily clad females. One of the three was also the lead singer and she had a very good voice. The show *and* the people in the audience were interesting to watch.

Richard was gone all day yesterday with Sonny, to clear us in. He seems to have stepped comfortably into Naomi's role as Sonny's butt-wiper. Both Mark and Ray make some pretty nasty comments about the two of them.

Saturday, April 5 - 5:25 A.M.- I found out yesterday afternoon that "Sail" is buying my article and some of my pictures! I am *really* excited! I was able to get Internet access here at the yacht club, and found that I had an e-mail from Peter Nielsen, the editor. He said that I did a nice job on the re-write and that he would like to buy the article and any pictures that they use, for $500. I would have hoped for more money, but I'm certainly not complaining! Selling your *first* article is something that can only happen once in a lifetime and I can't believe it happened to *me* yesterday! I sent back an e-mail accepting his offer, and asking if he knows when the article might be published.

Other things went well yesterday, too. I cashed traveler's checks, bought six phone cards, called and had a good conversation with Maureen, bought, wrote, and mailed post cards, bought new fishing line (with a spare) and a couple of lures, and did some exploring in the Old Recife and Sao Antonio barrios. Mark and I both found Old Recife to be pretty ratty once you get away from a few blocks around Rua do Bom Jesus. That area has been renovated and is nice, but they have a long way to go with their restorations. There, and in Sao Antonio we found that you can buy almost anything you want from street vendors and you don't have to go to them. They come to you, selling everything from combs and toothbrushes to small magnifying glasses, to reading glasses. Music in the form of CD's is sold by guys with pushcarts that have boom boxes playing the music as they walk down the sidewalk, or in some cases, the middle of the street. You see some of this in every city, but more here than anywhere else.

We wandered through a large outdoor market in Sao Antonio, and into an open, cobblestone courtyard, or square, that fronted two large churches. We walked over to one side where there were shops, food stands, and so forth, and bought ice cream bars from a man with a pushcart. I started eating mine, and as Mark was taking the wrapper off his an old lady walked up to him and wanted his ice cream. When he told her no, she stood there and *peed*, making a splashy puddle on the cobblestones between her feet! She was holding several lottery tickets in her hand.

On the down side, Mark was still feeling sick from his cold, or dengue fever, or whatever he had, and didn't feel like celebrating with me over the news from "Sail". He did, however, sit with me on the veranda here at the yacht club while I had four beers and a nice *Chicken Cubano* dinner. The whole thing cost me about $7.00 including two Sprites for Mark.

We didn't see any of the others all day but while we were on the veranda we saw Sonny and Richard get off the boat, go for showers; then get dressed complete with long pants, and head out for the

211

evening. As I said before, Richard has slipped right into Naomi's role!

7:15 A.M.- Ray is in a *good* mood this morning. He told Mark and me that he spent yesterday afternoon and early evening with a young blond hooker named Fabriana. He said that she is the same one who tried to hit on me Thursday night as we were getting into a taxi to come back to the boat. He said he paid her 35 reals, or about $11. U.S., which was the last of the money he had at the time. If she *is* the same one, she is nice looking, and at least looked *clean*, but I still think that is *very* risky business these days; something I wouldn't risk even if I was single and desperate!

Sunday, April 6 - 5:10 A.M.- My body thinks it is still doing night watch. It wants to go to sleep early in the evening, wake up around 2:00 A.M., and stay awake. I usually manage to go back to sleep for an hour or so some time between two and five o'clock but I stay awake a lot. I have even read some in the middle of the night the last two nights. Part of the problem may be that it is so beastly hot here- I sweat like a pig and my sheets and pillowcases get wet.

I am in a mood of anxiety this morning for no apparent reason, except maybe all the uncertainty regarding the coming summer, my prospects for consulting work, money, cars, the people at the condos, our boat, and so forth. Come to think of it, I guess there *are* reasons.

Ray didn't come home last night. I think he is in *love!* I went out on foot with him yesterday morning to find and buy some battery terminals, and when we got back, he got some more money from Sonny and immediately set out to find Fabriana. He said he was going to the beach with her but around 2:30 or 3:00, Mark and I were on the boat and here he comes, bringing her to show her the boat. I took their picture together, and then he takes her to the pool here at the yacht club where we, ourselves are guests! Then they leave, him carrying an overnight bag and telling us not to wait up for him. I swear he is like a teenager with a new girl friend, who just got laid for the first time. And this is a guy without two nickels to rub together! She seemed nice enough, spoke a *little* English, is supposedly 25 years old and has a nine-year old child who lives with her Mother in Sao Paulo. Maybe she *is* only 25, but she has been awake for a long time!

We got diesel fuel yesterday morning, got our filled propane tanks back, and Sonny and Richard did provisioning so *if* Sonny can manage to get us cleared out today, we can sail for Barbados early tomorrow. Mark felt better yesterday- varnished the toe rails on the boat, but still didn't feel like going far so we had drinks and dinner here at the yacht club. I had "feijoada", a Brazilian specialty stew of black beans, rice, and several kinds of meat, along with pineapple and orange slices, all for 10 reals, or $3.00. It was *outstanding!*

Sonny and Richard seemed to do a good job of provisioning- got lots of things we like- much better than when Naomi was here pinching pennies. Mark and I put things away so we know what is here *and* where it is! Sonny and Richard also went out for the evening again, all dressed up in their long pants!

I checked the Internet and still have no news about when my article will be published. I did have a nice conversation with Maureen, but nothing new there either. She is less aggressive than I am in bringing things to conclusions.

With Mark not feeling well, I have spent more time sitting around on the boat here than I would have liked. I wasn't interested in accompanying Ray, or Sonny and Richard last night so I just sat around, waxing philosophical, and worked myself into a down mood. Although I have no inclination to do what Ray is doing, at least he is *experiencing* Recife while I am more or less *enduring* it. When he thinks back on his visit here he will have something to remember, if it doesn't kill him. I really feel like I have sort of missed out here.

8:30 P.M.- We leave at 7:00 A. M. tomorrow. We still have to clear out with the Port Captain, as they were closed today but that is sort of on the way, and shouldn't be a big deal. We are ready to get on with the next passage, and with the trip.

I started the day in poor spirits but my conversation with Maureen this morning perked me up, and it turned out to be a reasonably good day. The weather improved through the day too, from cloudy this morning to bright and sunny. Mark was sick again this morning so I went to Sao Antonio and Old Recife by myself- took a bus without knowing exactly where it was going, but it worked out well. As it turned out, I needed to get rid of about 100 reals. Almost nothing was open, this being Sunday. I stumbled across "Restaurante Leite", an old and somewhat famous restaurant here where I had a really nice lunch of beef tongue, for 32 reals including a beer and the tip. That meal was *very* good. Then there was an arts and crafts market down along Rua do Bom Jesus with about 200 booths. I saw them setting it all up this morning, and in the afternoon I went back for some successful shopping. After that, I bought a few items at a drug store that happened to be open, and I was set. I came back to the boat and it was hotter than blazes, so I went to the pool to cool off- it worked!

Ray survived, and seemed to enjoy his night with Fabriana but has said good-bye after discovering that he was not in love after all. He said he decided that she is not very smart; in fact he doesn't think she can read very well. When he got back to the boat yesterday he reached in his pocket and discovered that he had her keys. He borrowed three reals from me for bus fare, to take them to her. He is stone-broke! Again! Every time we get to a port he gets some money from Sonny and within a day or two he is broke again, hooker or no hooker! He needs adult supervision!

Monday, April 7 - 9:35 A.M.- Well, we are aground! Stuck here until at least the next high tide at 7:00 P.M.! We cast off our lines at Iate Clube Cabanga at 6:35 A.M., and by 6:50 we were *hard aground*! No more than two miles from the yacht club, and in almost the *same spot* where we ran aground on the way in Wednesday! We knew that the water outside the channel is very shallow; in fact some of it dries at low tide, but we were leaving at *high* tide, so no problem. So we *thought*! The tidal range here is about four to six feet; right now, about four or so. We were motoring slowly up the channel, which is marked by two rows of sticks but the sticks don't go all the way out. Sonny was at the helm and several small local fishing boats were fishing in, and alongside the channel so we were taking a few pictures. Sonny had his video camera. We came to one fishing boat that had a long net out, that paralleled the channel, inside the channel for a while before curving away to starboard. Sonny wasn't watching, and almost ran over the net. I was sitting next to him and said, "Turn left; turn left." and he did; missing the net and steering parallel to it with it being on our starboard side. We were pretty close to the net and I kept watching it. Then I said, "It's about to curve away to the right", and then said, "You're clear of the net; it has curved away to the right." The dumb ass was still shooting video footage, paying little or no attention to where he was steering, and followed the net as it curved away to the right. I said, "You don't need to follow the net; you need to go straight ahead". In fairness, the sticks had ended so he didn't have them as a guide, but he just kept shooting his Goddamn video, paying no attention to me. I saw a brush pile sticking up out of the water, marking the place where we went aground Wednesday (we managed to get off that time), and asked him "What's your depth?" Right after that, we stopped moving, hard aground! We tried powering off, and that didn't work. Then, two fishermen in a good-sized boat with a diesel engine tried to pull us off: forward, backward, and sideways, with no success. Then we tried to take an anchor out in the dinghy to try and kedge off, but no movement. *So*, here we sit, with the boat tilting severely to starboard as the tide goes out. Ray took Sonny ashore in the dinghy, where Sonny is trying to find somebody to come and try to pull us off tonight at high tide. We shall *see* how it goes! The boat is tilted so much now that I can't stay in my bunk so I am sitting, braced in the cockpit as I write this.

To make matters worse, I feel poorly this morning. The yacht club was closed last night for a private party so Mark and I went into Old Recife for dinner. As I often do, I ordered a local specialty without knowing what it was. I have had a *lot* of *good* experiences doing that, but this time was an exception. It was some kind of stuffed onion with ham and cheese, baked in corn meal, dry as a bone, and *not good*! I was up eating Pepto Bismol tablets during the night, and still feel like crap.

As I have been writing this Ray came back in the dinghy and got into the boat, and promptly let the dinghy and outboard get away, blowing downwind. Fortunately, he is a good swimmer, and caught up with it but the guy is a *disaster!*

20 – WATER, WATER EVERYWHERE

Tuesday, April 8 Lat.-8 degrees, 19 minutes south; Lon.-34 degrees, 12 minutes west

9:05 A.M.- We were aground for almost exactly 12 hours. A guy from the yacht club, who operates a SCUBA diving business used his boat and managed to tow us free at 6:50 P.M., just before high tide. It wasn't easy, as several attempts failed before we finally tied the towline to our main halyard and he pulled the top of our mast over enough to lift the keel off the bottom and get us free. We were *very* relieved, as the tides will not be this high again the rest of the week and we were afraid of being stuck here for several days. Sonny knew that he had screwed up, and acted so humble that none of us felt like rubbing it in. The tidal range here is about five feet and at *low* tide, the boat was resting on the keel and starboard side of the hull, *almost* high and dry! We were right across the channel from a restaurant/ hotel/tour boat/dive boat business so I went ashore with Ray and hung out there most of the day. Nobody was around so I managed to take a nap on a picnic table. In addition to the meal Sunday night, I walked too much around Recife so my legs and hip bones ached, and the other day I strained my back a little while taking bags of canned provisions from the bow of the boat to the galley. All in all, I felt like crap all day, but right after we were pulled free I started feeling better. Mark and Richard stayed on the boat through it all, even tilted over that far. Mark is still pretty sick and we are all a little worried about him.

I felt no sentiment upon leaving Recife, even though that also means leaving South America, very likely for the last time. That is probably because of the grounding, and being so happy to get free. One observation- it was really frustrating to be in Brazil and not speak *any* Portuguese after getting by pretty well in Spanish. There is a *little* overlap between Portuguese and Spanish, but not much, especially in regard to pronunciation. It was a pain in the ass being unable to communicate. If I ever again go somewhere that I don't know the language, and have any prior notice at all, I will buy books and tapes, and try to cram as much as possible so that I at least know some basics!

We cleared the Recife breakwater at 7:50 last night and headed for Barbados, 1,970 miles away. The wind was blowing at 16 knots, right out of the northeast, where we wanted to go so we sailed southeast all night to get offshore and give ourselves room to tack. We changed tacks just before the end of night watch since by then the wind had come around to east-northeast and we had gained enough room offshore to clear the point just above Recife. This morning the wind is from just about due east, so now we are sailing north, heading for that corner, where we will turn northwest toward Barbados. I feel like that turn will be rounding third base, and heading for home.

Wednesday, April 9 Lat.- 6 degrees, 5 minutes south; Lon.- 34 degrees, 37 minutes west

9:45 A.M.- Good news and bad news! The good news is that we are burning up the ocean- Mark and I made 28 miles on night watch and Ray and Richard have made 30 on their watch that is just about to end. All this in winds ranging 16-22 knots, over and just aft of the starboard beam allowing us to steer the course we want. We are doing this under the jib and *reefed main*! Imagine that! I guess this boat is not so slow if you sail it right. We just weren't "shifting into high gear", so to speak.

Now the *bad* news: The water maker quit working last night. To make matters worse, we left port with only 25 gallons of water in the tank, and only had 30 when the water maker quit! We were *supposedly* told that the water at the marina in Recife wasn't potable, and the only way to buy any was in gallon jugs at the grocery store. *Common sense* says that you don't sail on a 2,000-mile passage without a full water tank, and that we should have gone ahead and bought enough to fill up, but the water maker had been working fine, so we didn't. Mark and I skipped showers yesterday, thinking it prudent to let the tank fill up some just in case something like this happened, but the others didn't, and Ray even washed out some clothes. Anyway, Sonny and Ray are trying now to get the water maker working. If they are not successful we will have to go into port somewhere and get water, which will add two or three days to an already long passage.

Everybody was moving kind of slow all day yesterday, keeping to their bunks a lot. I think the grounding incident took a lot out of all of us. Sonny is being more personable than he has for a long time. I think he is grateful for us not rubbing it in about the grounding. He knew he had screwed up big time, and was *very* humble about it.

217

More good news- I have slept great the last two nights and pretty well feel 100 per cent again. Also, I have re-rigged the fishing rod with the supplies that I bought in Recife- no success trolling yesterday though. Sunset yesterday and sunrise this morning were unspectacular, but nice. We did have another freighter silhouette itself against the setting sun last night, this one only about two miles off the port beam.

Thursday, April 10 Lat.- 4 degrees, 17 minutes south; Lon.- 36 degrees, 7 minutes west

9:25 A.M.- We are headed for Fortaleza, Brazil! Fortaleza is a city on the north coast of Brazil and the reason we are going there is that we were *stupid* enough to go to sea on a 2,000-mile passage with only *25 gallons of water in the tank*! After working on the water maker all morning and early afternoon, around 2:00 P.M. Sonny declared defeat and pronounced the water maker dead. It therefore became necessary for us to find a port and go in for water, and Fortaleza is the least out of our way. Still, it will likely add two or three days to our passage. This also means that we will have no water maker for the rest of the trip; two long passages, each on 145 gallons of water! Add this to the fact that we are sailing through the tropics with no refrigeration and you can see that the comfort level is going to be pretty low. To make matters still worse, the weather has turned shitty, with rain and highly variable winds all afternoon and all night. We got rained on pretty good on afternoon *and* night watches. I got really depressed, and pissed about it all. The weather and my mood are both better this morning.

We are, and will continue to be in a 1 to 1.5 knot favorable current, which greatly helps our progress, and *might* make this passage quicker than we expected. Hopefully, we might get in and out of Fortaleza in a matter of hours, getting water and topping off the fuel tanks.

I stopped a few minutes ago to take pictures of what I will call the "Fortaleza Chili Party" (ala the Boston Tea Party!). Before the trip Sonny, or Naomi had bought a *lot* of gallon-sized cans of chili, probably because it was *cheap*. We tried it twice early in the trip and after that, *nobody* would eat it- it was *that* bad, and I am pretty tolerant when it comes to stuff like that. It has been just sitting in the food bins taking up space, but as we left Recife we started smelling something stinking, and couldn't figure out what it was. Finally this morning, Mark couldn't stand it any more and went on a search. He found that at least one of the cans had rusted through and had maggots

218

on it, stinking to high heaven so he threw them all overboard. Good riddance, I say!

Ray was in a shitty mood last night too, and didn't cook. I was so pissed and depressed that I didn't feel like eating anyway, but I made myself eat a bowl of corn flakes for dinner. This morning I am fine, as I had a bowl of corn flakes at six o'clock, and after my morning nap I had three scrambled eggs and two pieces of "skillet toast" with tangerine marmalade and a cup of green tea. I am given credit for inventing skillet toast. Our toaster (like many things on this boat) never worked right and you had to flip on the inverter to use it, so I never bothered. After a while it quit working altogether. Then somewhere around Buenos Aires I started buttering two slices of bread and throwing them into the skillet as I am finishing scrambling my eggs- just push the eggs to one side and throw the bread in, letting it get just a little brown on each side. Now, everybody is making and eating skillet toast.

Friday, April 11 - 9:35 A.M.- Well, here we are in Fortaleza. We arrived 20 miles offshore in the middle of the night; then motored in slowly to time our arrival with daybreak. Since we hadn't planned to come here, we had no chart so we wandered around for a while, trying to find a marina. Sonny bounced us off a *marked* underwater obstruction on the way in, nearly getting us stuck again because once more, he was *not paying attention* as two guys on a pier were waving their arms, signaling us to stay away from that marker. There are no docks at the "Iate Clube do Fortaleza", so we finally anchored there just before nine o'clock. Sonny went ashore to the Port Captain's office alone, in the dinghy and hopefully, can minimize the time we are here- just get water and fuel and be on our way. He has a way of turning things that should be simple into big deals, so we will see. If we are on our way before dark I will be happy, although sooner would be better. *If* we don't get hung up here and *if* we continue to match our recent progress we *could* still make Barbados by April 23, and Key West *possibly* by May 10. I'm not getting my hopes up, but it *is* possible.

My first impression of Fortaleza is that it is much larger than I expected, with a lot of tall, modern-looking buildings. There is a sizable fleet of fishing boats moored here in the harbor with the tall buildings of the city in the background. Some of them are small sailing vessels with hulls shaped like jon boats, but not deep inside- more like rafts, with flush decks. The sails are unique too, with spars that look like small trees, or more likely, bamboo. They have very long booms, large triangular main sails, and teeny little jibs. It is all very picturesque.

Saturday, April 12 Lat.- 2 degrees, 50 minutes south; Lon.- 39 degrees, 9 minutes west

7:40 A.M.- We *did* manage to get in and out of Fortaleza in a day, but just barely, and it was an adventure! When Sonny went ashore to the Port Captain's office the hope was that we wouldn't have to clear in, but could just get water and fuel, and go; however such was not the case. He came back after half an hour and said that we all had to go to Immigration, after which he had to go back to the Port Captain to clear in. After that, we could go and get our water and fuel; then repeat the process to clear out. Also, the "Iate Clube" had no fuel or potable water so we would have to go to another marina at the Marina Park Hotel, about five miles away, for that. That seemed strange to me, but what can you say?

We all went ashore and walked about half a mile to Immigration (Policia Federale) only to find that the office was closed, and wouldn't open until 2:00 P.M. We found out the opening time because the security guard and I both spoke enough Spanish to communicate. Well, Sonny sat down and started settling in to wait until 2:00 - it was 10:30 A.M. at the time. I looked over at Ray and quietly said "God, give me patience – and I need it *now*!" He laughed so hard he nearly fell out of his chair.

After a few minutes I suggested, and then insisted that we go back to the Port Captain's office, tell them what happened, and try to get them to work with us. Sonny didn't want to go, saying, "they don't care", and "they don't want to help", and so forth.

I finally said, "If you don't want to talk with them, *I* will", so we went. To help make a long story shorter, this guy too, spoke a little Spanish and I was able to convince him (it wasn't hard) to let us go and get our water and fuel, and come back later to take care of the formalities.

Then, we went back to the yacht club and found an employee named Joe, who spoke a little English and a little Spanish. He was trying to explain to Sonny how to find the other marina. The channel to get there was tricky, with a couple of reefs along the way and was tucked in behind a breakwater, where it was hard to find. Sonny was obviously struggling in the conversation, asking questions like "Can we find it by ourselves?" when I spoke up and said, "Can you come with us and show us how to get there?" He quickly said yes, and he not only showed us how to get there, but also helped us find the fuel that we needed – it was not on the premises- and saved our asses when we tried to dock there. In that marina they dock Mediterranean style, with an anchor out in the middle and the stern to the dock. The theory is that you find your spot, drop your anchor, and then back in to the dock, paying out anchor line and snubbing the anchor as you go. Just as we got there the wind started piping up, coming from the starboard side, and kept blowing us off from our spot. We circled twice, nearly hitting several other boats before I dropped the anchor on the third try. Then the wind nearly blew us into another boat as Sonny tried to back us in. Sonny is poor at handling the boat under power. He decided that Ray would take a line ashore in the dinghy so we could pull the stern in, but when he was half way there the dinghy outboard quit and wouldn't start. The next thing I knew, Joe had jumped in the water and swam the line ashore!

It took a while, but by four o'clock we finally had our water and fuel, so we took a taxi to Immigration. They were open this time and the guy spoke enough English to understand our situation, so he cleared us in *and* out. Then we walked to the Port Captain's office. On the way there Sonny discovered that he had forgotten the boat documents and we thought we were screwed, but this time we were lucky enough to talk with the port Captain himself; someone with authority to make a decision that was not "by the book". It took a while but he finally understood our situation and cleared us in and out at once.

By then it was nearly five o'clock and we were five or six miles from the boat. We couldn't find a taxi right away so we took one of those "gypsy cab" mini-vans instead, and that was an adventure. We asked first if they went to the Marina Park Hotel and they said yes, so we got in. We covered a good part of the city at a high rate of speed, stopping frequently, with this guy driving like a kamikaze pilot, but he was a *very good* driver! Then, he reached the end of his route, where he put us on *another* "gypsy cab" that finally got us to the boat about 5:30. It was already starting to get dark, and we knew that Sonny wouldn't leave there in the dark (I wouldn't either), so we jumped on the boat and hurriedly got under way about 5:45, just before dark.

Now I understand why it takes Sonny so damn long to clear in and out of ports. He isn't very smart, and doesn't know how to be politely, diplomatically assertive, and *get things done!* He also is not decisive, like the situation with Joe, the guy from the yacht club. It's hard to think about all this without the word "incompetent" coming to mind!

Fortaleza is a nice, *large* city with modern buildings, a long, pretty beach with clean water, and a picturesque fishing fleet. It looks to be larger than Orlando, especially the downtown area. It seems like a very interesting city that I wouldn't mind visiting if I had some time.

In *this* case, "happiness was Fortaleza in my rear-view mirror".

Winds are southeast at 12-18 knots, coming from way back on the starboard quarter, giving us a "rolly" ride, but we are making good progress and the weather on night watch was clear, with lots of stars. When we went up for night watch at 2:00 A.M. we were in the middle of an oil field, with as many as 11 platforms visible at one time and once again, Sonny had the radar turned off. The other day I even heard him chiding Ray for referring to the radar.

Sunday, April 13 Lat.- 1 degree, 9 minutes south; Lon. 41 degrees, 5 minutes west.

9:10 A.M.- Ray is in a great mood and is cooking like crazy! Yesterday afternoon he made pizza, and for dinner last night we had curry chicken. Both were excellent.

We should cross the equator before the end of the day today, returning to the northern hemisphere for the first time since November 25. If this was any other boat there would be some kind of celebration or ceremony, to add some fun to the trip and be part of the adventure but we had nothing heading south in the Pacific, and we won't now. Mark and I talked about having a bottle of wine to celebrate, but nobody else was interested so we gave it up. Sonny just isn't a fun guy! I have seen no indication that he was having fun the entire voyage.

Night watch last night was nice. It stopped raining just as we went on watch and skies cleared, giving us a good, starry night. Wind stopped after the rain and we motored just over an hour before it started again. When it came back it was right over the starboard beam and settled at 14-15 knots which was just about perfect. A good-sized bird roosted on the mizzen boom so we waited for it to wake up and leave before we finally raised the mizzen at 5:15.

We continue to make good progress, helped by the current. In the 24-hour period that ends at 10:00 A.M. we will have covered more than 160 miles! If by some miracle we could maintain that pace we would reach Barbados the evening of April 21 but that is *highly* unlikely. The morning of the 23rd is more realistic.

My trolling has been unsuccessful, so I think it is time to try another lure. This one is new, and to me it looks just like a little fish swimming along but the fish must not see it that way.

I recently read a book called "Streets of Laredo", by Larry McMurtry and was impressed by a quotation regarding one of the characters, an old Texas Ranger named Woodrow Call:

"Call considered that he had always been able to draw on more

222

will than most men possessed. He could keep riding longer and keep fighting harder than any man he had worked with. He had never considered himself brilliant, and as a rider or a shot he was only average. But he could keep going in situations where others had to stop."

To me that quotation is the best description I have ever seen - of me; what makes me different from other people. Earlier I wrote that the difference between me and most other people is that they aren't willing to do whatever it takes to go out and get life. I think this says the same thing. It seems to be summed up in one word: "will". Out here I think I have gained a greater understanding of myself than I ever had before.

Monday, April 14 Lat.-0 degrees, 33 minutes north; Lon.- 43 degrees, 59 minutes west

9:45 A.M.- We crossed the equator at 9:08 P.M. last night. I woke up, lay there a few minutes, and when I looked at my watch it said 9:11. I guess I woke up when we hit the bump!

Yesterday afternoon's watch was strange. For the first two hours we had beautiful, sunny weather with winds of 12-14 knots, and still making a speed of five knots. Then at 4:00 it turned ugly with rain, gusty winds in the 16-24 knot range, and lots of clouds. The wind shifted so much once during a gust that reached 30 knots, that Mark, at the helm, came about accidentally. The autopilot had just stopped working during another shifty gust, so he was steering manually. None of this was a real problem, but just served to liven up the watch.

We have at least temporarily lost the current that was helping us. It may have something to do with the fact that we have started to pass the vast delta at the mouth of the Amazon River, dumping such a great volume of water into the ocean that it may create a current of it's own. Whatever the case, we are still making very good progress and I am confident that we will pick up the current again. Also, once we clear the doldrums we will pick up the trade winds, which will be more reliable, and should produce stable weather. Right now the weather is still partly sunny and partly rainy, with benign seas no more than eight feet and even those are mainly low swells, with only a little chop.

Ray has taken to sitting around all day in his underwear the last two days. These aren't boxers, either, or even standard jockey shorts. They are not exactly bikinis, but they are pretty brief. It's not a big deal, but is something that I would just as soon not see. I'm not sure what prompted this but I hope it is something that passes.

By the way, Ray seems quite proud of himself for his liaison with Fabriana in Recife. He even said that if he was rich he would fly down and shack up with her for a while. I guess he really was taken with her after all! I heard him telling Richard that he, Ray, got a much better deal with her than Richard did with his hooker in Panama. I didn't hear what Richard said, but he seemed to agree.

Tuesday, April 15 Lat. 1 degree, 59 minutes north; Lon.- 44 degrees, 51 minutes west

9:25 A.M.- These afternoon squalls seem to be becoming a pattern and yesterday was the worst yet. The first two hours of afternoon watch were not too bad, with a little sun, a few sprinkles, and gathering clouds. Then, right at four o'clock a squall hit with winds up to 30 knots and rain by the bucketful, and it lasted a full hour. We were under the jib and mizzen with the jib unrolled all the way but we left the sails alone. If the wind had risen above 30 knots we would have rolled up some of the jib. As it was, we sailed fast- over seven knots in a drenching rain. Around five o'clock it let up and the wind dropped to the point where we motored for a while. Then, at 5:30 the rain came again, but without so much wind. All in all, it was *not* a comfortable watch. Night watch was much better with beam winds that averaged 15 knots and partly cloudy skies that allowed the moon to perform. It looks like maybe two more days to full moon, and it's nice to think that the next time the moon is full I will be home.

Ray is back to wearing regular shorts. I don't know what the deal was with the underwear. He is still in a good mood, and cooking every night, too.

Figuring that we're roughly half way through this passage, I changed sheets and pillow- cases this morning. With the heat, I am only using the bottom sheet anyway so if this one gets smelly I can put on one of the top sheets.

I am still having no luck trolling. I think maybe the unsettled weather is affecting it.

When I woke up at 1:30 this morning, it was with a troubled mind that stayed with me pretty much throughout night watch. Like so many nighttime goblins, it seemed to go away with the darkness when daylight came.

Wednesday, April 16 Lat.-3 degrees, 32 minutes north; Lon.- 46 degrees, 45 minutes west - 8:45 A.M.- What a HELL OF A FISH! Just before five o'clock yesterday afternoon I caught the biggest fish I have ever caught! I was trolling off the port side and was sitting just aft of the cockpit getting some sun when the fish struck. For once I had the drag set just right; pretty tight, but loose enough that the fish could take a little line, in short bursts. When I got to the rod I couldn't lift it out of the holder at first, so knew I had something *big*. We were sailing at nearly six knots at the time, so Ray loosened the jib sheet to slow us down and give me a chance to fight the fish. I *gradually* tightened the drag so that it wouldn't take all the line, and pulled on the rod until I got enough slack to lift it out of the holder. Richard, who had been napping below, heard the commotion and came topside to watch. Almost every turn of the reel came with considerable effort and as the fish tired, so did I. By then the boat had slowed to about two knots, or I would have had no chance to land the fish. After a while it came to the surface about 30 yards behind the boat on the starboard side and I saw that it was *really big*, but still couldn't tell what it was. After a few more minutes it was 20 yards directly behind me and I saw the bill. I thought it was a marlin, but then I brought it a little closer and saw the magnificent dorsal fin, or "sail"! It was a sailfish! Its colors were a shiny silver and a dark, almost "midnight blue", with that awesome dorsal fin; something that I *never* thought I would see on the end of *my* line. I knew that I was going to let it go, but wanted my lure back so when I brought it alongside the boat Richard stuck the gaff in it's gills and lifted it up. I could have reached the lure, as the hook was in the top of the bill but just then I remembered hearing how those fish use their *very sharp* bills to cut through schools of small fish when they are feeding. Even hanging there on the gaff the fish was still very lively and when I looked at it's right eye, I swear I saw not fear, but malice! I decided not to risk a grab for the lure, and didn't want to harm the fish any more so I asked Ray to cut the line. When it fell back into the water it took a couple of seconds to realize that it was free; then was gone in a flash.

When the fish was gone, I just sat there staring for a few minutes, physically and emotionally drained. When it was hanging from the gaff we could see that it was nearly as long as we are tall, putting it between five and six feet including the bill. All of us, including Richard who lifted it, agreed that the weight was about 40 pounds, though I'm not sure how good any of us are at estimating weight. I will never forget the way that fish looked as it was alongside the boat fighting for it's life, exhausted but never giving up, even when it was hanging from the gaff. I think that fish showed more courage than any *person* I know!

I still can't believe that I had such a FANTASTIC fishing experience!

Some people spend lots of years and lots of money trying to catch a sailfish, and here I luck up and catch a *big* one off the back of a sailboat that is under way.

The weather has improved - three dry watches in a row - and we have picked up our friendly current again. Winds are still on the starboard beam and are up to 16-18 knots. We had enough clouds on night watch that the moon and stars provided little entertainment.

Thursday, April 17 Lat.-5 degrees, 0 minutes north; Lon.- 48 degrees, 45 minutes west

9:10 A.M.- We are officially out of the doldrums! We reached five degrees north latitude at the end of our night watch, and now have less than 800 miles to go to Barbados. Almost on cue, we picked up the trade winds, blowing from the east at 17-22 knots giving us *great* sailing at a speed of six to seven knots. We have made 150 miles or better each of the last two days and with any luck at all, we should be able to maintain that pace. If so, we will reach Barbados on Tuesday, the 22nd.

We have pretty well adjusted to life without the water maker and are using water sparingly these days, doing dishes in sea water, showering only every two or three days, and so forth. It's not what you would prefer, but tolerable for a relatively short time. Sonny has started to voice some concerns about water on the next passage, and mentioned making a water stop in Jamaica or someplace. We want to do whatever we can to dispel that notion. We *really* don't want to make any more unplanned stops.

So much for our streak of dry watches. We had two rainsqualls on night watch. It was nothing severe, with top wind gusts of 34 knots; just wet. I rigged a fishing lure yesterday that I thought looked pretty good, but had no success trolling. The interpersonal dynamics are quiet right now, and everybody seems to be in a good mood.

One of the things I will enjoy when I get home is living in a clean environment, where things don't stink. Things get pretty gross around here and you notice smells coming from various places. We wash and dry dishes, and wipe up the galley with rags and sponges that you wouldn't allow in your *house*, much less your kitchen. I think Mark and I are the only ones who ever heard of the concept of squeezing out a sponge, or spreading out a rag so that it will dry. It was just as bad when Naomi was here, too.

Clouds stole the show from the full moon last night, but it did make an occasional appearance.

Friday, April 18 Lat.- 6 degrees, 31 minutes north; Lon.- 50 degrees, 55 minutes west

8:50 A.M.- Sonny had a breakthrough yesterday. He sat down and looked at the chart and discovered that the trip from Barbados to Key West will be nearly 400 miles shorter if we go through the Mona Passage between Puerto Rico and the Dominican Republic, than if we go around the west end of Cuba, as planned. Why he had not done this before is a mystery to me. It's kind of like his startling discovery of how far out of the way Punta Arenas, Chile would have been, which resulted in our going to the Falklands instead- LACK OF PLANNING! He should have been *totally* familiar with all that before we ever left Mobile! In any case, what that means is that we *could* get home two or three days sooner than I had thought possible, *conceivably* as early as May 6 or 7.

I am at a loss to explain the dearth of birds in this part of the ocean. Somewhere between Rio and Recife the birds sort of went away, and now we rarely see one. Any time I have ever been on or near the ocean, including throughout this voyage, I have always seen lots of birds. Even when we were nearly a thousand miles from the nearest land we saw birds. In the Pacific, at night we would often see a white bird, or sometimes two, flying along with us, riding the currents of wind coming off the sails. But not here, and I can't imagine why.

Night watch was really nice last night. We only got sprinkled on for about five minutes and the rest of the time we had *super* sailing, with quartering winds of 17-22 knots giving us a speed of around seven knots. The post-full moon played hide-and-seek through the clouds for the first three hours before coming out and doing a solo show the last hour. It occurred to me that in all likelihood this is the last full moon I will ever experience at sea. I'm glad I am sensitive enough to realize that, and fully enjoy it as it happens.

No success trolling again yesterday, so it may be time to change lures. Also, I think our speed and the wind and sea conditions have something to do with it. I *still* can't believe the sailfish!

Saturday, April 19 - Lat. 8 degrees, 18 minutes north; Lon.- 53 degrees, 5 minutes west

9:00 A.M.- We had a blow-up between Sonny and Ray yesterday afternoon. I was at the helm and didn't hear all the particulars but I heard Ray yelling the "F" word a lot. It seemed to start over whether a hatch in the salon near Ray's bunk should be open to provide ventilation in this heat, or closed due to spray coming in. It escalated from there. I guess a lot of other shit came out including the reason why Sonny and Naomi quit talking to Ray, Mark and me- it seems that Richard was running to them and telling them things that we said. I don't *give* a rat's ass, as I never said anything about them that I wouldn't say to their faces if the occasion arose. I guess most of this had to do with us being glad she was leaving. Somehow Mark got drawn into it, and told Sonny straight out that he was in fact, glad when she left and that she had no business being on this boat. I am still keeping my mouth shut unless I am drawn into it by Sonny, which I doubt will happen. I don't know how he feels about me overall, but he acts like he has a fair amount of respect for me. In any case, if we're lucky, three weeks from now we'll be home.

We are continuing to experience trade wind sailing at it's best, and I am not allowing any of this other crap to spoil it for me. Winds are consistent, on the starboard quarter at 17-24 knots, giving us speeds of six to seven knots and we have averaged over 150 miles a day this entire passage if you don't count running aground and the water stop. Now it is looking like we will arrive in Barbados around mid-day on the 22nd.

During the row yesterday some mention was made of Ray leaving the boat in Barbados. I don't think that will happen because Ray has no money to fly home, and Sonny needs him to finish the trip. Still, I know Sonny is fed up with Ray's mouth and temper as well as his negative attitude. It is some consolation to me to feel that Sonny is having a miserable time. Only Sonny is having anything to say to Richard now. Mark said that to call Richard a weasel would be an insult to weasels everywhere! It is *very* awkward between Ray and Richard on watch together, too. As for me, I am still enjoying myself, even though I will be glad to get home

Sunday, April 20   Lat.- 9 degrees, 50 minutes north; Lon.- 55 degrees, 17 minutes west

9:00 A.M.- It's Easter, and I am homesick! I remembered all those Easter sunrises over at the beach with Maureen, and imagined her there this morning with Molly. Later today Molly will experience her first Easter egg hunt, and I know she will be a pip!

This sure is some *fine sailing*! This may be; probably is, the best of the voyage, challenged only by that spectacular downwind run between Easter Island and Puerto Montt with those awesome 30 foot following swells. That probably was better for seven or eight days, but this has lasted for ten days, and counting. *Nothing* is detracting from my enjoyment of this sailing. Swells have built the last couple of days to the 6-12 foot range with an occasional 15 footer rolling through, but nothing even resembling a problem so far.

I am in a rotten mood this morning, with my moody personality on a downswing. It started during night watch and I thought my morning nap would make it better, but it got worse. Sometimes I think too much, and let things overwhelm me. I did take a shower and put on clean underwear this morning, and that helped a little.

I was surprised at how much cooler it is since we crossed the equator. The sea temperature dropped from 84 degrees to 80 and the air temperature now is very comfortable. I don't even sweat-up my bunk now. I expected it to remain hot, with any change being gradual but it happened noticeably and quickly. I need my black anorak on night watch, and almost need a top sheet when I sleep.

Monday, April 21 Lat.- 11 degrees, 3 minutes north; Lon.- 56 degrees, 48 minutes west

8:25 A.M.- The fine sailing has gone away. At mid-morning yesterday the wind dropped to the 12-15 knot range and came around almost behind us. Then for most of the day we picked up a counter current that slowed us down nearly a knot. At least the counter current is gone now but we are dragging along at four knots- not too bad in the overall scope of things, but poor when you are anxious to get somewhere, and have been accustomed to six or seven knots. Our estimated time of arrival in Barbados has backed-up for the last 24 hours, and that is discouraging as now we are hoping to get there Wednesday. At least the weather is nice from the comfort perspective.

During the afternoon my rotten mood took a turn for the worse and I started waxing philosophical about life in general, and my life in particular. It was nothing worth writing down here, but I ended up sulking the rest of the day.

Tuesday, April 22 Lat.-12 degrees, 22 minutes north; Lon.- 58 degrees, 35 minutes west

9:25 A.M.- We had canned hot dogs and pineapple for dinner last night, but we *could* have had Mahi Mahi! Toward the end of afternoon watch I caught a really nice dolphin. The only problem was that it was too big, and too damned pretty! I might have gotten past the "pretty" part this time but it was nearly four feet long and I guessed its weight at about 20 pounds. Since we have no refrigeration, we would have had to throw away probably 70 per cent of the meat. I just couldn't bring myself to kill such a big, beautiful, spirited fighter of a fish and then

229

throw away most of the meat. I really *thought* about it, but I couldn't do it. Once I decided to let it go I didn't want to damage it by lifting it out of the water with a gaff, so I asked Ray to cut the line; sacrificing yet another lure. This fish too, gave me a fantastic fight, jumping twice, making several runs back and forth behind the boat, trying to pass the boat on the starboard side, (I was on the port side) and to head out to sea off the port side. Near the end of the fight the reel handle came off again but I was still able to bring him alongside and lift his head out of the water to where he could have easily been gaffed and lifted aboard. I say *he* because it had the iridescent blue, yellow, and green colors of a male. This morning Mark fixed the reel handle again, so we are back in business.

Just before noon yesterday Sonny started the engine and we have been motoring ever since in winds less than 10 knots. It seems that the doldrums have moved north! We also lost the adverse current and picked up a favorable one so with that, we have been motoring at six knots and it looks like we will reach Barbados tonight after all.

Oh yes, the lure that caught the dolphin was one that I bought in Buenos Aires, and modified. It was a pink rubber squid-like lure with two hooks rigged trailer-style and some tinsel mixed in with the pink and white of the skirt. The head was hollow, and it was too light- would skip across the surface when trolled. I found two small "egg" sinkers, stuffed them in the head to give it weight, and ran the leader through them to keep them in place. It worked, because I had one other strike on it before I caught the dolphin.

Sonny told Mark yesterday that he, Mark, is leaving the boat in Key West even though Sonny is taking the boat to St. Petersburg to sell it. Mark was planning to get off in Key West with Ray and me anyway, and had no interest in sailing a few more days with Sonny and Richard, but being *told* that seemed to hurt Mark's feelings. I don't blame him.

21 – BARBADOS

Wednesday, April 23 - 6:05 A.M.- We *did* make it to Barbados last night after all. We tied up at the Customs dock at 6:20 P.M., completing the 1,622-mile passage from Fortaleza in exactly 11 days. We even got cleared in before dark. Even counting the 24 hours that we lost between the grounding and the water stop, we made the 1,970 miles from Recife in 15 ½ days. That's the *good* news.

The *bad* news, at least so far, seems to be that we came to Barbados at all! From all first impressions, it is a very overpriced, glamour tourist trap destination that appeals to people with more money than brains.

It seems that there is no marina with docks here, so after we cleared in we came back to an anchorage that we passed on the way in, and managed to pick up a mooring in the dark. The anchorage is right off a beach complex called The Boatyard that has a nightclub, restaurant, and showers. We took the dinghy ashore about 8:30 to get dinner and a beer, and got a case of "sticker shock" when we saw the prices. To make matters worse, they tell us that this is one of the less expensive places! Mark had a cheeseburger (in paradise?) for $10. U.S., and Ray and I had flying fish sandwiches for $9. Banks beer, the local brew, comes in roughly nine ounce bottles, and was $2.75. The prices in Latin America really spoiled us! The worst part though, was the music. It was some sort of disco-Caribbean crap that was blaring so loud that you could barely have a conversation, and it *never stopped*, as one song went right into the next. I am pretty tolerant when it comes to music, that it was really a *horrible* sound. For many years I have heard that Barbados was very populated, touristy, and pricey which is why it was never an option when we were taking vacations to the Eastern Caribbean every year. I think I have now confirmed what I have always heard. It may get better, but the initial impression is bad.

Oh yes, while we were eating last night they were rehearsing on the beach for a "Pirates of the Caribbean" show that they do on Thursday nights, complete with guys on stilts in pirate costumes, wooden swords, and pirate girls. It looked like a bad imitation of Disney World! Also, the swimming area off the beach even has a fake iceberg- in *Barbados*!

Sonny said on the way in that we will probably be here until Sunday but with all the things I just mentioned, he might decide to move that up a little! Stay tuned.

Thursday, April 24 - 5:25 A.M.- After a full day here I still think Barbados is an overrated, overpriced tourist trap, though I am somewhat less negative about it now. The people we have met have been very nice, friendly, and helpful. The beaches and water are beautiful and with this being the lee side of the island there is really no surf, making it look like a giant swimming pool most of the time. Ray, Mark and I did a *lot* of exploring of Bridgetown on foot yesterday and found it fairly interesting. It is large enough to be called a city, and even has a river running through it with two bridges. One bridge is considered historic, though I don't know the history, and is closed to vehicular traffic. It has an interesting archway at the south end, and is the site of a fruit and craft market during the day. We ate lunch at a "locals-type" restaurant called Leon's, where we found the food good and the prices reasonable. I had fried chicken, red beans with rice and gravy, green beans, tomatoes, and a beer for $5.00 U.S. That was one of the rare bargains we found all day. We wandered around so long that we were left with few choices for dinner. We ate at a Chinese place that was pretty decent, with prices that were fairly reasonable. I had lamb with chilies- hot, but not *too* hot.

I had a very good telephone conversation with Maureen this morning. She has accomplished a *lot*, getting us all set with jobs and accommodations in Montana for the summer, did our income tax return, our self-employment tax, and so forth. She also told me that we don't have to start work in Montana until June 1, so I can finish the voyage with no problem! I really appreciate all she has done.

I also found out that my article will be in either the July or August issue of "Sail". I am *very* excited about it, and still can't believe it. I still haven't told Sonny or Richard about it, and don't intend to.

The music here at The Boatyard (if you want to call it music) went on until 3:00 A.M., very loud, and probably will every night. It bugs all of us to some extent, but especially Sonny. He is talking about leaving here Saturday morning, and that sounds good to me. I have looked at the pilot charts for April along our route and if prevailing winds and currents prevail, we *could* make the passage in ten days, getting us to Key West May 6!

Friday, April 25 - 5:25 A.M.- Mark fell into the water last night as he was trying to get in the dinghy to come back to the boat. There is no dinghy dock and the pier is high, to accommodate boats from cruise ships and party boats-"pirate ships"- that come and go. At the end of the pier there is no ladder, but a tire hanging about half way down and that is what you use to climb from the dinghy onto the pier and vice-versa. Somehow he climbed down onto the tire as I was holding the bow of the dinghy to the pier by the painter, or bow-line, and then missed the step into the dinghy. He didn't bounce off the side of the dinghy or anything, but just missed the whole step, going directly into the water. As he was going in he looked up, and his eyes looked *really* big! He wasn't even drunk, either, as he only had two drinks with dinner. He wasn't hurt, and it was hilarious except that he was wearing his camera on his belt and it is probably ruined. It is very similar to mine, and probably only cost around $100, but it was the only one he had with him. He lost the pictures on the film in the camera, and now can't take any more.

Yesterday afternoon Ray, Mark and I took a bus ride across the island to the community of Bath Sheba, on the east coast. It was an interesting bus ride through Bridgetown, across some countryside with lots of sugar cane fields, past a large sugar mill, across some low but steep hills, and down to a very pretty stretch of coast and beaches that is a destination for serious surfers. We went to a guesthouse with a restaurant and bar up a hill overlooking a rocky beach, and had a couple of beers. The beach was very pretty, sprinkled with huge rocks, the bases of which have been eroded by the sea so they look like giant mushrooms. The guesthouse caters to surfers and some were out on their boards. It was peaceful and relaxing. We stayed only a couple of hours because Ray had a bug up his ass to get back and use the Internet again. If I had known he was in such a hurry to get back I wouldn't have invited him to go because I would have enjoyed wandering around some more but it was a nice outing anyway.

Mark and I had dinner at the Waterfront Café down by the bridge. It was pricey but had a nice view and ambiance, and Mark wanted to go so I went with him. I had steamed flying fish that was good, but not outstanding.

Early the last three mornings while having tea in the cockpit, I have watched as a guy took his horses for a swim in the ocean. He takes one, while somebody holds the other one on the beach. They go into the water and swim together, out at least 200 yards and back. Sometimes it looks like he is on the horse's back and sometimes he swims alongside the horse. Then he leaves that one on the beach, takes the other one, and repeats the process. Not a *spectacular* sight, but a bit unusual!

Sonny is being very nice right now, and I don't know why. I still don't trust him at all. The music here has turned mellow by midnight the last two nights, which made sleeping a lot easier. Tonight is another party night though.

Oh yes, Ray is pretty sure that he has a boat to deliver from West Palm Beach to Long Island, departing around May 14. The timing is great for him, as he can pocket the money Sonny gives him for a plane ticket, *and* get paid for the trip. He is *very* happy about all that. He can stay with Tillie in Naples for a few days and then take his delivery north.

Saturday, April 26 5:15 A.M.- Today we sail for Key West, and home! The last passage of the trip and it stimulates *lots* of emotions. It's hard to describe. We are to leave the mooring at eight o'clock but still have to get water and fuel, and clear out through customs and immigration. Knowing how slow Sonny is, I will be surprised if we are actually under way by noon.

Yesterday was generally a good day; sort of a "farting around" day. We had to hang around during the middle of the day waiting for a guy to bring our clean laundry. He was late, but charged less than we expected- only seven dollars U.S. for two loads. Otherwise, we mailed post cards, shopped a little, did Internet stuff, ate another really good lunch at Leon's, and came back to The Boatyard for early drinks and happy hour. That early, 4:00-7:30, the music was tolerable, the people were interesting, and it was a fun atmosphere. At 7:30 Mark and I came back to the boat and Ray cooked pasta for us. We managed to spend all our Barbados dollars, so we are ready to sail. I had a really good conversation with Maureen during which we discussed arrangements for her to meet me in Key West. I told her to expect me no earlier than May 6 and no later than the ninth.

Yesterday was a day in which we enjoyed the "feel" of the island and like every other island, this one has it's own unique "personality". I still think Barbados is an overpriced tourist trap; especially in touristy restaurants and bars, but is not nearly as bad as my first impression. I could enjoy spending a little time here, and could do so at reasonable expense if I tried.

After dinner Ray left and went to an A.A. meeting. He had done some research and found one that started at 8:30. He hadn't been to an A.A. meeting for seven months, and felt a need to go. I have to say that he has been steadfast in not drinking in circumstances that were very tempting. He is still a bit of a head case though. When he gets a little money from Sonny he just can't *wait* to spend it. He is very generous, and in two days *or less*, he is broke again. When Mark and I were in the bar at The Boathouse, he came in and insisted on buying us a round of drinks. I mentioned all this to him and he readily admitted it. I really don't know how he manages to get by long term.

Sonny and Richard bought provisions yesterday afternoon, and then went out around six o'clock. We were in the bar ashore when they came through, went in together for their showers, and headed out for dinner, etc. Richard is such a trouble making suck-up, and a really bad hypocrite! Initially he was just as critical of Sonny and Naomi and that situation as anybody, but now he and Sonny are the best of friends after he ran and told Sonny all the things that Ray, Mark and I had said about them. Personally, I don't care but he really hurt Mark's feelings with his babbling on to Sonny. Mark is *very* bitter now and though he has had the adventure of a lifetime, he can't wait to get away from Sonny and Richard.

22 – THE EASTERN CARIBBEAN

Saturday, April 26 - 6:40 P.M.- So we begin the last passage of the trip, and with that beginning come lots of emotions, some of which are pretty intense. At about 7:45 A.M. we cast off from our mooring at The Boatyard and headed for the port to take on water and fuel, and clear out through Customs and Immigration. At 10:55 we finally finished that process and got under way bound for Key West, 1,454 miles away. The most intense emotions are happiness and excitement to be headed for home after 6 ½ months, and sadness because this is the beginning of the end of the greatest adventure of my life, knowing it is *highly* unlikely that I will ever do anything comparable. Then there was thankfulness, or gratitude for having the opportunity to do something like this and the courage and will to actually do it! I *still* feel like this has all been a fantastic dream and I am going to wake up at home in my bed any minute. I can hardly accept or believe that I have really done this!

Ray, Mark and I went ashore for final showers early this morning and I had another good telephone conversation with Maureen.

I spent a little time yesterday making fishing lures from components that I bought in Bridgetown, and promptly lost one this afternoon, at least somewhat through negligence. We are sailing fast, at six knots or better so I was trolling with the drag set pretty tight to avoid having a fish take all the line before I could get to it. I trolled through afternoon watch and when I went to bring the lure in at six o'clock I noticed that there was quite a bit less line on the reel than usual. As I reeled it in I noticed that yes, it *was* out a lot further than normal and then discovered that the lure was missing and the wire leader broken. We never saw a strike so it must have happened when we weren't paying attention. My theory is that when a big fish took the lure, the tight drag along with our speed created a lot of pressure as it took line off the reel. Then, with nobody fighting it, the fish was able to shake back and forth until the wire leader broke. I am annoyed at myself for not paying closer attention.

When Sonny and Richard bought provisions yesterday they didn't get any cokes or other soft drinks so I will just have to do without them for ten days or so. What they *did* get however, was five boxes of "Total", the first we have seen since Belize. They also got whole wheat bread!

Tonight Ray made what was probably his best pasta sauce of the trip, with corned beef, sautéed onions, a can of whole tomatoes (cut up), spices, and a little sugar. I don't know why, but this afternoon and tonight I have had a really bad case of gas. It is so bad that even *I* can't stand it so I just ate a couple of Pepto Bismol tablets to see if that will help!

We are back in the mode of *great* trade wind sailing with east-southeast winds 16-24 knots, just aft of the starboard beam with seas running four to eight feet. I don't think many things could detract from my enjoyment of this and I realize how lucky I am to be experiencing it.

Sunday, April 27 - 7:50 A.M.- I am writing this while sitting on the stern trolling and watching Martinique fade in the distance behind us, about nine miles away. At the beginning of night watch we were just before entering the St. Lucia-Martinique Channel and the lights of St. Lucia's northeast coast were eight miles off the port beam. We passed as close as six miles to St. Lucia as we sailed northwest and at daybreak the southwest point of Martinique was three miles off the starboard beam. It was a pretty sight, with the mountains silhouetted against the morning sky. That sounds pretty neat- running the channel under sail, at night, diagonally between St. Lucia and Martinique! Even after all the places we have been, I still find the Caribbean to be pretty exotic stuff! Also, it has a kind of homey, familiar feeling to it; not quite but almost, like "home waters".

Monday, April 28 Lat.- 15 degrees, 47 minutes north; Lon.- 62 degrees, 50 minutes west

8:40 A.M.- We are sailing as close to downwind as we can, as the wind is southeast and we are trying to sail a course of 319 degrees, or almost directly northwest. We can't sail straight downwind for three reasons. The first is that we don't have a spinnaker because Sonny chose not to buy one for this voyage. "No problem" you say; just use the whisker pole to hold the jib out. We *do*, in fact, *have* a whisker pole, but the second reason is that Sonny doesn't seem to know how to use it and won't let anybody else try. "Well, there is a third option" you say; "just put up the main, let it out all the way, and tie it with a preventer". Well, the third reason is that in addition to Sonny's apparent fear of *flying* the main (still!), if you let the main out very far it chafes against

237

the shrouds. I don't know whether Sonny doesn't *know* about anti-chafing material that you can put on shrouds and spreaders, or he made a conscious decision not to install any but whatever the reason, we don't have any. So there you have it; our three reasons for being unable to sail downwind!

Yesterday sailing was great almost all day. The wind died about 11:00 A.M. so we motored for an hour and a half, but then it piped right back to 20 knots, right over the starboard quarter. We averaged upward of six knots all day, with bright sunshine and seas that stayed in the four to eight foot range. About 4:30 P.M. a pod of dolphins, maybe 30 or 40 in number showed up; seemingly from all directions at once and gave us about a 15 minute show, jumping out of the water and swimming all around and under the boat. They were small dolphins like I have seen in the Eastern Caribbean before.

I am taking pictures of "life on the boat", as requested by Peter Nielsen of "Sail", and will send the good ones to him as soon as I can. I *finally* sat down yesterday and read the manual that came with this camera (duuhhh!) so now I think I can take even better pictures. Too bad I didn't do that sooner!

Oh yes, the handle finally came off the tea kettle; the latest thing to break. It had been showing signs for a few days and we were handling it carefully, so nobody got burned but this morning we were lifting it with two potholders to pour water for coffee, tea, or oatmeal. Mark had been working on it and seems to have it repaired, but we will still be very careful when we handle it.

Tuesday, April 29 Lat.- 16 degrees, 45 minutes north; Lon.- 64 degrees, 41 minutes west

8:35 A.M.- I was wrong yesterday- we *do* have anti-chafing material on board! Ray said that he offered to install it before we left Mobile but Sonny said no. Why? Who the *hell* knows? Maybe he knew then that he wasn't going to fly the main much and considered the anti-chafing material unnecessary. Whatever the case, this is the only boat I have ever been on that was unable to sail straight downwind and we fart around a lot when the wind is on our tail. Anyway, we are *still* trying to sail downwind, with the same results.

Yesterday about noon the wind dropped below ten knots so we motored all afternoon. Going downwind in very light winds made the day seem really hot.

I lost another fishing lure yesterday morning. I got a good, hard strike, and then the fish was gone along with another lure. Another wire leader had broken! I recently found an unopened roll of galvanized

238

wire in the trash, and thought, "wow, this stuff is great to make wire leaders"! It was easy to work with, and everything seemed great, but IT BREAKS! That *really* pissed me off as I have now lost two good lures and two good fish because of it. I have now learned, so there won't be number three.

Mark's repair of the handle on the teakettle works fine. We are seeing quite a few ships as we approach the Mona Passage, but Sonny still doesn't use the radar on night watch. Early this morning we saw our first sailboat on the high seas, of the entire trip. All the others have we have seen have been in or near ports. This one was a multi-hull, heading southeast. Ray tried to call them on the radio, but got no reply.

Wednesday, April 30 Lat.-17 degrees, 40 minutes north; Lon.- 66 degrees, 43 minutes west - 9:15 A.M.- The negative side of my moody personality is asserting itself again. It started during night watch and has continued through my after-watch nap, shower, and breakfast. Maybe writing will drive it away.

We are making crappy progress right now. The wind is still behind us and this morning we were sailing 40 degrees off course on Ray and Richard's watch, to "get in position for our run through the Mona Passage". Yesterday we motored for ten hours and then Mark and I motor-sailed for three of our four hours in following winds of 10-16 knots. The wind stabilized at 14-16 knots the last hour so we stopped the engine. At that point we were sailing ten degrees off course to starboard, but Ray tacked and went 40 degrees off to port- a little much in my opinion. He just tacked again, and now we are just about on course but we are getting nowhere fast. With this lousy progress, getting to Key West May 6 seems out of the question. The seventh seems doable, with the eighth a worst case at this point.

Yesterday Sonny expressed some concern about fuel consumption and was talking about where we could make a fuel stop but I think I got his attention enough to convince him that it is way too early to worry about that. I pointed out that we still have 140 gallons, which is enough to motor 700 miles and it is only 1,000 miles to Key West. Also, he was thinking that the Dominican Republic was our last option to get fuel since we can't go to Cuba, but I pointed out that Great Inagua Island in The Bahamas is right on our way; just opposite the east end of Cuba. He had never noticed it on the chart, or even *heard* of it and seemed to feel better after I pointed it out. And this is a guy who circumnavigated Cuba just last year!

I had no success trolling yesterday even though I used two different lures, and conditions seemed perfect. Ray continues to amaze us with his different pasta sauce creations, each with a little different taste. We are having pasta every night nowadays. I *really* need to catch some fish!

I almost forgot to mention that when we came on night watch we could see the glow of lights on the south coast of Puerto Rico. There were four distinct glows, one of which was quite large and which I assumed to be the city of Ponce.

Thursday, May 1 Lat.- 19 degrees, 8 minutes north; Lon.- 68 degrees, 17 minutes west

8:45 A.M.- At 2:00 A.M. we altered course from north-northwest to northwest, marking the end of our run through the notorious Mona Passage. We completed the run in good, calm weather and without incident. We entered the south end at roughly 1:00 P.M., so the passage took about 13 hours. At the south end are some relatively shallow banks that have a lot of fish traps- the kind that rest on the bottom, and have two floats connected by a short line- and we managed to snag one without knowing it right away. We were in 20-knot winds at the time, buzzing along at a speed of six knots when we suddenly slowed to four knots for no apparent reason. We looked off the stern but couldn't see anything so we were not sure what was going on. This went on for about ten minutes and Sonny was getting ready to go in the water to check things out when it worked free and the floats came bobbing up, right behind the boat.

About three hours after entering the passage we reached an interesting area of convergence where winds and seas that are coming around the north and south sides of Puerto Rico in the prevailing easterly winds, come together to create a brief "dead zone" for winds and confused area for seas. That was between Mona Island and Puerto Rico as we passed diagonally through the passage from southeast to northwest. As we approached that area winds had dropped to 12 knots and seas were no more than four to six feet but I can imagine how nasty it could be with high seas and winds that quickly shifted directions by 90 degrees or more. When we entered the "dead zone" the wind was south-southeast and when we left it the wind had shifted to north-northeast. We passed Isla Desechao at the end of afternoon watch, marking roughly half way through the passage. We continued on the same north-northwest course well after we were through the actual passage, to give ourselves room to

240

get around Cabo Cabron, in the Dominican Republic.

Winds stayed relatively light and at 5:30 we put up the reefed main; the first time it has flown in a *long* time. Then, about 6:30 Ray and Richard took out the reef and we were under *full sail*! *All three sails, fully deployed*! It didn't last long though, because the wind died down at the beginning of our night watch and we had to motor, so Sonny had us furl the main and jib. Again, he ran around the deck in the middle of the night with no life jacket; let alone a tether. As we did so, he said, "The main shouldn't have been put up in the first place!" I have *never* seen anybody so afraid to fly a sail as he is to fly that main. He is in *love* with the jib! In retrospect, if he hadn't been so enamored with the Goddamn jib, he *might* not have lost the one at Cape Horn-flying a piece of the jib in 50 knot winds when he had a perfectly good *storm jib* hanked on and ready! If you don't use your storm jib in 50-knot winds, when *do* you use it?

Lately I have been sitting on the stern for a couple of hours every morning, fishing and getting some sun. That non-skid deck is rough, and even though I don't move around much, my ass is sore! Mark sits back that way getting sun too, and mentioned that he has the same problem, so it's not just me.

We are sailing again now but the wind still hasn't stabilized to the 15-20 knot northeasterlies that we're expecting so we have been motoring, sailing, and motor-sailing. We are making pretty good progress though, covering 130 miles in the last 24 hours.

Friday, May 2 Lat.- 20 degrees, 13 minutes north; Lon.- 70 degrees, 25 minutes west.

8:20 A.M.- We are *buzzing* along! Since about noon yesterday winds have been in the 18-24 knot range, still right behind us. At least now we are tacking back and forth instead of going straight downwind, and that makes sailing a lot of fun in these winds; a pleasant change after slogging along for a couple of days. We are making a speed of between six and seven knots, and with just over 700 miles to go, a May 7 arrival in Key West seems very likely!

We are skirting the coast of the Dominican Republic, about 15 miles off and yesterday afternoon we could sometimes see the mountains as shrouded images through the clouds. It has been clear at sea but a combination of clouds and haze hang over the land.

Late yesterday I discovered that I had not screwed the cap on my water bottle straight and since I store it horizontally on the shelf above my bunk, it had leaked on both my pillows and the head of my mattress; the first time my bunk has been wet the entire trip. I got things *somewhat* dried out, but slept damp before night watch. I was *really* pissed off at myself. Everything is pretty well dry now, but the pillows still smell like mildew, as they have for a while.

We saw two sailboats yesterday and Ray had a brief radio conversation with one of them. It was a South African boat, headed for the Dominican Republic, and then to Newport, Rhode Island. We went 14,000 miles without seeing another sailboat on the high seas, and now we have seen three in the last two days.

I have had no success fishing the last few days; one of those "dry spells". The fact that we are going so fast may have something to do with it.

With any kind of luck we should only have five days to go, and I am excited. This will have been roughly a 200-day voyage. The Indy 500 race is 200 laps, so each day is sort of like a lap. I see myself as a lap ahead of the field with five laps to go - all I have to do is avoid a crash and not run out of gas and I will have succeeded in what I actually set out to do! I have always set high standards for myself, and success has not come easily or frequently in my life but I will consider completing this voyage to be a *major, major success*! I know that sounds stupid, but that's the way I feel.

Saturday, May 3 Lat.- 20 degrees, 32 minutes north; Lon.- 72 degrees, 44 minutes west

8:35 A.M.- We continue to skirt the north coast of Hispaniola Island and are now about 25 miles off Haiti. We are near Ile Tortuga, famous for being a pirate stronghold during the days of Henry Morgan, Francis Drake and the like, and more recently one of the settings for Jimmy Buffett's book "Where Is Joe Merchant?".

After a fine, sunny day at sea yesterday the sky is totally overcast this morning- the first such morning that we have seen for a long time; probably since leaving The Falklands. The wind died about noon yesterday and we have been motoring ever since. The sea is flat and glassy, with a bit of debris that looks something like lawn clippings, and some sticks and tree limbs, though not really any trash.

We did have a whale sighting this morning. About eight o'clock I went topside with my tea and Ray, at the helm, first spotted it some 50 yards off the port beam, just hanging out on the surface. We couldn't tell what kind it was, and it went under after about 30 seconds.

We are seeing lots of traffic (relatively) in this area, as Mark and I saw four other vessels during afternoon watch and four more on night watch, one of which passed just over a mile off the starboard beam as it overtook us. It appeared to be a small freighter. Between watching them on radar and visually, that kept us busy throughout night watch. Of course Sonny didn't have the radar on during his 10:00 P.M.- 2:00 A.M. watch!

My fishing slump continues so I will try yet another lure tomorrow. Meantime Ray continues to amaze us with his pasta sauce creations-pasta every night since we left Barbados.

Ray told me that he has decided to ask Richard to crew for him if he gets that delivery job from West Palm Beach to New York. The destination will be near the New York-Connecticut border, not far from Richard's home. After all the bullshit and conflicts he has had with Richard I can't believe he would even *consider* that, but he said he doesn't know anybody else to ask. I told him *nobody* would be better than Richard!

Even with all the interpersonal crap, and despite being anxious to get home, I still don't lose sight of where I am and what I am doing. The sailing is still great when we have wind, we are sailing along the north coast of the Greater Antilles, the sea is still that deep, inimitable blue, and the swells still look like moving hills. I will enjoy, and fully appreciate that, right to the end!

Sunday, May 4 Lat.- 21 degrees, 10 minutes north; Lon.- 74 degrees, 57 minutes west

9:05 A.M.- A small freighter passed less than half a mile off our port beam on night watch, just before 4:00 A.M. I first spotted it when I turned on the radar at 2:00 and it was straight ahead, 26 miles out. By 3:00 it was 12 miles out and still straight ahead. About a quarter past three we made visual contact when it was eight miles away. We were under sail at the time in light winds that were almost right behind us, but just slightly over on the port quarter. I was at the helm, and my intent was to pass starboard-to-starboard. My reasoning was that with the existing winds I could easily turn to port if necessary to get out of his way, with him on my starboard side. If we were port-to-port and I needed to turn to starboard to get out of his way, I would have to jibe, and may not have time to do so. Then, just before 3:30 three things happened. First, Mark noticed that it was about teatime, as we usually have tea/coffee between 3:30 and 4:00. When he started below to the galley he found Ray there. Ray, who had insomnia and was awake reading, had decided that would be a good time to make corn muffins. During all that, the wind dropped below ten knots and our speed dropped to three knots, making our maneuverability problematic, and with a ship coming right at us, I decided that would be a good time to start the engine. By this time, the ship was four miles out and closing *fast!* When I started the engine the electrical system blinked, and when it came back on, the autopilot was off and I didn't know it. I noticed it after only a few seconds but by then the ship, which *had* been slightly off my *starboard* bow was now slightly off my *port* bow! One of the most dangerous things you can do, *especially* at night, is to confuse another vessel's helmsman about your intent so I decided quickly that it would be bad to turn back across his bow again. What I did instead, was to alter my course ten degrees to starboard and gun the engine a little, giving him plenty room off our port side.

It all worked out well; the corn muffins were good, and we had our tea and coffee a little bit later than usual. We got past him with no problem, got back on our course, and everything returned to normal. It was just a little exciting at the time.

Yesterday's overcast didn't last long. By 9:30 skies were clear, the sea was glassy and beautifully blue, and there was not a puff of wind. Finally, between 4:30 and 5:00 P.M. the wind came up a little from the northeast so we unrolled the jib and motor-sailed the last hour of our afternoon watch. About 6:30 the wind was 15-18 knots so Ray stopped the engine for the first time in 30 hours. It didn't last though, as the wind came around behind us and then dropped on our night watch so we are still motoring this morning.

This morning we are 20 miles off the north coast of Cuba near the town of Antilla, and approaching the Old Bahama Channel. Yesterday we crossed the Windward Passage between Haiti and Cuba, and then passed between Great Inagua Island and the eastern tip of Cuba. Great Inagua is one of those "far away places with strange-sounding names" that I have wanted to visit for a long time. Too bad we are in a hurry- perhaps another time!

Early yesterday afternoon we stopped the engine for Sonny to check the oil. The sea was glassy, there was no wind, and it was hotter than blazes. I just mentioned the possibility of stopping for a few minutes for a swim but nobody else was interested. I know we are in a hurry, and me probably more than anybody but five or ten minutes wouldn't have made any difference. I didn't press it since I have pushed for us to make good time but a quick swim would have been really nice.

Still no luck fishing, even with yet another new lure. I am surprised, as I thought fishing would be good in this area. Pasta again tonight!

Monday, May 5 Lat.-22 degrees, 4 minutes north; Lon.- 77 degrees, 0 minutes west

8:30 A.M.- A Wednesday arrival in Key West appears less and less likely. We need an average speed of 5.5 knots to get there by dark Wednesday and all night we made about 4.5 in winds of 9-18 knots. Sonny doesn't want to run the engine unless the speed gets down to 3.5, so there we are. That would be understandable in a normal passage but when you're trying to get home at the end of the voyage, and you have plenty fuel, it doesn't make any sense. Right now we are making 5.0, so it is still possible, but less likely every hour. If we are still on the boat Wednesday night, I am going to be pissed!

We're entering the Old Bahama Channel near Cayo Guajaba, Cuba, still about 20 miles offshore. We saw no glow of lights on night watch but we did see five ships; one of which passed within two miles. There is still a cloudy haze toward Cuba. On afternoon watch yesterday we saw two large cruise ships, one right behind the other, emerge from the haze five miles off our port bow heading east toward the Windward Passage.

The fishing slump continues–pasta again last night!

Tuesday, May 6 Lat.- 22 degrees, 57 minutes north; Lon.- 78 degrees, 55 minutes west

8:45 A.M.- Sonny's refusal to motor-sail has pretty much assured that we will not make Key West tomorrow night. If we could have averaged 5½ knots, even from 6:00 A.M. today forward we could have made it, but our speed is ranging between four and five. On yesterday's morning watch Ray was running the engine to keep the speed up but at ten o'clock Sonny stopped it, and that was that. He *really* pissed me off.

On night watch we actually averaged about 5½ knots in tail winds that were 16-24 knots. We had to alter course 15 degrees around four o'clock. to avoid a ship. I had watched it come in on radar from 20 miles out, and when it was four miles away I concluded that he was headed straight for us, closing fast, and *not* altering *his* course. He passed just two miles off our port side. The night was absolutely gorgeous. The moon had set, and the stars were about as bright as we have seen them. I saw one shooting star. We could also see the glow of some shore lights as we came to the west end of the Old Bahama Channel.

Afternoon watch yesterday was also beautiful as we skirted the Cuban coast about eight miles off. We could see trees on some barrier islands off Cabo Romano all afternoon. This may be the closest I ever come to actually visiting Cuba. I deeply resent the fact that for my entire adult life, my government has forbidden me from legally visiting Cuba, just 90 miles from the U.S. Whatever your political convictions, it seems pretty obvious that our "sanctions" haven't exactly brought the Castro government to it's knees! Somehow it all just doesn't seem right.

I didn't feel well yesterday afternoon and early evening - a slight but persistent headache and my stomach wasn't exactly right. Two aspirins didn't work so after dinner I bombed it with an ibuprofen and two Pepto-Bismol tablets. I went to sleep, but woke up at ten o'clock and it was still there so I bombed it again; this time using *two* ibuprofen and two more Pepto-Bismol tablets. That worked, and I felt fine when I got up for night watch. I thought it was just aggravation with Sonny, but then remembered that at lunch I ate some peas from a can that was bent, and I think that they may have been bad. Anyway, I am O.K. now; just pissed off. I am trying to hold my temper and my tongue, and have this trip end on a positive note but it is not easy.

In spite of all this I am still enjoying the sailing, and the adventure of skirting the Cuban coast. It is pretty neat stuff, and I'm not letting *anything* spoil it for me.

Still no success fishing- pasta again! Ray continues to make good sauces but we are getting *really* tired of pasta. That cheap-ass Sonny didn't buy anything else decent to eat for dinners and *he* doesn't even *eat* pasta. I'm not sure what he does eat but it's nothing anybody else will eat. At least we *do* have plenty of canned fruit, and Mark and I have some for dessert every night.

6:35 P.M. - We have had two consecutive watches of great sailing. After a great night watch last night, we did even better this afternoon, averaging over six knots. There have, however, been some slow times in between and the latest plan is to get to Key West early Thursday morning. Sonny's story now is that he was afraid we wouldn't get there before dark tomorrow, and he doesn't know the way in at night. I think all that stuff he said early on about his experience running charters in the Keys was greatly exaggerated! He doesn't seem familiar with the Keys at all, and didn't know the name of *any* marina in Key West. I have resigned myself to getting there Thursday morning and am enjoying the nice sailing. We got occasional glimpses of the Cuban coast again this afternoon.

Wednesday, May 7 Lat.- 23 degrees, 57 minutes north; Lon.- 81 degrees, 0 minutes west

8:50 A.M.-

"My home town's coming in sight;
If you think I'm happy, you're right!
Six days on the road and I'm gonna make it home tonight!"
Dave Dudley

"Now Key West is coming in sight;
If you think I'm happy, you're right!
Six months on the ocean and I'm gonna make it home tonight!"
Me

Miracles *do* still happen! We were planning to turn west-southwest at Cay Sal, toward Havana, for 50 miles or so and then turn directly north to Key West, taking us straight across the Gulf Stream and getting us there tomorrow morning, but at the beginning of his night watch Sonny changed his mind. We were about even with Cay Sal at the time, and he set our course straight from there to Key West, diagonally across the Gulf Stream, a distance of only 75 miles. Maybe it was because of the great 16-24 knot winds that we had all afternoon and evening; maybe he overheard some of the rationale in discussions that Ray had about that subject and then looked at the chart and saw that we were right; or maybe he heard me bitching about taking an extra day to get there - I don't know, but I am *delighted*! It's still not a guarantee that we will get there before dark tonight but at this point it looks *very* likely!

I lost a lure fishing during afternoon watch yesterday and am not sure why. When I reeled it in the end of the line had that curly "pigtail" look that says, "knot failure". I had made sure I left plenty "tag end" out of the knot but maybe I didn't pull it tight enough, or maybe it broke along the knot somewhere. We didn't see a strike - maybe not watching closely enough - but it must have been the pressure of a fish that did it. *So*, pasta again!

12:35 P.M. - Right now the wind has dropped to 12-15 knots but when we slowed to 4.5 knots, Sonny started the engine so we are motor-sailing west along, and 10 miles outside the reef, some 30 miles from Key West. I am excited, and so are Ray and Mark! We pretty well have all our stuff packed. Mark asked me this morning if I am still going to confront Sonny about lying to us regarding the "Captain" business. I said, "No, I am going to let it go. I want to

247

have the trip end on a good note".

All through night watch I kept thinking "This is probably my last night watch, in all likelihood, ever". Then I started reflecting on the whole trip, but there is just too much. I'm sure I will do a *lot* of reflecting on it and dissecting it over time. As it is, right now I just think of what a *fantastic* and *unbelievable experience* it has been, and I can't wait to get home!

23 – KEY WEST

We continued westward for what seemed like an inordinately long time, until we were absolutely sure we were directly south of the Key West ship channel. The chart indicated some shoal water near the entrance that would be a hazard if we made the turn too soon. Running aground at this point was the *last* thing we wanted, so we forced ourselves to be patient. Finally, around mid-afternoon we made the turn north, and shortly afterward we passed the sea buoy marking the entrance to the channel. Everybody was excited as we motor-sailed up the channel, and high spirits prevailed. We took pictures of the shoreline, of channel markers, of Coast Guard ships and launches navigating up and down the channel; anything that might help us remember this moment at the end of the voyage.

We actually reached Key West just before sunset, and the street performers' shows were under way at the Mallory Dock. The "Sunset Cruise" business is healthy there as we saw several boats heading out as we approached - from large sailing catamarans to "pirate ships" all full of tourists drinking rum punch and margaritas (this *is* Margaritaville, you know!). Maureen had told me that her Dad was coming down with her and Molly to meet me so I looked for the three of them in the crowd as we passed Mallory Dock. I didn't see them, but knew they were in the neighborhood.

Sonny had told us that he wasn't staying in Key West, but was just going to drop off Ray, Mark and me before heading on to St. Petersburg with Richard so he was looking for the first available marina with a dock. He was getting a little cantankerous by this time but we paid little attention, as we were too happy to be getting home. He approached the first marina that we saw, right next to Mallory Dock, but it was part of a hotel and appeared to be private, so he turned away. He didn't see another one right away so he circled, and pulled up to the cruise ship terminal and told us we were getting off there. The top of the pier was six feet above the deck of the boat and we would have to climb up with our bags, over a giant rubber dock fender some three feet in diameter that was there to keep the cruise ships off the concrete pier. I was taken aback and almost speechless, but said "Sonny, you could at least put us off on a real dock".

"Quit bitching Charley", he said, "and go get your stuff".

"No", I said. "This is chicken-shit!" He just ignored me, and we all started bringing our bags up form below, preparing to get off there. Just as we were bringing the last of our things into the cockpit a security guard showed up and told Sonny that he couldn't tie up there; that they were being especially careful because of concerns about terrorists. Sonny first tried persuasion, telling the guy that the boat would only be there for a few minutes. When that didn't work he tried bullying, and that didn't work either so he reluctantly started the engine and left. We motored back past Mallory Dock and around a point, where we were happy to see a marina not more than 200 yards away. By then the tension was pretty high, but Ray, Mark and I were just anxious to get the hell off the boat and away from Sonny. He seemed just as anxious to get us off the boat.

He pulled up with the starboard rail alongside the fuel dock and we hurriedly threw our things over the rail in a pile on the dock. He couldn't seem to get us off the boat fast enough so we quickly climbed onto the dock and began sorting out our belongings. Richard walked over, shook my hand, and was saying something about what a great voyage it had been when Sonny started making a speech. He started by saying how he hoped he would never see Ray, Mark or me again, and how poorly we had treated Naomi, when I interrupted him.

I had been trying *really* hard to keep my mouth shut and end the trip on a positive note, but I was *not* in a mood to listen to any bullshit from him. "*You* started it all" I said, "by lying to us about that *captain* business".

A smirk came to his face and he said, "I didn't lie. Read your contract. It says that I will furnish two captains. One was Ray and the other was me."

"I know what's in the contract", I said. "I also know what you said to me *on the phone,* you lying son-of-a-bitch."

"*Son-of-a-bitch!* You're calling me a *son-of-a-bitch?* You're insulting my *Mother?*"

"I'm not insulting your Mother", I said; "I'm insulting *you!* This has nothing to do with your Mother."

"*No; No*" he said. "*You insulted my Mother!* You take that back!" Then he started slowly moving toward me. He climbed slowly over the rail onto the dock as I said again

"I'm *not* insulting your Mother; I'm insulting *you,* and I'm not taking anything back."

He kept slowly approaching me, as if everything was happening in slow motion, still saying, "You called me a *son-of-a-bitch. You insulted my Mother!*" He walked right up in my face. I was so taken aback that I just stood there, not believing what was happening. Then he put both hands in my chest and pushed me backward. When he got that close, I braced myself, and was more or less ready, so I didn't fall. He seemed determined to start a fight but instead of hitting him I pushed back, trying my best to push him into the water, figuring that would end it. He stumbled backward, but caught himself at the edge of the dock and approached me again.

I still just stood there, but by then I was prepared for anything. At that point he reached out with his left hand, grabbing the front of my shirt, my gold chain, and a few chest hairs while drawing back his right hand in a clenched fist. I may not be very smart, but his intentions were clear so before he could swing at me I hit him hard with my left fist, along his right cheekbone. He released his grip on my chest and stumbled backward a step or two, leaving himself open and I hit him several more times with my left fist, along the right side of his face and his mouth.

I think he was getting desperate by then, so he rushed at me and grabbed me. When he did that, I grabbed him and had the leverage to pick him up and throw him down from my left to right. He pulled me down with him and we fell between two fuel pumps with me sitting on top of him. I had his right arm pinned with my left knee and was holding his left hand with my right. He was looking pretty bad by then, with blood coming from his nose and the right corner of his mouth, but he was still struggling. He was in a helpless situation and I could have beaten him until my arms got tired but for some reason that I will probably never understand, I didn't want to pound him any more. I asked "Are you ready to quit?"

"No", he said. "You insulted my Mother. You take it back!"

He kept struggling, trying to get free and I remember thinking "I'd better say *something* to placate this idiot or I'm going to have to beat him completely senseless". I sat there on top of him for what seemed like a long time but was only a few seconds, and then said "O.K., I'm sorry if you think I insulted your Mother. I take that back; I was only insulting *you.*"

With that, he stopped struggling. I slowly stood up, getting off him very carefully, wary that he might come after me again. I was in control, but very pissed at that point, and as he got up I said "*You'd better get on your FUCKING boat and get the HELL out of here!"* I was standing between him and the boat so he circled counterclockwise around me and went aboard the boat without saying a word. I made sure he was in front of me as he went, not giving him an opportunity to try a "sucker punch". As he started the engine and Richard loosened the lines, the wind blew them off the dock and they started slowly motoring toward the aftermath of a colorful sunset.

When it became obvious that they weren't coming back, Ray, Mark and I just stood there looking at each other, mouths hanging open, amazed at what had happened. Mark was the first one to speak, saying "After watching you work out with your weights every day for six months, I can't believe he was stupid enough to start a fight with you."

As for me, I couldn't believe that the fight was so one-sided, or especially, that it happened at all. He never hit me, but when he rushed me he scratched my forehead enough to make it bleed a little. That was the extent of my physical damage.

As the shock began to abate we gathered our bags and walked off the dock to find a taxi. We were lucky enough to find one that was a van, with enough room for us and all our bags. He took us to the Blue Marlin Motel on Simonton Street where Maureen had agreed to meet me.

The trip was over, and I was home.

Coming Home From the Sea

A long white schooner drifted in
With yesterday's high tide;
I wondered where she might have been,
And someone softly cried

"We're coming in from Mandalay,
And there, from Tripoli.
We're looking for a place to stay;
We're weary of the sea.

We've seen a thousand stormy days,
And lonely, starless nights;
We've seen our sails ripped from their stays
And wondered if we might

Be going soon to Davy Jones,
Or drowning in the rain;
But each time we came safely home,
And sailed right out again.

We've seen men die in Boer Wars,
And Boxer Rebels, too;
And yes, we have our share of scars,
But now all that is through.

We're tired of skirting rocky reefs
And dodging sandy shoals;
Now we'll just sit in quiet relief,
And thank God for our souls.

We'll sit and dream of winds and sails
When we were young and free,
And maybe spin a few tall tales
Of life upon the sea."

    Charley Hester

GLOSSARY

Aft At, near, or toward the stern, or back of a vessel.

Aground The vessel is resting on the bottom; usually caused by navigating into water shallower than the draft of the vessel.

Astern Directly behind a vessel

Backstay A rope, cable, or wire from the top of a mast toward the stern, for the purpose of bracing the mast in place.

Beam Right angles on either side, to the direction the vessel is heading.

Beam Wind A wind at right angles to the vessel's course.

Bearing The direction of another object from the vessel; usually expressed in degrees of the compass, with north being 0 and south being 180 degrees.

Beating to Windward Making progress against the direction of the wind by sailing close-hauled or making a zigzag course upwind.

Bilge The lowest, curved part of the inside of a vessel's hull, where the sides and bottom meet.

Bimini A canvas roof, supported by a metal frame over the cockpit of a small vessel.

Bitter-End The end of an anchor line, or rode, that is not attached to the anchor.

Boathook A wooden or metal staff with a hook at one end, used for fending off or holding on.

Boom A wooden or metal spar, perpendicular to the mast, used to extend the bottom, or foot of a sail.

Bow The forward, or front end of a vessel.

Bowsprit An extension forward from the bow, or front of a boat.

Bridle A span of rope with both ends secured; usually used for towing or for deployment of a sea-anchor.

Broach To be thrown broadside into waves or surf.

Capsize To overturn.

Cast Off To let go, as in casting off mooring lines.

Catboat A small sailboat with the mast stepped well forward and carrying only a mainsail.

Center Cockpit A vessel with the cockpit at or near the middle, or center of the ship.

Chafe To wear by rubbing.

Chop A short, steep sea, or wave.

Cleat A T-shaped fitting of wood or metal, with horns, used for securing lines.

Close-Hauled Sailing close to the direction the wind is coming from with the sheets controlling the sails hauled in as tight as possible.

Cockpit The area of a vessel that contains the wheel or tiller and the helmsman, usually with seats for other crew members.

Companionway The main hatch and stairway leading from the cockpit to the main cabin of a vessel.

Course The point of the compass toward which the vessel is steering; can be expressed in directions or degrees.

Displacement The weight of the water displaced by a vessel.

Dodger A windshield-like device made of transparent plastic with a canvas framework that is used to protect the helmsman and crew in the cockpit from weather and sea-spray.

Draft The depth of water to a boat's keel, or the depth of water required to float a boat.

EPIRB Emergency Position Indicator Radio Beacon. An electronic device that, when activated, transmits a continuous signal with it's exact latitude and longitude, thus aiding search and rescue efforts.

Falling Off Altering course away from the direction of the wind.

Fender A device, usually made of rubber, hung over the side of a vessel to protect the vessel from chafing against docks or other vessels.

Forward At, near, or toward the bow, or front of a vessel.

Furl To gather up and secure a sail.

Gaff A spar to which the head, or top of a sail is secured.

Galley The kitchen on a vessel.

Genoa A large jib which overlaps the mainsail.

Gimbals A pair of rings at right angles to each other, that support items such as compasses and stoves and keep them horizontal through the motion of a vessel.

Ground Tackle A term used to include all of the anchor gear.

Gunwale The upper edge of a vessel's side.

Halyards Ropes for hoisting sails up masts.

Hank A clip used to hold a sail to a stay.

Hawse Pipe A hole through the deck of a boat near the bow, that leads to a locker in which the anchor line is stored when not in use.

Head The bathroom/toilet on a vessel.

Head-Sails Sails forward of the main mast.

Headstay A rope, cable, or wire from the top of the forward-most mast to the bow; used to support the mast and to hold head-sails.

Headway Making progress moving ahead.

Heel The tilting to the side of a boat, away from the direction of the wind as a result of pressure of the wind on the sails.

Helm The wheel or tiller, used for steering the vessel.

Helmsman The person, male or female, who is steering the vessel.

Horseshoe Buoy A horseshoe-shaped float, usually mounted on the stern, for the purpose of being thrown to someone who falls overboard to keep them afloat until they are rescued.

Jib A headsail set on a headstay, forward of the main mast. The angle of the sail is controlled by a *sheet*, or rope leading from the lower, aft corner of the sail to the cockpit.

Jibe Changing the sailing direction by turning so that the stern of the vessel passes through the wind, from one side to the other.

Ketch A sailing vessel rigged with a main mast set just forward of midships, and a shorter, *mizzen* mast set between the main mast and the stern, just forward of the rudder.

Knockdown The situation of a vessel where it is listed over by winds and seas to the extent that the mast touches the water.

Knot One nautical mile (6,080 feet) per hour.

Lee Shore Land on the downwind, or leeward side of a vessel.

Leeboard A board to keep a sleeper in his bunk when a boat is heeled.

Leeward The direction away from the wind.

Leeway The sideways drift of a vessel, caused by the wind or tide.

Lifelines One or two lines, attached to vertical metal posts called stanchions, running along the outer perimeter of a vessel for the purpose of keeping crew members from falling overboard.

List The tilting to one side of a vessel at rest, due to an excess of weight on that side.

Mainsail The sail that is attached to the main mast and spread by the main boom.

Mast A vertical spar, supporting the booms and sails.

Mizzen The secondary, shorter mast and it's sail on a ketch, set between the main mast and the stern, just forward of the rudder.

Mooring Buoy A buoy fitted with a ring, floating in a body of water and used for mooring a boat.

Painter A short rope attached to the boy of a small boat, or dinghy and used for towing or securing.

Pitch Pole To turn end-over-end in the surf or breaking waves; usually not recoverable.

Point To sail close to the direction from which the wind is coming.

Port The left side of a vessel, looking forward.

Pulpits Framework, usually metal, on the bow and stern of a vessel, to which the lifelines are attached.

Quarter That portion of a vessel's sides from the beam back to the stern.

Reach Sailing with a beam wind.

Reef To reduce the area of a sail that is deployed; usually by securing a portion of the sail to a boom or stay.

Rigging Ropes, cables, and wires securing masts and sails.

Rode The anchor line of a vessel.

Rudder A flat device of wood, metal, or fiberglass, fitted on or near the stern, that controls the direction of the vessel.

Sea Anchor A drag device, usually parachute-shaped, that is secured by a bridle and deployed over the bow in heavy weather, to keep the vessel pointed into the wind and seas.

Sheet A rope used to control the angle of deployment of sails. It is attached directly to the lower aft corner of head-sails, and to the boom of boom sails.

Shorten Sail To reef, or take in some of the sails.

Shrouds Ropes, cables, or wires from the top of the mast, sideways to the rails on either side for the purpose of bracing, or securing the mast.

Snubbing Tightening the anchor line (rode) at intervals to dig in the point of the anchor when backing off the boat to set the anchor

Spar A pole supporting a sail or other gear.

Spinnaker A light, triangular or scoop-shaped sail, deployed as a head-sail for the purpose of sailing in following winds. Commonly used as a racing sail.

Spreader A horizontal spar fitted to a mast and used to spread the shrouds.

Squall An intense storm, usually brief, that arrives suddenly and usually brings strong winds and heavy rain.

Stay A rope, cable, or wire running forward or aft, that is used to support a mast.

Staysail Any sail that is set upon a stay; commonly one that runs from the mast to a point between the mast and the bow.

Stern The after, or back end of a vessel.

Stow To store, or put in place.

Tack The lower forward corner of a sail. That corner points in the direction from which the wind is coming; thus the terms "port tack" and "starboard tack". Changing directions or headings, in relation to the wind direction, is called "changing tacks", or sailing on a different tack.

Tiller A short piece of wood, metal, or fiberglass that is attached to the head of the rudder, and used to steer the vessel; used in lieu of a wheel on some vessels.

Weigh Anchor To raise the anchor of an anchored vessel in preparation for departure.

Windward Toward the direction from which the wind is blowing.

Charley Hester was born in Natchez, Mississippi in 1944 and graduated from the University of Southern Mississippi with a B.S. in Psychology. He is married and has three daughters, ages 39, 35, and 3. He learned to sail on "sunfish" in 1981 and subsequently took several "bareboat" charters in the Florida Keys, the Bahamas, and the Eastern Caribbean before buying a Cape Dory 28 sloop in 1992. He took early retirement from a career in Human Resources in 1999 and since then has worked as a Human Resources consultant and a fly-fishing consultant. He lives with his wife Maureen and daughter Molly in Indialantic, Florida and West Yellowstone, Montana.

Printed in the United States
50534LVS00004B/193-198

9 781595 940186